LEMONADES OF DESTINY

Paths into the Unknown

Liia Stash

I

The six-year-old girl's heart was filled with unbearable pain. Huddled in the corner of another room, she cried bitterly. At the same time, she was thinking about saving her sister. Once again, the father found a reason to punish his eldest daughter. During these horrible moments, his usual tool was always a belt. The loud crying of his sister tore little Miia's soul apart. Recognizing the urgency of the moment, she finally dared to act. Running out of the room, she grabbed the belt her father was about to swing at her nine-year-old sister. As he looked back, the stocky faced a defiant green-eyed gaze that pierced him with contempt. Swallowing hot tears and gripping the belt tightly with both hands, the girl screamed.

"Beat me instead of her." Her plump lips trembled with anger. "Don't you dare touch her."

The father felt embarrassed by his daughter's persistence.

Holding Jeanne by the elbow with one hand, he tried to pull the belt out of Miia's hands. She understood that as long as she had the belt, her sister was saved.

"Let go," the echo of his cry spread menacingly through the rooms.

"No." She squeezed the belt even tighter.

"Oh, stubborn girl," roaring like a boar, he let go of his elder daughter's hand and moved towards the younger one.

"Zhanna, run!" the girl screamed.

The father slowly approached the child, slapping the belt on the arm. Her heart was beating faster and faster.

Suddenly, Zhanna ran up to her father and pushed him so hard that he was thrown backward.

"Miia, faster," Zhanna said, grabbing her hand, and she pulled her sister to the front door of the house.

Without looking back, the girls ran out into the street.

"Girls, return!" the father demanded.

The girls hurried to hide from the cold.

"Let's put on our shoes and hurry to our mother. It's freezing." Zhanna said, looking back towards the yard.

Seeing her daughters in only sweaters, tights, and boots, the mother understood everything.

"Galina, when will your Vlad stop his tyranny?" With horror and pain in their eyes, the mother's colleagues met the sisters. Mother took the girls to the store's utility room. She wrapped them in blankets that were always there, gave them hot tea and cookies.

Father's menacing voice came from the store's hall:

"Are mine here?"

"Vlad, get out of here," the colleagues answered almost in unison, "they're not here."

"Where are they?" Banging his fist on the table, he wanted to go into the utility room.

"Listen, don't bang. Maria, call the police officer." Aunt Stefania always had a stern and confident voice when she didn't like something. Knowing her temper, Father stopped.

"Go home, get some sleep, and then we will talk. Why don't you, idiot, understand that you need to protect your wife?"

"Stefania, don't start teaching me how to live."

Aunt Maria went into the utility room. She picked up the phone to call a police officer, and, putting her finger to her lips, whispered:

"Quietly".

The customers entered the store. Father stood, thought, and left. Through the window, it was visible that he was moving towards his street.

"Did you have time to eat at home?"

"No," the girls were so hungry that even tea and cookies couldn't satisfy them. "Mommy, he beat Zhanna again."

Miia looked at her sister, who was sitting quietly and silently. Tears welled up in her mother's eyes. She hugged and kissed her daughters.

"I'll bring you some food right now."

As soon as he left, a policeman entered the store.

"Girls, what happened here?"

"When are you going to restrain Galina's Vlad somehow?" Aunt Stefania asked demandingly.

Miia ran to the door and began to watch through the crack. It wasn't the first time she had seen a policeman. He had often been to their house, but mostly he came to his father on personal matters.

"What again?" he asked, showing concern, turning to his

6

mother, whose face expressed disrespect for this man.

"I'll kill him someday," whispered mother.

"And then what?" he interrupted her. "You'll orphan the girls, and that's it. What happened this time?"

"Ivan, aren't you ashamed to ask such questions?" Aunt Stefania intervened in the conversation. "Children are running around the village without clothes in the cold."

"Stefania, I didn't ask you. And the children need to dress before going outside."

After these words, the mother shook her head and was just about to say something when Miia ran out of the utility room: "Go and see how he beat Zhanna again," she started shouting, "we ran away," the girl's voice trembled.

"Miia, calm down, baby," mother said, hugging her.

"Did he beat her? Let's go and see." Having come to his senses, he moved into the utility room.

Everyone was horrified by the marks of the belt on the skinny child's body.

"Is this today?" he asked, sitting down next to her. Zhanna nodded in response. She was in pain.

"The girls came running twenty minutes ago." Maria's aunt said in a low voice.

"Where is he now? I am his," the investigator's jaws trembled. "Galina, sit down and write."

Mother was writing a report. Miia, hugging Zhanna, looked at the police officer from under her forehead.

"You will forever remain bad for me if you do not explain to my father that you cannot beat children. And you cannot beat a grandmother." Miia shouted, "Forever bad."

He stood silently and looked at the girls. His face showed both despair and anger.

"Now start concluding, comrade lieutenant," Stefania's menacing gaze pierced the policeman through and through. "Vlad is your friend. Analyze his behavior at the party meeting. Explain to him thoroughly that there will be consequences. If you slow down again, I'll turn to your superiors with a statement about your inability to fulfill your duties." Her hands on her hips confirmed her determination: "Ivan, I'm not kidding."

"Stefania, I said I would figure it out," taking the statement

7

from my mother, he said in a completely calm voice, "Galina, I'm going to your home right now. You and the girls go with me?"

"They'll be with me today," Stefania interrupted him, "And if necessary, tomorrow and the day after tomorrow."

"It will be better this way. Galina, we will meet tomorrow." And having said goodbye to everyone, he left the store.

Later, the grandmother said that he was very strict. The next day, he called a meeting at the village party center and warned his father that the next time, the district party leadership would communicate with him. A day later, his father apologized to his mother and the girls right in the store. He promised that he would never repeat what he had done. Of course, no one believed him. But they knew that for a couple of months, the family would live in peace.

Despite a strict childhood, Miia grew up to be a generous and kind person. But not everyone could count on it.

One dreary November day, on her way home from school, Miia gazed at the orphaned branches of the trees, which, to her, looked sadly like they were reaching up to the sky in search of the sun. Her thoughts hummed a song about lost sunny days.

"Don't be sad. The sun remembers that you are waiting for it."

Seeing the car in the yard, Miia felt scared. Several people had come to her father multiple times. Their faces and speech seemed strange.

Then she remembered how the children had said that there were people who ate dogs. "Maybe they are the ones who came for Boba and Toba," was the first thing that crossed the little girl's mind.

"Belli, come here. Boba, Toba," the girl called anxiously, running up to the doghouse. One by one, two pretty four-month-old puppies jumped out at her. They joyfully rushed to the little one, jumping and licking her:

"Hurry up, I'll hide you."

At that moment, the gazebo door opened. The father stepped out first. His guests followed them.

"Oh, Miia," the father called out, seeing his daughter near the booth, "call the puppies here."

8

"Why?" Her voice began to tremble.

"They came for them."

Hugging the puppies, Miia glared menacingly at her father and his guests, whose faces were lit up with fake smiles. The girl froze. Suddenly, she grabbed Boba with her left hand and Toba with her right and ran across the plowed garden.

"Where are you going? Stop!" her father shouted after her, hoping for "Stop."

What is "Stop!"? Stumbling over bumps, the child ran, holding the puppies tightly under her arms with all her might.

"Come back." His voice boomed like thunder.

Ehe girl didn't stop.

"I will not give them away. They will eat them." Tears streamed down her pink cheeks.

The puppies didn't even try to escape. At that moment, the little girl didn't care how her father might punish her. The main thing was to save the puppies. In the middle of the garden, knee-deep in mud, she stubbornly stood and looked toward the yard until the uncles got into the car and drove away.

The child wasn't scolded for this act. Instead, everyone laughed. However, two days later, she faced bitter disappointment. When she got home from school, Boba and Toba didn't greet her.

"Eat these candies yourself. You sold Boba and Toba for them," she shouted, then ran to her room to cry. Neither her mother's comfort nor her grandmother's explanation had any effect on her. She also told her father at length how evil he was for giving the puppies to those people. She didn't even touch the candies.

One of the most crucial household chores assigned to the sisters was herding geese. Each year, the flocks consisted of forty to sixty birds. The grandmother raised them herself, and the sisters enjoyed participating in this task. Alongside the grandmother, they went to feed and water the entire flock. They also collected eggs and carefully placed them in pre-prepared boxes. After a while, the grandmother put the selected eggs under the goose. For almost a month, the girls eagerly awaited the appearance of the first goslings. The happiest moments were when, in the middle of the night, the sisters were woken up by the soft squeak of the first goslings, which my grandmother usually took into the house. The girls hugged them and kissed them.

One day, the grandmother brought an egg in which the gosling was less than half hatched. After waiting for the grandmother to go out, the sisters attempted to help the chick break free from its shell. When they noticed the first drops of blood, they ran to the grandmother in fear and tears, shouting, 'Save him!' However, the grandmother gently reassured them, explaining that such efforts were unnecessary. Nature has a plan, and God gives the tiny chicks the strength to hatch on their own. The time spent inside the egg is vital for the proper formation of their bodies, and human interference can disrupt this natural process. The sisters carried this lesson with them for the rest of their lives.

The worst thing was being alone with the flock's leader. Usually, it was a proud, beautiful giant goose who protected his entire family from uninvited guests. More than once, the girls saw him chase away not only cats and dogs, but also their grandmother and mother. Because of this, the sisters never went into the pen alone.

But, leading his large family to the pasture like a chieftain with his majestic figure, the giant goose was proud of himself. It was enough for him to spread his wings and caw, and the whole flock instantly followed him, flying away until their echoes spread around. At these moments, catching up with them and bursting into loud, joyful laughter, the girls believed that the geese were carrying them on their wings to the horizon.

In the pasture, the girls stepped carefully on the stubble so it wouldn't prick them. They lay on the warm ground and embarked on imaginary journeys through sandy deserts, endless seas, wide rivers, and steep banks, along with flowering gardens and fragrant meadows. This filled the children's hearts with peace and calm. "What artist, and with what colors, could paint such incredibly fabulous grandeur?" Miia thought again and again.

The geese had already gone back home on their own, and the girls, lying in the middle of the field, fantasized and enjoyed

10

the magical creations of God.

The girl's first love happened when she was seven. Her first-grade friends had already felt it. Vika loved the boy she went to kindergarten with. Nadia was in love with a neighbor's boy who often took her to school on his bike. The feeling of inferiority weighed on Miia, and she also wanted to be with the girls as an equal. Then, this day arrived. A handsome Italian actor and singer captured Miia's heart. She didn't even realize he was the idol of all women because she didn't understand much about it. She was just proud of her taste.

The girl grew up without any interest in the boys at her school. Many liked her, and each tried to get her attention in their own way. She ignored the messages from her admirers. She turned down their help if they happened to meet her in the library or store. Similarly, she paid no attention to the cyclists who constantly had something broken near her yard. When Miia turned fourteen, the brave young man gave her a record with new songs by Tetty, hoping that such a gift would catch her attention and that he would become the knight of her heart. But Miia thanked him for the luxurious present, kissed him on the cheek, put the rest of her pocket money in his pocket so she wouldn't consider herself a debtor, and ran home. Once there, she locked herself in her room, listened to her idol's songs, and imagined herself happy, walking along narrow stone streets somewhere in Rome or Milan. The girl saw photographs of the same streets in magazines. Architecturally, they were completely different from the streets of Soviet cities or villages, fueling her dreams of imaginary travels. The lack of opportunity to see them herself always made Miia want to cry, and she didn't hold back.

"What happened? Why are you crying?" the father asked, surprised as he entered the room.

"Oh, I rubbed my eye, and an eyelash got into it." This was the main excuse Miia used to justify herself when she was in tears.

The day finally came when the girl summoned the courage to tell her whole family she loved Tatty. She was tired of always making up new excuses for her shifting moods, which went from cheerful to sad. She also wanted to learn her idol's

11

favorite songs, but doing so without getting caught was impossible.

One day, while watching her granddaughter, the grandmother couldn't take it anymore and stepped in:

"Miia, you have already ruined that record by moving it to the same place for the thirtieth time."

"But I can't understand this phrase." The twelve-year-old girl was nervous.

Without being distracted from knitting, the grandmother quickly uttered the words from the song.

After listening to this passage again, the girl ran up to her grandmother and hugged her tightly.

"Thank you, grandma!" and left with a sheet of paper, cheerfully humming the words of an Italian song that she had just written down in Ukrainian letters.

II

Years passed quickly. In two weeks, Miia will turn seventeen. In the southern part of the country, real spring arrived at the beginning of April. After the spring school holidays, girls no longer wear boots, jackets, and hats. The start of the fourth school term was always the most anticipated time for every student, as it marked the beginning of the two months before the end of the school year and the long-awaited summer break.

It was a warm day in April outside. As usual, the schoolyard was filled with the lively activity of students who headed home promptly after the last lessons.

Not far from the school building, Miia's classmates stood with older boys. When she passed by, an unexpected address from one of them caught her attention.

"Have you started learning to play the guitar?"

The girl last heard his sweet voice three years ago, when he handed her a Tatty record with trembling hands.

"Started," she answered, without saying hello.

"I can help with the chords," Mark said as he approached her, looking her in the eye.

This proposal caught Miia off guard since she and Mark hadn't spoken in nearly three years. Even when they were part of the same friend group, Mark's behavior showed that he ignored Miia, and she acted as if she was utterly indifferent to his actions. The only typical interaction between them was arguing, usually whenever Miia asked to play her idol's songs. Each time, without hesitation, Mark would walk up to the speakers and deliberately change the record. This frustrated her. Usually, the boys cheered, and the girls scolded Mark, repeating the phrase, "You look like you're from a kindergarten class." But the boy stayed stubborn. Miia knew Mark liked her. She also liked him. But she pushed those feelings aside, convinced that her inner peace only came from thoughts of her distant idol.

"Are you kidding?" Disbelief flashed across her face.

"No. I'm serious."

"What kind of miracles?" the girl asked, narrowing her eyes with ironic curiosity.

13

"A dream," he said with a smile.

"Wow! Did I dream of you? With a guitar or an axe?" she continued playfully.

"Don't flatter yourself." He grimaced and added with the same irony, "I only dreamed once. With a guitar. And so, I don't dream of you with an axe, I decided to offer my help."

"And what will you ask in return, Your Acting Majesty? To dance a polka or a lambada?" Narrowing her eyes, the young lady continued to ironize.

"I see your Lambada at every disco. Polka at local concerts. Is there anything else on your list?"

He got so close that Miia could smell the chocolate scent of his breath. At that moment, her heart started pounding so loudly it felt like it might jump out of her chest if Mark moved even slightly toward her. They gazed into each other's eyes.

"I know you play well and could share skills, but don't waste your time on me." She felt she needed to pull herself together.

The young man was quiet. Moving away from the girl, he looked around.

Mark was two years older than Miia. He began playing the guitar professionally after starting to study at a music school at the age of twelve. This allowed him, after graduation, to attend a theater and art school. To please Miia, he learned a couple of Tatty Migelti's songs; he wanted to become like him. But he never dared to sing them. This secret was shared with Miia's friend Nina by Mark's closest friend, Illia.

"Lots of homework," and, looking into the distance, smiling, she continued. "Sleep well. With an ax in my hands, I promise, you won't dream."

At that moment, Mark took her left hand to look at her fingertips. There were blisters from the strings.

"I see you're trying. Does it hurt?" the guy asked gently, stroking her hand. Miia was silent. "It will stop hurting. Your fingers need to get used to it," and showed her the fingertip of her left hand.

Miia saw the guitarist's actual fingers, but she didn't dare to touch them. The friends nearby, although trying to create an atmosphere of active discussion about musical rehearsals, kept looking back at Miia and Mark with surprised expressions. The girl began to feel herself blush again, and her hand was squeezed even tighter in Mark's hand.

"Bye, Mark!"

Miia looked at her hand. The young man, with his characteristic artistry, bent down and opened his palm. The girl, without looking back, went to her friends who were waiting for her nearby.

"Mark, what role did we see in the rehearsal this time?" asked Illia, Miia's classmate.

"Othello," Mark answered coldly, looking after the girl.

"Don't even think about it, because it would be a crime." The guys started joking.

"Is she seeing someone?" Not paying attention to the jokes of his friends, the young man asked.

"Yes," Illia nodded, quickly replying in a serious tone.

Mark instantly turned to the guys with a frozen surprise on his face. A bitter lump choked the young man's throat.

"With whom?" he asked discontentedly, narrowing his eyes. The guys glanced at each other. The silence lingered. Everyone stayed silent.

"Well, with whom?" Illia looked at his friends. "Her heart is busy."

Mark's inquisitive gaze seemed to pierce his friends, who, with sad expressions on their faces, looked at each other. In those few seconds, Mark pictured a happy Miia with a neighbor's boy, who was older, well-mannered, and handsome. The young man recalled his stubbornness over Tatty's songs, which Miia enjoyed, and even acknowledged that he had been a complete fool for his behavior, arguing with the girl. Mark looked menacingly at his friends, demanding an answer.

"You have a serious competitor," Oleg said, scratching the back of his head.

"We were only gone for a month. Did we miss anything?" Timko asked, spreading his hands in surprise as he looked at Mark.

But his friend stood silently, as if frozen in place. He wasn't afraid of competition because he was confident that almost every girl would be eager to meet him. At school, girls often slipped him love notes. Naturally, this boosted Mark's confidence and fed his narcissism. All his efforts to showcase

15

his youthful charm always paid off. However, he often mocked the girls rudely, annoyed that the note wasn't from Miia.

The guy's loud laughter made Mark come to his senses.

"What's with the face, my friend? Relax! We don't think that Tatty Migelti is your serious competitor." Illia blurted out, still laughing.

"Damn comedians." Mark, walking up to him and giving him a push on the shoulder, exhaled with relief. Threatening his friend with his fist, Mark continued, "Tell me, thank you for not hitting. I thought, sinfully, that the lucky one was Yura, the grandson of her neighbor."

"The one who's a military man? He's about to get married," Illia hurried to reassure his friend.

"Mark, I don't know, but it seemed to me that you weren't indifferent to her after all." Mark's eyes lit up. "What about Mila?"

"Mila," Mark repeated, smiling. "I am not a monk..."

The warm rays of the sun played with the breeze as if competing for dominance in nature. The blue sky smiled down at the fluffy, curly clouds drifting across it. Blooming gardens released gentle fragrances. The beautiful green cover of the earth was proud of its beauty and tenderness. Birds chirped joyfully, carrying dreams and hopes on their wings. Spring is always so wonderfully magical. Without rushing anywhere, the girls let their dreams take them into the distant future, where they imagined themselves as happy, successful, and famous. And the stormy fantasies of reaching their goals slowed down their flights, causing only laughter.

"We stop because of such considerations." Taking a breath after another humorous statement, Miia eagerly inhaled the fragrant air and, closing her eyes, whispered, "What magical days have come with April?"

"I watched your conversation." After a long silence, Ksenia's voice rang out like thunder in a clear sky. "What was that? What happened to him? Did you see Timko and Illia's eyes?" She made circles with her fingers around her eyes, mimicking her friends' eyes in surprise.

"No." Miia's voice radiated calm. "I only saw Mark," she

16

laughed out loud. "Oh, my Tatty! I feel so safe with you. It was enough for me to cry bitterly to your songs. And now?" laughing even louder, the girl continued. "Cry to Mark's songs? Where did he get his?" Miia parodied in an angelic voice. "He got me."

"Admit it, do you like him?" Vera's voice was both warm and cunning.

"Who is?"

"Mark. He's handsome, and many girls like him." Xenia's phrase sounded like a warning.

"I know, and what?" Miia's tone became icy.

"How, what? You can meet him."

"Are you serious?" the girl interrupted her.

"Why not?"

"Do you think he's reliable for the meeting?" Miia hesitated at first, then continued confusedly. "Listen, I'm sixteen; he's already nineteen."

"So what? You're almost seventeen," stated Xenia.

"Seventeen," repeated Miia. He studies in one city. I plan to study in another." Stopping, and with a pretentious expression on her face, Miia asked. "What will we do with each other? He is in the east; I am in the west."

"Write letters." Her friend did not stop. "And come home on weekends."

"Xenia, you noticed that he is not at home every weekend. I am sure that he is not sad there." Miia felt a slight irritation: "He does not study at the theological seminary."

"And what is the theological seminary for?" Her friend blocked the way and looked at her inquisitively. "And... I understand... How do you manage to do it like that? Oh, character." With an essential expression on her face, Xenia nodded at Miia.

"Do I have a bad character?" Miia looked at her friend and smiled, surprised.

"I didn't say bad, by the way. You have the character of a rebel. You would have been shot during the revolution." Guilt flashed across Xenia's face.

"I know. And in the Middle Ages, I would have been burned at the stake for disobedience." Miia added.

Loud laughter engulfed the girls.

17

"You like him. Noticeable!" Xenia was always straightforward.

"Oh, my God!" Miia raised her hands to the sky. "Girls, the topic is the castle. Yesterday's incident with the historian still bothers me," she sighed, shrugged her shoulders, and continued. "Why did she give me a two-point grade? I told her everything about the lesson topic and pointed out that Lenin had nothing to do with it."

Xenia and Vera exchanged glances. It became clear to them that continuing to talk about Mark was useless.

"She is a passionate communist. Sparks seemed to fly from her eyes when you revealed everything about Lenin." Vera didn't hesitate to comment.

"In general, the era of glasnost and democracy has arrived. We have the right to openly and freely share our thoughts," protested Xenia.

"That's what I'm saying? Lenin brought along criminals, idlers, and drunks who lived and waited for permission to kill, steal, and take others' property. Of course, there were factory workers among them who believed in the proletarian idea. But in their bloodthirstiness, they are no different from all the other Bolshevik crowds. Lenin called the West "decadent," and he lived in the countries of the same "decadent West." Breaking the silence, Miia repeated her speech, which caused great anger in the history teacher. As a result, the student was kicked out of the classroom with the words 'Don't come to my lessons anymore,' and she was given a two on her report card.

"You told her everything so boldly and confidently that it irritated her." Vera looked at her friend. Miia noticed the anxiety in her eyes.

"I can't do it like you. I'm calmer," said Xenia.

"You had a calm childhood; that's why you can't do it like that." Miia's tone evened out. "My father is a communist. And what? An exemplary person? Therefore, it's more anger than courage," she interrupted herself and turned to her friend. "By the way, Vera, I believe you didn't tell Claudia Ivanivna at home about the argument with the historian."

"Of course not." Her voice was confidently firm.

Vera's mother worked as a school principal. She was kind, sensitive, and fair as a person and a very talented and dedicated teacher of mathematics, algebra, and geometry. The students found her lessons to be the most interesting.

"Vera, I beg you, promise that you will remain silent. No, swear that you will not tell." Blocking her friend's way, Miia looked into her eyes even more demandingly.

"But what will happen if she finds out?" Xenia asked.

"Whatever happens, Miia answers without thinking."

Vera assured that she would not discuss the incident, explaining that she did not understand the implications of her mother's actions as the school principal. She said goodbye to the girls and went home along her street.

Walking along the dam that separates the last street of the village where Miia and Xenia lived, the girls remembered how, during the February thaw, forty-centimeter snow began to melt quickly. They strolled along the same road in sneakers with wet feet up to their knees. That day, they were in such a rush to get to the volleyball practice that they forgot to pick up their boots from the school locker room in time, the key to which the cleaning lady took home with her. In the morning, they went to school in the same sneakers. Back then, having spare boots was considered a luxury. But the girls didn't even think about it. So, with pride and laughter, they bravely walked that path in front of many residents, who were surprised and delighted by the sight. Glancing at their sneakers to justify themselves, the girls hurried to share the stories of their boots' adventures. After cheerful memories, Miia said with a sad tone in her voice:

"You know, Xenia, I go to school for two days with the same textbooks."

"What again?"

"Yes, we spent two nights at Katrina's. I'm going to her again."

"And when will you go home?"

"Grandma will tell me when I can come back."

A wave of helplessness washed over Miia. For a moment, she remembered how often she, her mother, and her older sister had to spend nights at her mother's workplace, where bags of sugar or cereal served as their beds. She recalled hiding in one neighbor's then another's, while their father, holding a belt, searched for them, threatening the neighbors

19

who always insisted no visitors came to their place. When returning home in winter, they would constantly look up at the chimney. If there was smoke, it meant they could safely go home because their father was sober and had lit the stove. She also remembered how many times their grandmother met them in the middle of the street, holding books in her hands, telling them, 'Go to Katrina' or 'Go to the Kovalevs,' fully aware that their father was already drunk.

The trouble was that his father's drinking was not enough for one day. Three or four days became the norm, so girls had to wander around the neighborhood. One day, his older sister packed up her things and went to live with relatives. Their daughter was a classmate of her sister. Her father tried to bring Zhanna home, but she was unyielding and only returned a month later.

"She's my favorite teacher, too," Xenia said with pride in her voice. "What? You'll say it in physical education? Well, you know what to say."

"Yeah, I'll have to make it up." Miia laughed, winking.

"History tomorrow," Xenia said after a moment of silence.

"I'm not going. And I'm not going to come to those damn communists' lessons until the end of the year." There was firmness in the girl's voice.

"Wow. You surprise me." Xenia couldn't help but believe her friend's words. "And the certificate?"

"Whatever happens, it will happen."

"Does mom know about the incident with Galina Markivna?"

"Yes, I told her."

"And what does she think about this?"

"You can't expect anything good from the communists," Miia repeated her mother's phrase verbatim. "I confessed to her because I knew she would support me."

For a while, the girls walked in silence.

"Regarding Mark."

"Don't start again." Not letting Xenia continue, Miia interrupted her. "At the moment, this is not something that should worry me."

At the intersection, the girls said farewell and went their separate ways.

III

A month and a half passed quickly. Preparing for final exams took a lot of time and effort. Every day, the excitement grew stronger. The only outlet that kept Miia afloat during the intense exam routine was the guitar.

Miia recalls the day Zhanna entered the yard with a brand-new six-string guitar. At that moment, Miia's breath was taken away by just one glance at the musical beauty.

"Don't even think about approaching her." Zhanna's eyes lit up menacingly.

Their father had an old seven-string Cuban guitar. However, these guitars are no longer played by modern youth. Miia made all kinds of suggestions to her sister so that she would let her study too. Her sister's icy heart melted, and she agreed, but on one condition: when Zhanna was at home, Miia would not pick up the guitar. In exchange for keeping this promise, Miia would receive new chords.

Happiness was endless. The girl started to dream of singing the song 'The prom is over; let's say goodbye to it forever' at the school celebration, and she began preparing carefully for that performance.

And then that day arrived. The children eagerly gathered in the classrooms, anticipating the start of the solemn ceremony. Everything around them exuded a festive atmosphere. Miia felt panic take hold of her. Her breathing grew faster and faster. She tried to find her strength, but she realized it had left her.

"And now, in honor of our school family and all of us, the 10th-grade graduate will sing a song," the host said.

Miia felt the gaze of hundreds of eyes shining with kindness. The only eyes that burned her with their fire were Mark's eyes. Anger and despair overtook her. At some point, it seemed to her that she hated him for being there because she was sure that on this day, he should have been studying in the city. And so, every step toward the microphone started to feel like a step on a razor's edge into the abyss.

Meeting Klaudia Ivanovna's eyes, Miia began to regain her self-control. She grabbed the guitar. Both microphones were already set up. The girl felt worried. Her mother's loving smile and the teacher's two raised fists gave her confidence. The first chord sounded, then the second. With the opening words of the song, some people started to wipe away tears. 'Oh God, don't look at them,' flashed through the girl's mind. 'Don't look!' Her fingers skillfully strummed the strings. Miia's mother was crying. No matter how hard her daughter tried to hold back, she couldn't. The girl sensed her mother's sadness, and tears filled her own eyes.

"Sorry." The lump in her throat kept her from saying a word. The school principal approached her and, hugging her, said: Don't worry, child! Today, you are truly like birds from a song – you have grown up and are flying away from your nest. So let these tears be the last, and may success, joy, happiness, and love be with you always.

After the formal ceremony, teachers, relatives, and friends started to approach the graduates with congratulations. The sadness faded, and the lively noise sounded like birds chirping.

"You, smart girl," like thunder in the middle of a clear sky, Mark's voice sounded. The girl was stunned. She felt his hot breath. Taking her hand, the young man turned her to him.

"I admit, I didn't think that in such a short time, you would be able to learn the song." Mark looked intently into her eyes. She attempted to put out the fire burning inside her.

"I'm diligent." His mysterious smile puzzled her.

"Mark, we're waiting for you." Mark's younger sister, Nona, appeared next to them.

Looking around, Miia saw that Timko was standing nearby, having recently started to appear with Nona. Miia's classmate Mila was standing with him.

"What happened? Go, I'll catch up with you." And turning her sister around by the shoulders, he pushed her toward Timko and Mila.

Anger and rage surged through Miia. She finally understood, unexpectedly, Nona's friendship with Mila.

'Oh, don't be ashamed... Control your emotions!' an inner voice commanded the girl. She couldn't afford to show weakness or jealousy. She knew that doing so would leave her defenseless in front of him. She can`t humiliate herself.

"Mark, I don't want to keep you. Go, they're waiting for you."

22

"They'll wait," his face flashed with displeasure.

"I don't understand you... Go!" she said, and she walked towards her classmates, who had already started discussing the prom.

The first three exams resulted in one grade of five and two fours. In terms of academic success, the girl always maintained a balance. Therefore, her exam results were well justified. History remained her subject of choice, which did not cause her any anxiety. Her knowledge of history was at a high level. However, her principled nature took precedence. Only God knew how everything would turn out. That day, Miia woke up before sunrise. She didn't want to sleep. The fairy-tale magic of the morning fascinated her with its mystery. Distant stars, one after another, dissolved into space. On the other side of the sky, the transparent moon still smiled. Tired from night concerts, crickets fell silent in the grass, and frogs quieted in the reeds. Somewhere far away, nightingales were still singing and larks were singing. Waking up, the roosters started crowing nonstop, and the sparrows chirped under the roof. Everyone greeted the new day!

Miia stood in the middle of the yard and admired the enchanting morning scene. The first rays of the sun softly touched her face. Closing her eyes and feeling their warmth, the girl smiled gently. Her soul was filled with divine light, and her heart with kindness. At that moment, it felt as if invisible wings had lifted her and carried her through the endless universe, filling it with energy. From all this power, her thoughts became clear. The girl didn't know what a new day held, but she appreciated it for such a magical beginning.

"Are you ready?" Vera asked her as she met her on the way to school.

"Always ready!"

The examination committee members took their seats. The classroom was filled with the charming scent of peonies. The tickets, stolen from the red tablecloth, were already waiting for the first five brave participants. The students were called into the room. The seating arrangements for the examinees were designed so the committee could easily monitor each one. The others waited at the back of the classroom. Some reread their cheat sheets, while others quietly rustled

23

the pages of their textbooks. Meanwhile, two of the head splitters started playing Sea Battle, and watching them was impossible not to laugh.

Miia remembered how, back in seventh grade, a geography lesson was disrupted. The behavior of those two troublemakers caused complete chaos among the students. To get everyone's attention, the teacher lined up the entire class in the school's central hall so that everyone could be seen, then had them loudly repeat, 'Be disciplined!'

And it began... 'Be disciplined. Be disciplined.' Thirty-two voices blared continuously for ten minutes until the lesson ended, and then there was a ten-minute break. Teachers and students from all over the school started to converge. They all laughed at the seventh graders like they were clowns in a circus. It was a shame.

Returning to her memories, Miia noticed that gradually the number of students waiting for their turn was decreasing. When she and Vera were left alone, Miia calmly asked her friend:

"Who's next?"

"So that you don't end up last, you go."

Approaching the examiners, Miia greeted them politely. An arrogant, impudent smile appeared on the history teacher's face. The girl's eyes flashed with hostility towards this person.

"Well, Miia," said Klaudia Ivanovna, "Be bolder."

At that moment, Miia felt a strange lightness take over her soul. Without taking her eyes off Galina Mykytivna, she calmly said, "I won't take the exam," and left the classroom. The principal ran out after her.

"Miia, what just happened?" Catching up with the girl in the corridor and grabbing her hand, the principal asked excitedly. "What happened?" She looked around and turned to Miia's classmates. "I'm asking you. What's going on?"

But everyone was silent, their heads down.

"Why are you silent?" Tatiana Mikhalivna turned her gaze to Miia. "This is the final exam. What are you doing?" she turned to her classmates again. "Vera, Tania, Sasha." Everyone was silent.

Miia realized that she was putting everyone in an awkward

24

position.

"Ask Galina Mykytivna." She nodded toward the office. "Let her explain first."

Without waiting for further explanations, she said goodbye and left the school. Driven by an unknown determination, the girl immediately began working for her mother.

We need to let her know about the act. I am sure that Klavdiya Ivanivna will ask her mother about her daughter's behavior, the girl said to herself, crossing herself.

On her way home, she didn't want to think about anything. She only wanted one thing: to pick up her guitar and quietly play, strumming the chords. She didn't care what mood her father was in. She wasn't afraid. The desert of silence inside her mind swallowed all the excitement.

"May I congratulate you?" Surprisingly, her father was sober.

"Yes," she replied, looking at him attentively. He remained silent, surprised. Miia was gazing at him intensely. "Zhanna doesn't want to come home on weekends because of you. Aren't you tired of vodka?" Such a question made her father feel embarrassed.

"What, is it because of me?"

"Listen, we're adults now. You can't even imagine how ashamed we are. Oh, my God! Don't you comprehend that your alcohol consumption has deprived Zhanna and me of a peaceful childhood and my mother of a happy family life? When will you stop?

"What are you talking about? I'm not a drunkard."

"Do you believe that? Do you even remember how proud you once were of your membership in the Communist Party? How many years have gone by since you were expelled from it? Six. And have you counted how many times my mother left you? Do you even see how unhappy your grandmother is?" Miia's eyes filled with tears. "Zhanna is seeing a guy. She wants to introduce him to you. But how can she introduce someone to you, especially someone like you were yesterday?" Despair filled her heart.

"Wait".

Miia wanted to keep going, but her grandmother stepped in, and the girl didn't want to continue the conversation in her

25

presence.

"I went to play the guitar."

In the evening, my mother mentioned, but without details, her conversation with the school principal. Miia knew that her mother's stance perfectly reflected her own. 'First, let the teacher explain his words and actions.' Principle was not an inherent trait of Miia`s mother's character. She always prioritized compromise and taught her daughters the same lesson.

Two days later, Miia was rushing to school for a meeting about the graduation ball. The physics teacher's car was approaching and stopped next to her.

"Good afternoon, Mykola Viktorovich!"

"Good afternoon, Miia! I have something to tell you. But first, give me an answer. Is your stance on the history exam firm and unchangeable?" Miia was silent. He looked at her with a probing look. "You are silent, so you are firm. However, think carefully."

Miia realized that if Mykola Viktorovich is discussing this, then Claudia Ivanivna is aware of the incident.

"I won't go," she thought for a moment and replied.

"Then, listen. The main thing is to understand everything clearly and keep it private. Without passing the history exam, Galina Mykytivna refuses to include grades in your certificate, which accurately reflect your knowledge. She wants you to come." He looked at the girl closely.

"Mykola Viktorovich, your family knows very well what the main problem in our family is." The girl began to get irritated: "The trouble is that people like Galina Mykytivna have not responded for decades, despite all our requests and hopes. I know that they will demand an apology from me. But I have nothing to apologize for. In my opinion, which I shared in that lesson, it has not changed; in fact, it has even strengthened my confidence in my judgments. Therefore, I see no reason to contact her."

"Without taking the exam, the school administration can only give you a three."

"I will be sincerely grateful for that!" the girl sighed with relief.

"But you understand that this will affect the average score of

26

the certificate," he said.

"It will be as it will be." Miia blushed, either from joy or from shame, because her principled stance led the school administration to make a decision.

"The main thing is not to regret it. You're planning to go to the institute, right?" His gaze was curious, but there was no judgment in it. The girl nodded her head. Mykola Viktorovich looked at her and smiled, then continued: "You have a passing score for entrance. Good luck to you!"

Feeling a sudden wave of relief, Miia smiled happily, thanked him, and cheerfully walked to the school. In the classroom, Vera hurried over to her: "Listen." Her eyes were intense, her breath was quick, and her voice trembled so much that Miia felt confused just looking at her. "My mom, Klaudia Ivanivna, comes in and starts questioning me about why you refused to take the exam. I told her I don't know anything. Then, Dad joins her." It was clear from Vera that she was nervous. "They cornered me like a rat and threatened that they wouldn't let me out until I told them." Miia started laughing.

However, quickly shifting away from feelings of resentment, Miia smiled and showed her friend the certificate.

"Vera, I wonder what would have h appened to Galina Mykytivna if I had told her, in detail, about the baptismal ceremony I experienced." Her face lit up with a sly smile, her mysterious gaze fixed on her friend. "I can't imagine," she finally said, but was silent for half a minute before continuing with a smile, "You never told me about it, partisan. When was that?"

"In April 1986. In Kakhovka. Grandma and mama took me with them to the church. After my mother's brother died, they performed a ceremony to protect his grave from evil spirits.

"How does that work?"

"It's when you take a handful of earth from the grave, bring it to the church for a special prayer service, and then scatter the earth in the shape of a cross on the grave when you return. Until this ceremony is done, it's believed evil spirits might try to take over the deceased's body. The cross of earth, blessed in the church, acts as a talisman."

"Sounds like a spooky fairy tale about the afterlife..."
"Which we can't see with our eyes; we can only feel."
"Do you have godparens? What do you know about them?"
"Yes," the girl started to say, "my godmother's name is Maria, and my father's name is Mikhail. My grandmother wanted me to be baptized for a very long time. But what were those times? My father is a communist, my mother and grandmother are honored workers of socialist labor, my sister is a Komsomol member, and I am a pioneer. With such baggage, you can't go to church... The time has come. Father reads prayers. We are standing. There are five of us. A young man with cerebral palsy, about seventeen. Two twin sisters. They are around nine years old, a boy, six years old, and I. Then the father started approaching each of us to perform the ritual of anointing with holy oil. I was the last person he reached. At times, I found myself standing there without really understanding why I was there. I wanted to laugh, then cry. Especially when I remembered my uncle's funeral, I remembered his body in the coffin, which sat in the middle of the hall, and how we were afraid to go in because it seemed like he might get up and speak to us. And how the prayer songs filled the air. They filled the soul with the bitterness of wormwood, then with the scents of linden. I didn't understand their words, but the melody surrounding them was so enchanting and soft that it felt like they were melodies from Heaven itself, given to us by the Creator for our humility and repentance." Vera stood deep in thought. Was a moment of silence. Then, c rossing herself, Miia cheerfully continued. "The peace of my soul disappeared like mist in the sun when the priest approached me. 'Your name, servant of God?' First, I was confused by the word slave instead of child. I replied that my name was Miia. He responded by chanting 'Maria' over and over while reciting the prayers. I didn't understand, so I repeated, "Miia." After reciting the prayers and crossing himself three times, the holy father bowed to my feet. But I couldn't calm down, because I wasn't Maria. I stood there, confused, not fully appreciating the sacredness of the moment. ' Maybe he's

28

deaf, calling me Maria?' I thought. So, I said again, loudly, so he could hear: 'Oh, Father, my name is Miia!' He stopped, looked at me with pity, crossed the backs of my hands, and bent down to anoint my feet. Then he i nterrupted the prayers and continued in a chant: "Servant of God Maria, don't argue with the priest, but rather take off your socks." After that, I gave up on myself."

"Why take off your socks?"

"To anoint your skin with holy oil, not the fabric of your socks. Everyone else was standing barefoot. I also thought they were fools. And it turned out I was like that myself. The name Maria is my baptismal name because, among church names, there is no Miia. My baptism story didn't e nd there. Two days later, on Tuesday, an inspector from the district education department visited the school. His visit interrupted the geography lesson. For fifteen minutes, he talked about atheism and religion as poisons for humanity. At the end, he asked, 'And tell me, children, which of you or your friends is baptized?' I stayed silent.

"I remember something like that. That day, our geography lesson was in the biology classroom because the glass in the geography classroom was being replaced. And that guy had such an unpleasant, cunning face and a disgusting, hoarse voice."

"He was a classmate of my mother. In his youth, he had courted her. But my mother frankly wanted nothing to do with him. She was afraid. His father and uncles served in the NKVD. Her mother told my mother that all the villagers hated them. They were cruel to everyone, regardless of gender or age. One of the stories is the most terrible. They were looking for an enemy of the people. They decided that he was hiding among the Roma. So, t hey organized and personally participated in the murder of several Roma families, along with children, women, and the elderly. They quietly crept up at night. They left no one alive. Someone was shot, and another was stabbed. Thirty-four people were killed that night, and t hose they were looking for were not found.

And so that there was something to report upstairs, they

arrested my mother's uncle instead. He was convicted and sent to the camps. What happened to him next? No one ever found out."

"Hm, Galyna Mykytivna needs to start getting baptized and asking God for forgiveness for the actions of her party members."

"First, she needs to believe in God."

IV

The summer is in full swing. But this summer, for Miia, became very stressful, both physically and emotionally. Preparing for the entrance exams to the agricultural institute at the economics faculty was pretty nerve-wracking. At her father's request, his cousin agreed to let Miia live with them, specifying the fee. The mother wasn't even surprised by this because everyone in the family knew that Aunt Irina was distinguished by her arrogant and selfish character.

For two weeks, while staying with them, Miia was not allowed to turn on the light in her designated room after ten at night to save money. You could only take items from the refrigerator in the presence of either your aunt or her husband. When asking their daughter, 'Why is there such a ban?' Miia received an answer she couldn't expect.

"Diet is more important than anything."

Uncle Lexey was a very well-mannered, polite, and kind person. One day, after taking his wife and daughter to the store, he came to Miia's room and said, "Child, when we are at home together, please feel completely free. I am not going to control you. As a child, my mother did not restrict me. And in your family, there are no restrictions on food."

"Thank you. My needs are simple so that I won't cause you any trouble," she replied with a smile. 'How does he live with that visper? And a daughter, just like her mother,' the girl thought, but she didn't dwell on her thoughts because she didn't feel good about herself, thinking poorly of the people who had given her a room, even though she had to pay for her stay. 'Nothing; I can manage three more days. One more exam, and I'll be home.' The ice cream lifted her spirits, and she kept taking notes on the preparatory exam material: 'The first exam in language and literature was passed with a score of four. Three days later, I had algebra and geometry.'

Thanks to Claudia Ivanivna, the girl had no problems with these subjects.

One evening, Irina's aunt's daughter, Valia, and her friend invited Miia for a walk. Their classmate joined them. It was impossible not to notice that Valia and Tania's behavior was not condescending towards Ivan. This caused unpleasant feelings in Miia, so she tried with all her might to protect the guy. But he did not react to their stinging words in any way and calmly continued talking to Miia. She was surprised by his self-control. The next day, Ivan invited Miia for a walk around the city. He said that he wanted to celebrate his entrance to the institute in this way. Despite the need to prepare for exams, Miia agreed.

Ivan and Miia spent almost the entire day together. They visited attractions, went to the horror room, took a walk in Central Park, and strolled along the embankment. Most notably, Miia rode a river tram for the first time. She was comfortable being herself because talking with Ivan was so easy. She also wasn't ashamed that she was born and raised in the village. Ivan was educated, intelligent, and wise beyond his years. There were moments when it seemed to them that they had known each other all their lives.

Returning home, Ivan offered her his help in preparing for the exams, and Miia agreed again. Over the next two days, they attended consultations at her university together. To avoid distracting Miia in the classrooms, he waited for her in the very top rows of the auditorium. Afterward, at the student café or in the university library, they worked through problems, equations, and theorems together.

On exam day, he arrived with flowers to pick her up. These were her first flowers, a gift from a young man. While she was taking the exam, he waited for her in the hallway. Afterwards, they went together to collect her things. That day, she was headed home.

"Aunt Ira, Uncle Lexey, I sincerely thank you for sheltering me." At that moment, Miia genuinely appreciated them, and it was visible in her eyes.

"Child, Ivan is a wonderful boy from a good family. He likes you. His father was interested in you." Miia was surprised by her aunt's revelation. "I wanted life to have more mercy on you than on your mother."

"And I want that too."

On their way to the bus station, Miia and Ivan were nearly silent. Both knew what the other was quietly thinking.

"In how many days will the entrance results be announced?" Ivan asked sadly.

"Next Thursday."

"You'll come, right?"

"Definitely."

"Then there's no need to be sad; we'll see each other next week," he said with a smile.

"I'll come." Cute smiles shone on their faces.

For a week, Miia felt cheerful and full of pleasant expectations. Her thoughts were occupied with memories of meeting Ivan, their walks around the city, and his support while studying for the exams. The only person she confided in about the young man was her mother. Ivan was not like everyone else Miia knew. And although they were the same age, in mind and actions, he was different from his peers.

"You'll know the results tomorrow." Entering the room, her mother hugged her daughter.

"Mommy, I'm so worried."

"Me too. I hope you get into a university similar to Zhanna's. Without higher education, it's hard to get a better position, where there's more respect and a higher salary."

"I want to study at a university myself."

"Let's go to bed since we have to be at the bus stop by five tomorrow. Good night!"

"Good night, mom!"

While reading through the lists of students enrolled in the first year, Miia couldn't find her name.

"Are you enrolled?" Ivan's voice asked.

"No," Miia replied, turning to him with despair in her eyes.

"I looked at the exam result lists; you have two fours. With those grades, you should have been enrolled."

"I suppose that." Miia looked at him thoughtfully.

"What?" the young man looked at her intently. "Let's go to the dean's office; we'll find out everything now," and, grabbing her hand, they left.

Ivan went in with Miia and, without letting her say a word, asked about her exam results.

"Yes, Miia Borko." The methodologist took the girl's case. "Ivan, I'm sorry. The exams were passed, but considering the average score of the certificate, half a point was not enough for admission." Turning to Miia, she asked? "Are you taking the documents now?"

33

"Yes," the girl answered firmly.

After waiting for the documents, Miia thanked her and left the office.

"Give me the certificate," Ivan said as he walked down the corridor. Looking at the grades, Ivan stopped her.

"Talking to you, I wouldn't say that history and social studies were the worst subjects for you at school."

"Until April of this year, it was like that."

"Listen, maybe we can still fix the situation with your enrollment."

Miia looked at him in surprise.

"Ivan, how does this woman know you?"

"I'll talk to my father today; ask him to influence the decision and get you enrolled."

"Father?" Miia was even more surprised.

"He's the vice-rector of this university," the young man answered modestly.

"Don't get your dad involved in something that neither of you nor he has anything to do with, Ivan. I knew what I was getting into. Promise me that you won't talk about me to your father."

"Why?" he exclaimed in despair.

"Because no!" Miia firmly emphasized.

They walked to the bus station. On the way, the girl told him about the incident with the history teacher and how it all ended. He fully supported her principled stance and confessed to a similar story that had happened to him, which had caused his father a lot of trouble.

"How hot we are." Miia smiled.

"I can feel it." His gaze seductively pierced the girl:

At the bus station, the driver invited the passengers to go into the bus cabin.

"I'm going to the village to see my grandmother for three weeks. Let's agree; when I get back, we'll decide something. For example, in December, you can apply for the preparatory department. The studies will start in January," he said quickly and emotionally. Then he took out a tram ticket and wrote his city address on it. "Wait for me! Please write to me when I get back. In three weeks. Promise to write."

With a sweet smile, she only thought, 'Ivan kept my tram

34

ticket…' He held her hands and then kissed them tenderly. The girl immediately responded and kissed him on the cheek. At home, Miia told her mother about Ivan's proposal. But to her mother, it seemed out of reach. She advised Miia to consider enrolling in a technical school in the same city.

"A new group has opened at this technical school. However, please hurry and submit your documents. You will also need to take two entrance exams: one in language with literature and another in mathematics. You are prepared for these exams."

"The two fours received when entering the institute are proof of this," the daughter responded without hesitation. "I agree. I'm going tomorrow."

She was even glad about this opportunity. 'If I'm lucky, I'll be in the city from September, which is much better than waiting until January. In three weeks, everything will be known, and there will be something to write to Ivan about.'

The father also supported this decision and volunteered to go with his daughter. The results were known within two weeks. Miia was enrolled in the first year of the commodity science faculty at the cooperative technical school.

"Congratulations, daughter! You understand the trade well, so studying will be straightforward. After graduating from the technical school, you'll be able to apply directly to the second year at the university." It was felt that the mother was happy.

"Thank you, mommy!" They hugged

"Although during this time, a lot of water can flow".

"How is that?"

"A lot can change."

There was only a week left before the start of studies. Girls and boys from their street gathered almost every evening in Miia's yard. Some were older, some younger. Every time, there was something to talk about, something to laugh at, something to dream about, something to mock, something to believe in, and something not to. The variety of stories was filled with fantasies. In particular, the fictions sparked the imagination about strange phenomena. Conversations about ghosts made the blood run cold. Thoughts about UFOs were especially intense. To make the dreaming even more exciting and to make the starry sky feel as if it were in the palm of your hand, the children turned off the streetlight on the pole in Miia's yard.

That evening, new news about UFOs was being discussed. The night was very dark, and it seemed like you could reach the stars with your hands.

Suddenly, footsteps echoed in the darkness. A silhouette started to form. Everyone froze. It was so silent you could hear a bug squeak as it crawled among the leaves.

The silhouette was heading straight for them.

"Stop, who's coming?" Sasha interrupted the silence with a guard's voice. "Living creature, stop!"

The tension turned into loud laughter.

"It's me."

"Oh, my God," Miia exclaimed, thrown into a frenzy. "What is he doing here?"

"Who am I?"

"Sasha, it's me."

Yes, it was Mark.

"Hi, everybody."

"Hi! What are you doing here?"

"If I tell you that I'm going around the estate, will you believe me?" the young man joked. "Is everything okay with you here?"

"Of course." Everyone answered almost in unison, except Miia.

"Mark, if you're here, maybe you'll play?" Vika said happily.

"I'll play! I need a guitar."

Everyone immediately looked at Miia.

"Zhanna will kill me if she finds out that I took her guitar outside."

"Oh, we'll eat our fill of pies." After Sasha's words, everyone laughed out loud again.

"You don't wait," Miia smiled, returning with the guitar. "Let's get out of the yard, because the neighbors are singing to us."

They went to the river, which flowed in a narrow stream through the gardens. Even as children, they loved to run there to swim. The fishermen's dissatisfaction with the children's gang seemed endless. The little ones never restrained their

36

playful noise, whether on the shore or in the water. They did not understand the importance of silence. The Little Mermaid and Neptune dove endlessly underwater, searching for the treasures of the Queen of Rivers at the bottom. Sailors rejoiced at the storms that the children themselves created on inflatable rings. The swimming contests to the other shore had a lot of meaning: the winner became the captain of their pirate gang. The silk willows admired the happy children, whose joyful chirping filled the heavenly distance with celebration. The wise Reed was also pleased. Like a loyal guard, he protected the secret paths of his little Cossack robbers from prying eyes.

The stars celebrated their beauty in the mirror of the night river. The evening was peaceful and warm.

Having sat down, the young men and women started with familiar songs – song after song. Mark was a true master. It seemed there was no song he couldn't perform. And no one worried about UFOs and ghosts anymore.

At some point, Miia felt that their communication with Mark was starting to show the first signs of ease and trust. She remembered her conversations with Ivan and wanted a similar connection with Mark. Having tuned in, Miia confidently asked him to teach her a new playing technique, and he happily agreed. She excitedly asked him to show her her new chords, and he gladly demonstrated. She boldly sat down next to him, and he playfully nudged her with his shoulder.

No one kept track of time.

Suddenly, there was the sound of a broken string. Miia found herself in an icy rain.

"I'm done for." The poor thing took a deep breath.

"I have an extra string. I'll bring it," Mark quickly reassured her, hugging the girl by the shoulders.

"Zhanna will arrive in two days."

"I'll bring it tomorrow and tune the guitar."

"Mark, do it," Vika said anxiously. "I know Zhanna. It will be a disaster for all of us."

The night gatherings were ending. Somewhere far away, half asleep, a rooster crowed. As great-grandmother used to say, it's the evil forces that go into the night and the forces of

37

light that are preparing to meet the sunrise.

Everyone quietly headed home.

Mark and Miia stopped close to her yard.

Mark suddenly announced, "I'm going to serve in the army."

"When?"

"In the middle of October."

"What troops?"

"Airborne."

"You wanted that, right?"

"Yes."

Mark suddenly approached Miia, hugged her, and, without hesitation, kissed her passionately. The girl didn't even have time to pull away.

"Wait for me," he whispered.

She couldn't push him away. She held a guitar in one hand, and the other was numb. A storm raged through her heart.

"Mark."

"Miia, I want..." The boy's voice trembled as his hands held the girl's slender body tighter and tighter. Sweet lips greedily kissed her face, hair, and neck. Her strength, on the other hand, was beyond her control.

At that moment, Miia hesitated, unsure whether to push away the one she had been waiting for. She had also longed for this moment, but couldn't shake the feeling of fear. The intensity of his eyes somehow made her feel lost in a captivating mystery.

"No. No need. You can't," the girl whispered. 'But his body... divine' flew through her thoughts.

Her whisper acted on him even more strongly.

In the first glimmers of dawn, the unbuttoned buttons on her silk dressing gown did not hide the beauty of her girlish breasts. He was going crazy. He was burning with the fire of determination and the desire to drink her to the fullest.

"No. Stop! Go away!" as if waking up from hypnosis, Miia shouted.

With one hand, the girl pushed him away from her with all her might. Her body trembled. With the same hand, she tried to get to grips with the buttons. But they were unruly.

Mark approached her. His eyes greedily enjoyed her.

"I'm going to break the guitar right now." Her body trembled

38

with fear.

"Let me zip it up," Mark said hoarsely. "Will you wait for me?" The girl looked into his eyes.

"Who else will be waiting for you?" She wanted to find the answer in the young man's eyes.

She thought about Mila and her close bond with his sister. She recalled how Mark and Mila always left the disco together.

"Nobody," he growled irritably, turned around, and walked away.

Miia watched him, her soul tingling. She realized she had just lost both of them – Mark and Ivan.

By morning, the girl could no longer sleep. Her blood was boiling in her veins. With every cell of her body, she felt Mark's presence. Her lips still burned from his first passionate kiss, and his strong hands roamed her body. The divine mystery of his body was driving her crazy.

She went to the large mirror. Slowly, she began to unbutton her silk dressing gown, one button at a time. She wanted to see herself as the young man saw her. Putting aside her shame, she revealed herself fully.

In the mirror's reflection stood a busty brunette with a slim waist and slender legs. Her hair fell over her shoulders, giving her an air of fragility. Every curve of her elastic body held a mystery. The girl admired her beauty. Today, she saw it for the first time.

The sun rose higher and higher.

During the day, Miia took care of household chores and yard work. She baked her favorite biscuits. She read a few chapters of 'Gone with the Wind.' And no matter how hard the girl tried not to think about what had happened, the broken string on her guitar rang out insidiously: 'Wait!'

The girl sighed and turned to the guitar, saying, 'He won't come.'

During the day, Miia reassured herself that guys don't handle rejection well, but she was thankful for not doing anything foolish.

She quoted the main character of the book, saying, 'I don't know what Zhanna will say, but I won't think about it now.'

By evening, the emotions had eased. There were no plans,

but she only wanted to sleep.

The sun had long set behind the horizon, and night had taken the place of day. Mom and grandma were finishing their chores in the summer kitchen. Dad was in his workshop, busy with another renovation.

Miia's room was filled with cosmic echoes in a calm melody. A candle burns down on the table, casting dancing shadows on the walls. Sleep took over.

"Miia, are you not sleeping? Come, your father is calling you," the girl snapped back to her senses from her mother's quiet voice.

"Why?"

"I don't know; he asked you to come."

"I was already asleep."

"No one knew that you had already gone to bed."

The girl yawned and stretched.

"What, did you go to bed late?"

"I didn't look at the clock."

"At three in the morning, you were still giving concerts."

"Hmm… We were by the river, weren't we?" Miia was surprised.

"Artists. Half the village heard your songs… I'm already going to rest. Good night!"

"Good night, mommy!" She put on her dressing gown, kissed her mother, and left the house.

On the way to the summer house, the girl wished her grandmother goodnight.

"Is Uncle Misha at father's?"

"I wasn't looking. You know he gets angry when he's disturbed."

"I know." She picked up the cat, which was gently rubbing against her legs, and quickly headed for the workshop.

Opening the door, the girl no longer heard what her father was saying to her.

"Hello, Miia!" Mark was sitting next to her father, a soldering iron in his hands. "The radio broke; I brought it so your dad could look at it."

Miia couldn't say a word.

"Miia, bring the cassette." It seems that the father repeated his request. "Mark, listen, we won't do anything today."

40

"Then I'll do without it." Mark quickly put the soldering iron on the table, stood up abruptly, shook her hand, and headed for the door.

He didn't take his eyes off the girl, went up to her, and took the kitten from her.

"Just like our little mischievous one," he said, looking at his father with a smile. "What are you standing there for, Miia? Mark didn't bring the cassette, and I need it in the morning." Opening the side covers of the radio, his father repeated what Miia hadn't heard the first time.

"I'll bring it now," she barely managed to say, coming to her senses. When the door closed, the young man grabbed the girl by the hand: "I brought it. Take the guitar with the cassette. I'll wait for you outside the yard."

As if in a dream, without feeling the ground beneath her feet, and without saying a word, Miia headed for the house. She did everything he told her. A few minutes later, the guitar was tuned. 'Why so fast?' she thought. Their eyes met. "I didn't want you to get hurt. I'm sorry!" There were notes of hope in the gentle intonation of Mark's voice. Silence fell.

"You saved me." She realized that she would have kissed someone else for this, hugged them, and chirped with gratitude. Someone else. Out of a million. Out of a billion. "I'm sorry," he whispered again, and after a short pause, added, "Your parents think you are home. Go."

"I'm sorry," she replied, barely breathing. The boy moved away.

"Mark." She confidently moved toward him. He was impatiently waiting for what would happen next. "Thank you for keeping your word." Her gaze radiated warmth and tenderness.

She didn't dare kiss him. Not even on the cheek. Smiling, she turned around and happily ran to the yard.

V

On the very first day, at the general meeting, an announcement was made that all first-year students from every faculty would be going to the collective farm to work. The meeting was scheduled for seven in the morning the next day. Hearing this, Miia panicked. She hadn't brought any work clothes or shoes with her, and she wouldn't have had time to go home and come back by seven in the morning.

The first couple of lessons focused on introducing us to the class teacher. She saw most of her classmates at the entrance exams.

"Do you hear, Miia? Do you have work clothes?" Natalka asked quietly.

The girls met on the bus as they were heading to take their first exam. They immediately clicked because their conversation started with humor and student jokes.

"No. And you?"

"No." Looking around the office, Natalka asked even more quietly, "What should we work on?"

Seeing her, Miia started to laugh. "What are you doing?"

Natalka herself felt amused. "I'm sure we're not the only ones who will be dragging boxes of tomatoes in dresses and sandals."

And the girls began to peer into the faces of their classmates, trying to find their kind.

"Miia, I see on the horizon two figures whispering, just like us, suspiciously."

"You continue the reconnaissance." Covering themselves with their palms, the girls burst out laughing.

"Why are you having so much fun?" Serg looked at those who had given him the cheat sheets with the answers to his exam tests.

"Do you see that ship over there?" Natalka glanced at the board. He turned around to look. "I don't see," he said, surprised. "Close your eyes. Open your eyes. Close. Open." Natalka spoke in a hypnotic tone.

Sergey turned around again to look: "Well, you, with your tricks. Do you have a needle and thread?"

The girls looked at each other.

"Will a sewing machine work?"

"Which machine?" Serg looked at one, then the other.

"A sewing machine," the girls laughed.

"When are you ever serious?"

"We don't need that right now," answered Natalka. "Did you take your work clothes?"

"No."

"Serg, we are consecrating you as a knight of the order. A dress and sandals. The order will provide you with a spare dress and sandals. You will faithfully carry boxes of tomatoes for the collective farm."

With her eyes closed, with her hand on his shoulder, and the other on her heart, Miia was acting out the consecration.

And then the stern voice of the classroom teacher rang out: "Middle row, last two tables, what kind of consecration do you have there?"

Serg immediately sat up straight at his desk, and the whole group turned toward him. There had been a steady hum of voices in the room before that. Disguising themselves amidst this noise, the girls were joking without noticing when they drew attention to themselves.

"In the knights of the order, Natalka tried to stay serious, holding back a smile.

"Oh, we have our order in the group?" Galina Semenivna joined in the fun. "What does your order want to achieve?"

The girls were beginning to feel nervous, but it was too late to back out. Their classmates were waiting to see what would happen.

Mia got up from the table, looked at Natalka, smiled, and quickly said:

To determine if anyone else arrived without work clothes.

"An important question." Galina Semenivna said it seriously and turned to the group. "Please raise your hands; who doesn't have work clothes?"

Out of thirty students, nine raised their hands. It turned out that all of them were from remote areas and had not received letters with updated information promptly.

"Will everyone be able to get home on time today?"

"Yes!" they answered almost in unison.

"Will everyone be back tomorrow?"

43

"Yes!" they answered almost in unison again.

"Will everyone be here by 1:00 PM?"

"Yes," they answered amicably.

Here's the plan. Who needs to go now? Please write a statement to the director stating that you will be absent today and will arrive at the technical school by 1:00 PM tomorrow. I will talk to the director to arrange with the head of the facility to send a bus for you.

The next day, everyone was in place by 1:00 PM. Galina Semenivna was right yesterday: twenty-seven students had gathered.

Having taken the most comfortable seats on the bus, specifically the back seats, Miia and her classmates made such a loud, cheerful noise that the driver turned around and asked them to calm down at least a little. The students didn't argue.

"Can we sing?"

"If the songs are good, then sing," the driver replied, smiling as he looked at them in the mirror.

"With the guitar," Miia chirped.

"With the guitar? Then let's play with the guitar. I'm listening."

"Wolf, give it to me."

"You play?" The classmates' eyes widened in surprise.

"I have many undiscovered talents." Smiling, Miia took the first chord for a moment. "Well, sing along."

Why didn't you come when the moon rose?
I was waiting for you.
Didn't you have a horse? Didn't you know the way?
Mother didn't let.

Everyone on the bus began singing. Even the driver. Then...
Oh, in the cherry orchard, there, the nightingale was chirping.
Eevee, tu-tu-tu, ay-ay-ay, oh-oh-oh.
There, the nightingale was chirping."

"Vova, it's your turn to sing next," Miia said, handing over the guitar, smiling.

"Father Makhno's favorite song."

44

They sang the whole way and didn't notice when the bus arrived at its destination: the workers' dormitory. At the entrance to the building, two men were talking animatedly. Under the influence of the cheerful singing, the students hurriedly began to get off the bus.

"Our plane was flying; the wings were rubbing.
You weren't waiting for us, but we were."

"We're here," Miia and Natalka sang as they approached the men.

The two interlocutors stopped their conversation, silently looked at each other, and carefully watched the group of young men and women heading toward the building.

"Does this mean that our truants have arrived?" said the older man. "Good afternoon, gentlemen! My name is Ivan Vasilyovich, and I am the commandant of the dormitory."

Everyone greeted back.

Good afternoon! My name is Mykola Vasilyovich.

"And your brothers?" asked Vova.

"What, similar?" both smiled.

Someone's voice was heard asking, "And why are we truanting?"

"Because all of your people work in the fields, and you sing songs here."

"Do we sing badly?" Natalka smiled.

"You sing well; the whole village heard it. We'll have to see if you can work just as well," said Ivan Vasilyovich.

"But we are interested in seeing," says Vova, scratching the back of his head, "how we know how to work."

Everyone laughed out loud.

"Now we will show you your rooms," continued Ivan Vasilyovich. "The guys live on the first floor, and come with me. The girls go up to the second, and Mykola Vasilyovich will show you your rooms. You are all from different groups, right?"

"Oh, no. We are like one family; we can live as one commune. Vova approached the girls and hugged them."

"I am the deputy director for educational work at the technical school." Mykola Vasilyovich said in a stern voice.

45

"I always demand that all students be disciplined."

"Oh!" with a serious expression on her face, Miia raised her finger. "Being disciplined is our everything. Only after."

Serg smiled and winked at the girl, saying, "You just surprised me."

"Serg." Miia winked at him. "Only after."

"After what?" the deputy dean asked, looking intently at the girl.

"But empty. Don't pay attention." Miia's sly eyes sparkled. "Although, if I have the chance, I'll tell you."

"Come on now," Serg demanded.

"I said if I have the chance."

"Now," the young man insisted, smiling.

"Come on, you leech." Natalka snapped at him, and they went to settle in their rooms. Soon, their classmates arrived back from fieldwork. They were tired, but thoughts of lunch and the end of the workday cheered everyone up, giving them energy for the evening festivities. Students from other schools also worked on the collective farm. After lunch, instead of resting, the students chose different activities. Not far from their rooms was the school stadium. The boys formed teams and went to play football. Miia and the girls made a separate team and invited girls from another group to play volleyball. They picked a referee and started the game. The score was sometimes tied because the teams kept defeating each other.

"Miia, come here quickly." Hearing Vova's voice behind her, the girl glanced around. He was standing with the guys from their group, holding two guitars.

"Where did you get the second one?" the girl asked, surprised.

"We need you here as soon as possible."

"Tamila, play instead of me," called a classmate and approached the guys. "Speak."

"I have a deal for you worth a million dollars, but I won't give you a million dollars right now," began Vova.

"Well, standard," interrupted Miia.

"We argued with the guys from Uman University that we could play Viktor Tsoi's songs better than they could."

"Wow, you've taken a swing. And when did you manage to argue with them?" The girl was surprised.

46

"Hold one guitar. I have the second one. They are tuned to the same key. Here are the chords and the beat that you will play. There is nothing new here. I'll take the solo."

"Oh, what a wonderful sound." Having played a couple of chords, Miia was overcome with pleasure by this guitar. Where did you get it?

"It's mine," answered a classmate. "My parents gave it to me, but I haven't learned yet. I'll study here. And you, I see, are such a good guy," he smiled. "Have you been studying for a long time?"

"In March of this year."

"Can you be learning it so quickly?" he was surprised. "Do you play by notes?"

"Dima, I honestly admit, notes are a thick forest for me. The chords are not difficult. But to play with joy, your fingers need to get used to it," and showed him the fingertip of her left hand.

"Wow, what calluses." He was surprised, touching it.

"Dima, don't worry," Vova was playing the solo of the song with which he aimed to win a bet. "With such a teacher, you will learn," he nodded at Miia with a wink.

"Don't listen to him, he teased me. You will, my dear, teach us." Turning his gaze to Vova, Miia winked. "I won't let go of you."

"Dude, you are just like Jimmy Page. Wow! Masterful!" Dima exclaimed with admiration, watching Vova's hands.

"Yes, this is my favorite musician." Vova was wholly absorbed in playing the melody. After playing a couple of times, he paused and looked at the girl intently. "Now you," and she began to show the chords with a beat, with which she should play a song she liked. "You play; don't stop. I will make adjustments."

"When is the bet?" Miia asked.

"They will come here in twenty minutes."

They started to be surrounded by students from other groups at their technical school. Seeing the gathering, teachers and students from Uman University also joined in. A large crowd formed. Everyone picked a favorite.

"Who goes first?" Vova asked his opponents.

Seeing the girl with the guitar, sly smiles flashed on their faces. Miia noticed this.

"Guys, you are gentlemen!?" she turned to them, narrowing her eyes. "You should start."

"Wish pleasure."

They had one guitar, but two sang

"Well done, well done." Miia thought. "I hope we are no worse."

During the perestroika era, Viktor Tsoi was the most popular singer and musician. Millions admired him for the courage and relevance of the ideas reflected in his songs. As a result, his performances anywhere and at any time always evoked feelings of respect and pride. When the guys finished, everyone clapped and praised the young musicians.

"Well done; I liked it." Without delay, she looked at Vova and began to play "I'm turning off the TV...". Vova's extraordinary solo was impressive in its skill. He didn't try to imitate a real performer, neither in voice nor mannerisms. Miia felt proud that, at such a young age, the two of them were becoming stars. The teachers' and students' enchanted faces showed evident admiration for their duet.

"We are amazed. Bravo. Encore." With applause and shouts of "Bravo," "Encore" turned into a genuine burst of emotion. "Let's do it again."

The Uman guys approached Vova, shook his hand, and admitted that he had won the bet.

"Lady," they turned to Miia, "I'm Mikhail, and he's Olexei. You are unmatched! And as true gentlemen, it would be an honor for us to kiss your hand."

Applause burst out all around. These moments in life are never forgotten.

After that, both gentlemen, settling their lost bet, began doing twenty push-ups on the ground. This excited the crowd so much that some supporters of the two losers also started doing push-ups.

"Vova, listen, I'm delighted you're doing great!" Miia's meticulous gaze pierced. "And if we lost, would I also do push-ups?" she asked him, nodding at Mikhail and Olexei.

"No. I would have to eat a whole stick of butter." Miia's face turned grim at that moment. "And you would kiss them both." He looked at the girl with guilty eyes.

"I'll kill you."

"But why are you?" he pressed her. "Maybe one of them is your future cavalier."

"The devil's matchmaker." She was just about to continue when she saw Mikhail and Olexei approaching them.

They asked the girl, "What's your name?"

"Miia."

"What an unusual name." Both were taken aback.

"Thank you, my mom," she said confidently.

Then Natalka, who was headed to the stadium exit with the girls, told Miia they were going to the store for ice cream.

"Yes, guys, hold the guitar." She handed the guitar to Dima and said, "Wait for me, I'm with you." The girl quickly got up and tried to leave.

"Take me with you." Miia looked around at Olexei's voice. "I want ice cream too."

"Let's go."

Seeing her friend in Olexei's company, Natalka smiled, and with the words 'Everything is clear with you!' she moved forward with the girls. Miia then started an interesting conversation with the new employee. He said that he was already in his third year at the Faculty of Economics. In his childhood, his grandmother mostly raised him because his parents worked in the far north and earned a substantial income, but doctors advised against living there. He has a younger sister who is now only seven years old. He shared his view of family life, emphasizing the importance of treating children equally. Miia was surprised by these words.

"And, equal. What does that mean?"

"It's when everyone treats the younger one like a doll."

"That's how it should be." Miia interrupted him, smiling gently, "She's only seven years old."

When I was seven, my grandmother scolded me whenever I didn't want to wash the dishes, clean my room, or fold my clothes. Not only did she scold me, but she could even punish me for it. She was pretty strict and always expected more from me than I was willing to give.

"What exactly?"

"Didn't let me play outside with the boys. Didn't let me watch TV. And always with a belt in my hands."

"Beat you?"

"No. Just threatened me."

"Has it been a long time since my parents returned from the north?"

"Five years ago."

"Have you been living with them since then?"

"Yes."

"And your grandmother?"

"She lives separately. When my parents returned, they immediately bought a big apartment and a car."

"Are you still offended by them?"

"Money shouldn't be more important than the children."

"I'm sure they went to work for you, too. And you never asked yourself whether they would have earned enough to buy an apartment and a car if they hadn't gone to the north."

"On my 18th birthday, they gave me a car. Do you think it was out of great love? No. They did it to make up for their wrongs against me."

Miia had no desire to continue this topic. She couldn't understand the young man. So, the rest of the way to the store, she stayed silent.

"And he is nice," Natalka whispered to her with a wink.

"Not all that glitters is gold," Miia said coldly in response. "He is strange."

"What?"

The girls saw that Olexei was approaching them.

"Later," said Miia, turning to Natalka.

"Girls, choose what you want; I will pay."

Hearing this, the girls were delighted, except for Natalka, who looked at Miia anxiously.

"Girls! You will have to dance away. Don't be ashamed." Miia said, looking intently at each of them, wary of the girls' behavior.

"I will seriously pay, girls."

"Olexei, don't worry," Miia smiled, trying to make Lida and Lora understand that she should avoid the guy's offer. "They haven't spent all the money yet."

But the girls agreed. Frankly, while flirting with the young man, Lida shamelessly asked him to buy them ice cream and the most expensive sweets. Miia began to feel uncomfortable

50

in his company.

Having caught up with Miia and Natalka on the street, Olexei insisted on hugging the girls by the waist and, with a sly fox smile, began to flirt.

"Your seriousness turns me on, beauties. Especially yours, Miia." and, grabbing her hand after the girls wriggled out of his arms, he continued. "I'm serious. I want to tell Miia something. Natalka, leave us alone, please."

His story was short.

"This is some kind of delusion." The girl looked at him as if he were crazy and, pulling her hand away, called the girls.

"Catch up!" she called out, turning toward her friend's voice, and they stopped.

"When it gets dark, I'll come," he managed to shout after her. "You just get out."

It was forbidden to leave the dormitory in the evening. So, everyone was chatting in their rooms like bees in a hive. After changing into her nightgown, Natalka went to Miia's bed and asked about Olexei.

"He is strange." Having listened to the story all the way through, she was surprised. "But he will probably come to you."

"I won't go." Miia was utterly stunned. "We also need to ask Vova where he found them."

"Yes, we must," her friend agreed.

"Girls, good night to you all!"

Despite the lights being off, a quiet commotion continued in the room. Miia was already drifting off to sleep. Suddenly:

"The gentleman has arrived. Hey, Miia, wake up. He's standing there by the windows," Natalka called out to her.

Miia jumped up quickly from the bed and hurried to the window.

"Oh, how quickly you woke up." Tamila mocked, supported by the other girls.

"Did you fall from the sky?" Miia looked around at them. "If anyone needs that miracle, I give it to you."

"Why are you like that? He's quite handsome. His car is like this." Yulia was surprised.

"What?" Miia answered, heading for her bed. "He's not to my taste."

51

"But Lida."

Mia interrupted her, saying, "Then let him take her." "Then you tell him you're not going out."

"I said that during the day. I see they didn't understand me," Miia muttered, walking to her bed. Morning came. There was a knock on the door in Mykola Vasilyovich's voice. Room ten! We wake up, get dressed, wash, brush our teeth, have breakfast, and gather downstairs; the bus will be waiting at 8:30.

VI

It would be strange to picture the exemplary behavior of the most mischievous students in the tomato fields. How can this happen in real life? Miia's class at school was the unruliest. All the students seemed handpicked. They could disrupt lessons amicably and just as easily win competitions. From the first days, Miia noticed that her group at the technical school was a mirror of her class in spirit. The only differences were first names, last names, and faces.

All the students from other groups and different educational institutions performed their work conscientiously and to a high standard, except for group number 212.

"Torpedo attack!" was shouted somewhere nearby.

"What, again? Natalka, we're falling!" Miia shouted to her friend.

Lying on the ground among the bushes, the girls could only watch as tomatoes flew over their heads from both sides.

Miia asked Oksana, "Did we miss something yesterday?"

"Yes, a joke," Oksana laughed and got up to see what was happening on the field.

And the tomatoes whistle past their heads, hitting their targets.

And now the time has come: "The torpedo attack is stopped." Raising their heads, the girls saw the guys from their group in tomato-stained clothes. Trying to pretend that nothing was happening in the field, they rushed to pick vegetables.

The village garden manager's car was getting closer and closer to their group. When she pulled up, the manager jumped out of the car and started shouting and threatening to complain to the college management. When asked who was causing the mess, of course, no one responded.

"Yesterday, they promised that they would not allow such a mess again. And when she left, they staged such a shelling twice more."

"Liars. Both laughter and sin."

Near the dormitory, the girls saw Olexei and Mikhail. They were standing by the car and smiling defiantly.

"Miia!" Olexey called her.

Natalka looked at Mia excitedly.

"Is this a new bet? I told you everything yesterday. Get away from мею." Irritation showed on her face.

"What are you like?" Mikhail had just begun to say something when Miia interrupted him and snapped at both of them angrily.

"Go to hell!" she said and ran to the dormitory.

In the room, Natalka called her to her window.

"Look." Smiling, Natalka turned her gaze to the window. "They'll probably get rid of you, for sure."

The other girls in their room also rushed to the window.

"Dreams come true!" Tamila declared with a smile, and putting her hand on Miia's shoulder, she continued. "You're left without a suitor."

"Thank God!" Miia folded her arms, raised her head, and closed her eyes. "It felt easier."

"Why are you like this?" Yulia asked completely seriously.

"How? He tells me, 'I liked you as soon as I saw you. You're bright, passionate, sensible, and beautiful. I want a wife like that.' I think this is not normal! And I don't care at all that his dad is a boss and his mom is an economist. By the way, they bought him this car. And he still can't forgive them for taking his childhood away from him and his grandmother. His parents earned money in the North." The girls stood with wide eyes and listened silently. "And in general, I'm only seventeen. A marriage not for me?" Exhaling, she went to change.

"Girls, can I hint to her somehow?" Natalka turned to the girls.

"Maybe, if she hears," Miia growled.

After waiting for Lida and Lora to return to their room, Miia, Natalka, Yulia, and Tamila went to the girls' room. They were busy doing their makeup and hair. "Oh, the whole delegation. What do you want?" leaning back in her chair, Lora turned to them irritably.

"Girls. You don't need to get involved with those guys," Yulia started.

Lida and Lora examined the entire company from head to toe.

"Jealous?" Lida said with a condescending smile.

"Lida, you just don't get that they don't care which girl runs

54

to them on a date." Tamila joined the conversation. "What do you know about them?"

"Girls, get out of the room." Lora and Lida said it almost in unison.

"I repeat, what do you know about them?" Tamila's cold, meticulous gaze pierced both girls.

"And I repeat, get out," Lida snapped condescendingly, pointing her finger at the girls at the door.

"Girls, let's go." Miia stopped at the exit and smiled. "Maybe I've tricked myself."

The workdays kept moving forward. In the tomato fields, the boys' behavior stayed precisely the same. The girls started to join them, and they were even waging tomato battles one-on-one. Due to the girls' agility, the boys were hit more often. None of the manager's threats had any impact since they were only spoken threats.

On the seventh day, the bus with the 212th group drove past the tomato field and stopped near the apple orchard.

"Now arrange your fights here!" With a sly smile, the manager waved her hand towards the orchard, then got into the car and drove away.

"Well, we'll have to work here. Let's go get acquainted with the area," one of the guys muttered.

The students were divided into different zones, and a large-scale plan was presented to them.

"Do you hear, Tamila?" Yulia called out from under the tree. "Working on tomatoes was more fun. It's too boring here, and the boxes are so huge."

"This is where we should torpedo," Miia and Natalka joined their conversation, laughing. Yulia took a couple of rotten apples and threw them on the ground. "How beautiful."

"No, you can't torpedo here. Because this same beauty will be on our heads," Miia laughed, imagining such a picture.

The autumn day was incredibly warm. Gentle rays of the sun, breaking through the smoky veil of air, generously endow everything around with a fairy-tale charm. The singing of birds enchanted the garden with its strange melody. It felt like no one was nearby. In the distance, a tractor rumbled, and the faint voices of boys could be heard.

At the start of the work, everyone was divided into groups of

55

four men, with six rows behind each group. After collecting seven boxes, the girls decided to rest. The four of them gathered under one tree. The grass beneath it was green, and there were hardly any rotten apples. Amid their calm, dreamy conversations, they didn't notice how they first lay down on the ground and then fell asleep.

"Steh auf! Schnell!" Like thunder, a formidable, loud voice raised the girls as if on command.

They opened their eyes and saw an unfamiliar man nearby.

"Who are you?" Miia asked, looking at him.

Natalka whispered, "It's good that there's no machine gun."

The man remained silent, staring closely at each of their faces.

"We need to run away." Yulia barely whispered.

"We're going to scream now," Tamila said in a frightened voice, and as if she were about to scream, "Help."

The man immediately burst out laughing.

"Calm down, girls! I'm a teacher. Starting today, I'm assigned to your group. My name is Sergiy Vasilyovich."

The girls instantly felt relieved. Laughing out loud, they realized what a mess they had gotten themselves into during their quiet hour.

"You, Sergiy Vasilyovich, should have said Hande hoch!"

"Miia half seriously addressed him."

Well done; you didn't get confused. I understand that you studied German in school.

"You know that you are the only ones who slept. Everyone is working. Some have already fulfilled the plan."

"So now we go quickly." Natalka didn't let him finish, "True, girls! Let's show that we not only know how to sleep." Grabbing the boxes, she headed for the trees. The girls hurried after her.

"The timer is on," the teacher shouted after them, glancing at his watch. You have an hour and a half.

For successfully exceeding the daily quota, despite the quiet hour arranged by the girls, Sergiy Vasilyovich praised them and offered to become their assistant.

A few days later, he asked for their help.

Girls, two students, Likaschuk and Kosovets, disappeared from the next room. In the morning, they told Mikola

56

Vasilyovich that they had a fever. Even the thermometers confirmed it. He left them in the dormitory. When everyone came back, they weren't in the room. Only work clothes and shoes were left.

"And what do the girls from their room say?" Natalka and Miia exchanged glances.

"They say they don't know anything."

Yulia and Tamila are back in the room now.

"Lida and Lora are not there." Natalka began. "In the morning, they said they got sick. And when everyone returned from the garden, neither they nor their things were there."

"I know that you may be more at home than anyone else," said the teacher, his piercing gaze as if he were reading each other's thoughts.

The girls looked at each other strangely.

"Sergiy Vasilyovich, we can talk now," Miia said, turning to him. "We'll tell you everything we know, or whatever becomes known. But please, give us twenty minutes."

"Okay. Will twenty minutes be enough?" he added by the door.

When the door closed, the girls fell silent for a moment.

"To begin with, we need Vovchik here. It's time to ask him about the story with the bet." Miia broke the silence.

"You think," she said, looking at her friend in surprise.

"What kind of story is this?" Yulia and Tamila didn't understand what they were talking about. But without waiting for a response, they ran out of the room. Their excitement made it clear where they had gone.

"Let him rush here at the speed of sound," Miia shouted after them, then, grabbing Natalka's hand, she quickly walked to Lida and Lora's room.

"Nadya, Olesya. Did the girls go with those scoundrels?" Mia looked each of them in the eye demandingly.

"We don't know." Shrugging their shoulders, they replied in unison.

"Have they spent the night here for the last week?" Miia's gaze pierced one, then the other.

"When Nadya and I fell asleep, they were in the room."

"And in the morning, when you woke up, were they also here?"

57

"Yes." Nadya and Olesya exchanged surprised glances.

The loud voices of Vova, Yulia, and Tamila echoed in the corridor. Natalka, as she opened the door, called them to come inside.

"Sit down, Vova! Five minutes have already gone by. Fifteen more to go." Now, Miia turned her inquisitive gaze to the young man. "Tell me quickly and briefly how you met those wandering singers and how you got into a bet."

"And what happened?" he asked, eyeing everyone with wide-open eyes.

Lida and Lora disappeared. Their belongings are also missing from the room," Natalka said.

"And why did you decide that they could have gone with those guys?" Vova asked casually, leaning back on the bed.

"How?" Miia moved closer to him.

"We were playing the guitar. They came over, listened, and then asked where we were from and when we arrived. We told them. Then Mikhail said I was playing it wrong, grabbed the guitar, and played it himself. We started arguing. That's how the bet happened," the young man blurted out in fear.

"Oh, right!" Miia said emotionally. "They were doing push-ups. And if you lost, you'd eat butter, and I would kiss them both. And overall, what the hell were you looking for?"

"I was looking for you because I knew that I wouldn't lose with you. And when I said that there would be a girl in the pair with me, then they suggested that you not eat butter, but kiss them." Emotions went off scale.

"Well, you're a fool," Natalka snapped at him.

"What's this?" he asked, turning away from her and looking intently at Miia.

"I'm after Sergiy Vasilyovich." Tamila ran out of the room.

They returned so quickly that no one even had time to regain their senses or ask anything else.

One by one, the students started to share what they knew.

"Do you know what kind of car he has and where the dormitory is?" the teacher asked, clearly surprised.

"He knows." Natalka apologized and pointed her finger at Vovchik.

"You three," pointing to Vova, Miia, and Natalka, "let's go."

On the street, teacher Tatyana Andriyivna joined them.

58

The small, two-story building where Olexiy and Mihail stayed didn't look like a typical hut. There was no car parked nearby, and no one was at the entrance. On the second floor, music was barely audible in one of the rooms.

Natalka asked anxiously, "Can we wait for you in the car?"

"Don't be afraid. Let's go." Tatyana Andriyivna answered calmly.

Having climbed to the second floor, the teachers started trying to open the doors, but they were locked. After walking almost the entire corridor, Sergiy Vasilyovich opened another door leading into a room. The sharp smell of alcohol and cigarette smoke filled the corridor. Inside, a half-naked Lora was sleeping in bed with two young men. When the door was opened, neither of them even woke up. What they saw caused Miia and Natalka to jump back from the door. Blushing with shame, they looked at each other, confused. Sergiy Vasilyovich and Tetyana Andriyivna entered the room.

"What will happen now?" the frightened Vova looked at the girls, who were silently staring back at him with equally scared eyes.

Suddenly, they heard a rustling coming from behind one of the doors.

"There's someone there." Vova's eyes widened.

But they didn't dare go in there alone. The teachers came out into the corridor with Lora, who was barely shuffling her feet. When asked, "Where's Lida? How did you end up here? Who are these young men?" she didn't respond at all.

"There's someone here," the frightened students whispered in unison, waving at the door.

"Hold her." Sergiy Vasilyivich immediately turned to them, nodded to his colleague, and opened the door.

"My God." Miia turned away. "Let's go outside. Hurry... Well, you girls, you are fools." Miia and Natalka grabbed Lora and dragged her outside to the car. Vova ran after them.

"Why are you shaking so much? What's going on?" Natalka asked her friend firmly.

"Some kind of brothel," the girl whispered. "Lida is also in the company of two."

The girls directed their menacing stares at Vova.

59

The terrified Vova blinked his eyes quietly. Natalka looked sternly at the boy. "Help me hold her. Miia, were those two suitors there too?"

"Both were." The girl's excited gaze lingered on Lora's face, which showed both a strange color and a strange expression. "Lora." She didn't react.

"They'll probably be taken to the hospital now, and we'll go to the police," Vova mumbled.

"Why are we going to the police?" The girls asked together.

"Are they eighteen?" he asked them.

"We don't know."

The teachers came out of the house with Lida, who was in the same condition as Lora.

"To the hospital now?" Natalka asked softly.

"Why?" Sergiy Vasilyovich's voice was not just stern; it was angry. "Girls, get in the car," and looking at Vova, he continued, "And we, let's go. We need to pack their things."

Returning ten minutes later and getting back behind the wheel, Sergiy Vasilyovich addressed everyone:

"Two of these scoundrels have stamps in their passports about their marriage to these beauties, dated today," and showed them six passports.

"Do you have their passports?" Tatyana Andriyivna asked in surprise. "How did you manage to do it?"

"You saw what condition they were in. I barely woke up the oldest of them to give him a note telling him where to come tomorrow." Vova laughed at that moment.

"And where?" Tetyana Andriyivna asked.

"To our dormitory." Sergiy Vasilyovich answered with a smile. "We will celebrate two of their weddings together."

"And the girls are already eighteen?" Natalka asked quietly.

"That's the thing, yes. One turned 18 at the end of August. The other four days ago."

"And what can they do so quickly to get married?" Miia was surprised.

"Maybe if they provided a certificate of pregnancy, for example. Our actions. We don't officially contact the police or the hospital. I don't think it will be necessary. They have a lot of alcohol and other things. But you don't need to know that. They celebrated the wedding."

60

Miia and Natalya sat with their heads lowered in shame.

"Sergiy Vasilyovich, when did you have time to check the passports?" asked Tetyana Andriyivna.

"I had time. The one I woke up, one of the so-called newlyweds, still dared to declare that we had kidnapped their wives and promised to return with the police." At these words, the teacher laughed. "I told them that the police are good and advised them to sleep well first. Tomorrow at nine in the morning, I will wait for them in the dormitory. By the way, this is the third marriage for one of them, and the second for the other."

"Are they so much fun? God, how old are they?" Tetyana Andriyivna didn't have time to ask questions.

"One is twenty-one, the other is twenty. The question is different, Tetyana Andriyivna – the girls' parents. I'm sure they don't know anything. But they are our students, for whom we are now responsible."

"We need to call the parents."

"Don't say a word to anyone. Miia and Natasha, please go to the room with these two, so they will ask you fewer questions. Tetyana Andriyivna will visit you. And I will ensure that all the students sit in their designated rooms. Vova, you will be with me. We will wait until morning."

Leaning on the railing and holding their knees with their hands, the girls sat in complete silence.

"Can't sleep? How are they?" Tetyana Andriyivna asked softly as she entered the room.

"They're sleeping," whispered Natalka.

The teacher sat down beside them on an empty bed.

"How old are you?"

"I'll be eighteen in April," Miia was the first to reply.

"I'll be eighteen in June."

"Looking at you, I understood that you had a shock." The girls were silent. "I'll talk to you like an adult. Have you already had sexual relations?"

"No," they answered quietly.

"And have any of the young men already made attempts?" The girls kept their eyes down and stayed silent. "I'm not asking you to reveal your secrets."

"They were," Miia answered shyly.

61

"Also." Natalka followed.

"Are these your friends?" the girls nodded, saying they were friends. "Have you known them for a long time?"

"We studied at the same school," they replied nearly in unison again.

"Do you like these young men? Do you think of them as adult men?" Hiding their gaze, the girls only nodded their heads.

Tetyana Andriyivna approached Lora and Lida, checked their temperatures with her palm, and then went back to her spot to keep going.

"Sexual life is a natural phenomenon. There is no need to be ashamed of its beginning. Of course, I do not support early sexual relations."

"So, we are old women already?" Natalka joked, feeling a certain relaxation.

"Oh, you're already starting to joke," she continued, smiling in response. "I don't know if these girls have had sexual relations before. Imagine that until today, no." The girls looked at each other and then glanced at the teacher. "I'm a married woman, married for more than ten years. My husband and I, like you and your boys, studied at the same school. He's four years older than I. We started having sexual relations as soon as I graduated from school. One day, he came to the dormitory and said, I don't want any scum to be found on your body." We got married two years later. She looked in the direction of Lida and Lora. "I'm not promoting immorality. These girls are having a wedding today. And what morality? I want to say one thing: if you have feelings for your boys and these feelings are mutual, it's better like mine than like Lida and Lora."

Silence fell. It was audible as the rain started outside, and its refreshing, enchanting scent filled the room. A strange awakening surged through every cell of Miia's body. She remembered her first kiss that evening. It was with the person she had dreamed of, yet feared in those very dreams. Her idol was just a protective shield, hung by her hand, naively hoping for the magic of her powerful protection. She wanted not only herself but others to believe in it. But eventually, all those barriers began to break down under the relentless

62

pressure of Mark's insidious persistence.

"Tetyana Andriyivna, I want to say something. You were there when Vova and I performed a song for two guitars."

"Yes, you were unsurpassed," she praised.

"One of those two came after me. On the way, he talked about his resentment toward his parents, about the evil grandmother who took care of him and then raised him. He confessed how much he liked me and that he would like to marry me." Miia looked at her with fearful eyes.

"And when we were in the store, he wanted to pay for all of our purchases." Natalka continued. "Miia refused. She told the girls not to agree, either."

"But Lida and Lora are happy." Miia looked at their beds.

"He paid for them," Tetyana Andriyivna finished the sentence.

"Yes."

"What happened then?"

"The next day, he wanted to talk to Miia, but she sent him away. And five minutes later, he was already whispering politely to Lida."

"We decided to warn them both. We came to this room to talk. But they didn't even want to listen to us. They kicked us out, accusing us of jealousy. Yulia and Tamila were with us, but they didn't want to listen to them either."

"Everything becomes clear." She got up and headed for the door. Pausing, she looked around at the girls. "What are the names of the young men who give your hearts no peace?" After hearing the names, she continued. "Well, they're better than some scumbags... Go to bed. Tomorrow is the decisive day. Are there free beds? I'll be with you until morning."

"We don't work tomorrow?"

"Tomorrow, you and Vova, you'll be needed here."

"Tetyana Andriyivna, what will happen to Lida and Lora?" Natalka asked quietly.

"I don't think they will continue their studies at our institution. The girls themselves probably won't want to. One of the people they celebrated with was a former student of theirs. What are rumors? You know."

VII

In the morning, all the students prepared to go to work. But before they started, Sergiy Vasilyevich held a brief meeting and announced that a dormitory rotation would be implemented from today until the end of the agricultural work. He also read the list of the first five students.

"Girls, is it because of Lida and Lora? Did something serious happen to them?" Yulia asked Miia and Natalka.

"Yes. However, today everything will become clear." Miia answered in an even voice.

"Where are they now? They're not here," Tamila looked around at the students.

"They are tired," Natalka smiled, took Miia by the arm, and headed for the dormitory.

"Well, you'll tell everything later, right?" Yulia and Tamila shouted after their friends.

"We are working!" they answered in unison, without turning around.

Everything in the corridor was so loud that the girls didn't immediately know whether they should go outside or stay behind the door of the room where Tetyana Andriyivna was trying to talk to Lida and Lora. They decided not to leave and listened carefully. "Girls, do you remember where you were yesterday? What did you do? Why did you leave the dorm without telling anyone? Can you remember how you got back? Do your parents know about your actions?" It was clear that all the questions would go unanswered.

Someone's voices were heard on the first floor. One was unfamiliar, and the other belonged to Sergiy Vasilyovich.

"And where are those girls?" the stranger asked.

"The senior teacher in practice is talking to them."

"You told those stallions to come at nine?"

"Yes."

"Will they come? Maybe they should have..."

"They will come."

"I have everything ready."

"We have too," and went to Sergiy Vasilyovich's room.

Miia and Natalka stood quietly, like little mice. They looked at each other and tried to leave the floor, but the creak of the

64

floor stopped them. They froze in anticipation.

"Where is Vova?" Natalka asked in a barely audible voice. Miia spread her arms. "But I know you don't know." The girls started to feel that, looking at each other, they were insidiously beginning to want to laugh. "Wasn't he at the meeting?"

"He was eaten," and Miia began to laugh, covering her mouth with her hands.

"Who?" Natalka also started laughing.

"Cannibals," Miia whispered in response, tears beginning to well up in her eyes from laughter.

Over the creaking of the floor, one could hear Tetyana Andriyivna walking silently around the room. Suddenly, the door opened, and, surprised by the presence of Miia and Natalka, she quickly stepped out and called them to the end of the corridor.

"The guys will come to them now. You go into the room and stay there. Calmly talk about anything. Just not about yesterday. You don't know anything. Under no circumstances should you leave them alone in the room."

"And where is Vova?"

"Go."

After standing for a moment, exchanging glances, and gathering their courage, the girls went into the room. Upon entering, they saw Lora crying. Lida didn't bother to comfort her; she looked at the girls with a blank face, surprised.

"What are you doing here?" she asked them angrily.

"Why are you so angry, Lida?" Natalka asked, shifting her gaze to her classmate. "Why is Lora crying? What happened?"

"So many questions." Lida stood up and began sorting through her clothes in her bag. "Where are our documents?"

"Lida, what happened to you?" Miia grew bolder and approached Lora, trying to sit beside her. But Lida immediately pushed her away.

"Go and mind your own business. Lora, where are our documents?"

"They should be in the bag."

Miia and Natalka just looked at each other. They already knew the end was near. Unsure of what to do, they started rearranging their beds.

65

You could hear Tetyana Andriyivna talking loudly with the young men in the corridor.

"First door on the left."

Miia and Natalya were full of excitement. To hide it somehow, Miia threw a pillow at Natalka, and Natalka responded. Just then, the door opened, and Olexiy and Mikhail entered the room. Seeing the girls all together in one room was very surprising.

"Oh, hey!" Olexiy smiled and approached Miia. "I'm glad to see you, my dear."

"Not mutual! Surprised?" she asked, moving away from him.

"Little girl, why are you so unkind?" he moved closer and closer. "I didn't deserve such treatment from you. Look into my eyes," the girl backed away. He approached her until the wall stopped her. Without taking his greedy gaze away, he whispered, "You'll see flames in them."

Everyone else in the room remained frozen in place.

"Why are you staring?" Miia snapped, her voice rising with anger. "Get away from me!"

"You're so hot." He looked at her like a predator on prey. "This turns me on."

"Listen, I'm going to hit you. You'll have to be treated for the rest of your life after this." Gathering her strength, she pushed him away. He grabbed her hand, but Miia quickly pulled it away. "Don't you dare touch me. Lida, take him away." Looking at Natalka, Miia saw that she had gone pale. Winking at her friend, Miia smiled.

Lida approached Olexiy and insistently addressed him:

"Where did you put our documents?"

"I just came to pick them up, and your teacher isn't here right now."

She glanced at him with wide eyes.

"The teacher?" Looking back at Mikhail and Lora, she continued. "I don`t understand."

"Don't worry, I'll take care of everything," he said and went to Lora. Leaning down, he whispered something in her ear. She sat on the bed and, covering her face with her hands, started crying. "Misha, calm her down," he growled, turning to Miia and Natalka. "Go for a walk." He winked at Miia

66

with a sly smile. "With you, little bird, I would be left alone."
"We have nowhere to go." The girls looked at each other almost in unison, growling in response, then started to sort through their things, remembering they had been told not to leave the room under any circumstances.

"Don't be cruel; we need to talk to our wives alone."
"Oh, so you've already found a wife?" Miia's smile faded. "How fast are you? When did you manage to do this?" Her ironic tone helped her cope with the excitement that was building up inside her.

"Yesterday." He hugged Lida and smiled cheekily in response.

"My God! I won't say that I'm happy for Lida, you. What are you showing off?" Grimacing in disgust, she turned away.

"Look at those beautiful photos from our wedding." He pulled out a dozen from his pocket, approached Miia, and began showing them. In the photos, both Lora and Lida were smiling in gorgeous dresses, holding luxurious bouquets. He kept showing them. When he reached the last one, he paused. Then he turned away from everyone and showed it to Miia.

"What a pity that you were not with me." Looking at the photo, Miia was overcome with wild rage.

"Oh, your vile pervert!" and with all her strength, she gave him such a slap that he was thrown back. "Girls, you are stupid; you don't even realize what a mess you've gotten yourself into," she shouted at them. "Your heads stuffed with straw? What were you thinking when you went to the registry office with these criminals? At that moment, he took out a lighter and set fire to the photo he was showing Miia.

"Bird, calm down," he said, turning to Lida from Lora. "And you, wives, love money, so know how to earn it. So, hurry; the car is waiting for us. We're going on our honeymoon to the sea," and smiling impudently at Miia, he rubbed the ashes from the photo on the floor.

"And this is the kind of monster your grandmother raised?"
"You're not the first to believe this fable."
"And what about the fact that dad is a director and mom is an economist, also a myth?"
"No, that's the truth," he smiled sarcastically, pleased with

67

himself.

"You are a criminal?"

"Don't exaggerate! No one forces anyone to do anything," he moved towards Miia.

"Don't come any closer." Miia grimaced.

"Listen, you're poorly brought up. We need to deal with you."

"The belly button will come untied!" Looking at Natalka again, Miia turned to Lora. "You don't want to go with them, do you? Yes?" The girl felt utterly safe, knowing teachers were in the dormitory and would probably arrive soon. That's why she allowed herself such daring behavior.

Looking around, Olexiy lay down on the empty bed and, waving his hand, called Lora over to him.

"Come here. Why are you crying? A wonderful family life awaits you with Misha."

But she stood quietly, her head bowed.

"Don't go to him, Lora," Miia ordered.

"Do you think she doesn't want to go with her husband?" Olexiy said, pleased with himself.

"I think you and your friend are vile bastards and trash."

"Listen, you two," Lida snapped at the girls. "What have you forgotten here?"

"I'm not talking to you." Interrupting her, Miia turned to Lora in a more commanding tone. "Answer!"

"Lora. Why are you standing there?" Lida yanked her hand with all her strength.

"She doesn't want to."

At that moment, a loud commotion erupted on the stairs. The door to the room swung open suddenly, and eight men rushed in. Olexiy and Mikhail were immediately handcuffed. Behind them, Sergiy Vasilyovich entered with a stranger. Everything happened so fast that the girls didn't even have a chance to react.

"Lida and Lora, you will be taken to a technical school. Your parents are waiting for you. And these two, to the detention center," Sergiy Vasilyovich said in a commanding voice, turning his gaze to Miia and Natalya, who were standing there blinking with frightened eyes. "You are already completely safe," he added, smiling at them. "Continue to

68

be as smart as ever."

Tetyana Andriyivna passed by, smiling, went to her bed, took a pillow, and gave it to the stranger.

"Sergiy Vasilyovich. It seems you didn't answer. Wer sind Sie?" Miia quietly addressed him.

"Police Colonel. Investigation Department," he saluted, turned around, and exited.

"Here you go and hande hoch ..."

The scene was silent as the girls exchanged thoughtful glances. Everything that had happened over the past week kept replaying in their minds. Surprise flickered in their eyes as they wondered what kind of inner strength had been guiding them, steering them on the right path, and shielding them from harm. All of it seemed like something out of a movie, but what they saw was a harsh reality.

Vova's appearance broke the silence.

"Where the hell were you going?" the girls rushed at him.

"They are not Uman students. They have been hunted for over a year. Olexiy formed a gang that tricked naive and trusting girls, married them, and then... Well, you and I saw it. The police finally arrested the photo studio, which secretly printed not only wedding photos." Miia was utterly shocked by these words.

"What?" Natalka asked, looking from him to her friend.

"Photo for adults," the girl answered her friend. "Too frank photos for adults."

"This is some sort of detective story," Natalka muttered.

"And you, Miia, you flint!" Vova looked at her with respect. "He broke his teeth on you!"

"They broke them on us. Her gaze froze on the white canvas of the wall," and, turning her gaze to Natalka, she added. "And you know, Tatyana Andriyivna is right."

"What are you talking about?" Vova asked in surprise, looking from one to the other.

"None of your business." Miia blushed and smiled.

69

VIII

Terrible news spread through the village: a young neighbor, Yurko, shot himself while on duty. Rumors circulated that his wife had left him, and he couldn't accept it.

Miia was left alone at home. Her parents and grandmother went to Yurko's parents.

It was raining. Although it was still the end of September and one could enjoy the autumn warmth, the evenings were cold.

In complete silence, the girl's thoughts about Yurko did not leave her.

Miia remembered when she and her sister were still young, he would take them snowboarding in the winter and cycling in the summer. They would all swim together in the river, and he would teach the kids to swim. She remembered when the neighbor's dog broke free from the leash, and Yurko saved Miia.

She remembered how, when he was a twelve-year-old boy, he scolded his father for walking around with a belt in his hand, looking for his daughters. It was so brave. She recalled the first time he brought his sweetheart. 'Oh, they won't be happy,' her grandmother would repeat. She remembered his wedding. The couple looked beautiful, but there was something fake about that beauty. It seemed to Miia that this madam needed to, as they say, cling to someone.

She remembered how Yurka's mother would come and cry, saying that he had started drinking. 'My mother's brother also committed suicide because of his wife. First, he started drinking, and then he committed suicide.'

Her thoughts were interrupted by a knock on the door. Wiping away her tears, she opened the door and almost fainted.

"I'm glad to see you!" she said softly, inviting him in. Her tear-streaked face concealed her excitement well.

"Your dad won't kill me?" the young man asked with a smile, looking into the corridor.

"My parents are at the neighbor's. And if he opened the door, what would you do?" Miia got bolder.

"I was ready to die," he said confidently, as he took off his

70

shoes.

"Another one."

"I heard what happened," realizing what he had blurted out "Should I make some tea?" Her voice trembled, and tears welled up in her eyes. "I can't believe it."

Mark started to wipe the tears from her cheeks. There was so much warmth in his eyes.

"I'm sorry. You cried a lot, I see. And this is for you," he said, pulling out a box of sweets and perfume from under his jacket, which Miia had been looking at the day before.

Miia couldn't say a word when she saw the perfume.

"How did you know?"

Mark gave a smile and a wink.

"Oh my God. I think I know."

At the moment she was looking at this perfume, Timko and his sister were in the store. Miia didn't hide her pleasant surprise. Her sweet smile was genuine.

"Thank you, Mark! I wanted this perfume," she said, and kissed him on the cheek.

He took her face in his palm and looked at it intently. Miia stood spellbound by his presence. A divine feeling of passion was reflected in his eyes. Her breathing quickened.

"Do you want some tea?" the girl whispered.

"I want you!" the young man said softly, gazing into her eyes as if seeking reassurance.

"We have candies."

"You are my sweetheart," he whispered.

The girl remained silent. Her heart ignited, her soul shone, and her inner voice insidiously echoed 'Time.'

"Miia, I want..." Mark started to kiss her face gently. Then he took the perfume and candies from her and placed them on the table.

"Your jacket." Her hands reached out to him to take off his jacket. Mark did it himself instantly. Then, at the same time, he took off his sweater.

"My God, how beautiful." A thick fog clouded her mind. "He is divine." The girl could barely hold back as Mark passionately kissed her neck, shoulders, and chest, holding her tightly.

Her robe softly slid off her tense shoulders.

71

"I never..." she barely said, panting.

"Trust me. You're charming," he whispered.

His passion captured a fleeting moment and all the beauty of her slender body.

Another short moment, and Miia's fragrant bed enveloped their burning bodies with its softness. The young man felt her arms hugging him tighter and tighter.

"No one..."

"What have you done to me? I'm going crazy."

Ardent passion consumed him more and more. His hands eagerly explored her supple body. He kissed her repeatedly. Her heavy breathing was in his hands, with each touch of her charming, girlish breasts, waist, and hips.

"How long I've waited... Long..."

A sharp pain pierced her body like fire. In another fleeting moment, the tenderness of her movements drew her closer to the secrets of the unknown, drifting further from the Miia she was just a moment ago. Mark took his time. He enjoyed her with each innocent kiss. She responded to each of his movements.

"Mine..." he whispered.

They are alone all over the world.

Just a quick moment...

"No..." Her consciousness sinks in silent screams.

The strength of his body forever kept her from herself, from which she would never return. With each of his movements, her powerless hands tried to push the young man away, then hug him with all their might. Even though she wanted to scream, she couldn't because he was kissing her so passionately and sweetly. And with every movement he made, the pain became increasingly bearable.

"Everything will pass," he repeated again and again with each movement. She believed him.

Whether it was her lost consciousness or the unknown divine unity of the two, it carried them into the infinity of worlds. It seemed as if all the stars in the universe lit up for them with their entire heavenly glow.

He didn't want to let her go. It felt like two young hearts had joined forever in a shared desire to beat as one. It seemed that two souls would always fill each other with blissful warmth, that two minds, side by side, would reach the heights of life together, not giving in to its storms. And two bodies would make love, sharing sweet passions of union.

"Thank you, little angel!" whispered the young man. He was happy to be there, and the girl stayed silent because she wasn't sure what exactly to say.

Time was in no rush at all.

"My parents may return soon," the girl said quietly and hurriedly moved to the chest of drawers to get her sleepwear.

"Yes," Mark gazed at her naked beauty with tenderness.

"Please, don't be sorry." Mark kept his eyes on her.

He stood up and hugged her tenderly.

"Look at me... Please, don't be sorry."

"I'm not sorry."

"I don't want to go anywhere. I want to talk to your parents."

"About what?"

"About us."

Miia stared at him with scared eyes.

"No. Now is not the time. You'd better go."

"You again. Don't be shy; look at me." Mark noticed her shyness, then hugged her tightly. "We'll all work it out; you just wait for me," he kissed her tenderly. "Just wait..."

"Get dressed. My parents won't be impressed by your frank appearance," she said, turning her head away from the attractive, nude man. "You have to go."

The rain kept drizzling outside. Dampness and cold surrounded her, and her only warmth came from her nightgown. Noticing this, the young man immediately wrapped her in his jacket.

"Do you have to go?" Miia took it off and handed it to the young man.

"We'll meet next Saturday. I'll come talk to your parents."

After a few steps, his silhouette vanished completely into the darkness, which was enchanted by the soft rustling of the rain.

"I had a dream," she whispered to herself.

But the crumpled sheet with wet, crimson drops was not just a dream.

Wandering thoughts kept her from figuring out whether she felt more shame or peace.

73

IX

The next day, the girl went to the city to continue her studies. All her thoughts were on Mark and what had happened. Her first husband was the one who burned her heart with a fire, and from the thoughts of him, her soul froze, rooted in the deepest desires.

She thanked the universe for her most daring dreams. But deep in her soul, like black darkness, a feeling of anxiety was feverish. And no matter how hard Miia tried to disperse this emptiness, it drew nearer with a menacing gait.

However, the educational process began to distract her from evil thoughts, and the fun that the girls constantly organized in the dormitory made her forget the word 'Anxiety'. This week has become very busy. After an unexpected proposal from the college leadership, toys in the game "Opa Panas" were suddenly replaced with active preparations for the concert.

"Girls, look." Sitting on the bed, Miia rubbed her knees, which were bruised.

"Yeah, I have the same ones." Tossing back the blanket, Natalka looked at hers. "Olena, do you have the same ones?"

Olena got out of bed and began to show off her bruises.

"You girls are chasing that the game "Opa Panas" down the entire corridor so much that I'm surprised your heads are still intact," Lusi laughed and suggested. "The concert is the day after tomorrow, so let's practice more."

"Let's," the girls responded in unison and began singing song after song.

Just then, Tamila rushed into their room and hurried to search the grocery cupboard.

"We need some eggs."

"Why do you need?"

"There's nothing to shoot back. There, the locals came and threatened to break into the dormitory and throw us off the fourth floor." Finding the eggs, she grabbed them and ran out of the room, slamming the door.

The girls instantly jumped out of their beds, still in their nightgowns and without shoes, and ran into the next room. A picture caught their attention. The girls, stacked one on

74

top of the other, peered out of the wide-open window in a row and teased the boys. Following their rude words, eggs flew through the air. Miia wanted to see what was happening outside, but she couldn't reach the window, so she had to stand on the table.

"Miia, what's up?" Natalka asked as she danced beside her. "There are about seven or eight of them gathered there."

"Oh my God, they're collecting stones."

"We're going to break all your windows right now," it was heard from the street.

Fear gripped the girls. As if on fire, they began to run away from the window, clinging to each other and falling.

"Natalka, hold me," Miia called, barely managing to grab the window frame. She shouted to the guys below, "Hi, handsome guys, wait," then jumped off the table and rushed to the windowsill. "You can kill me."

"Oh, and you weren't with them. Where are they? Call them."

She heard from behind:

"Miia, what negotiations? Let them go to hell."

Looking back, Miia noticed that only Tamila, Yulia, Natalka, Lusi, and Olena were in the room. The others seemed to have been blown out by the wind.

"Girls! They're about to break the windows now, and we'll all have to fix them. Is that what you want?" Miia looked at them seriously and then turned to the boys, who were already ready to throw stones.

"Guys, think smarter. You don't need to do that."

"What's this about?"

"That I won't move away from the window, and you'll have to throw stones at me. You're not going to kill me, are you?" They started talking about something in private.

"And where are the girls who threw eggs?"

"They hid. Stones aren't eggs."

"You weren't with them. Why are you responsible for them?"

"Because I'm older. Smarter."

"And how old are you?"

"Twenty." Looking around the room, Miia burst out laughing. "Guys, I'm sorry you can't see the girls' remorse. They cry bitter tears and beg for forgiveness on their knees."

75

Hearing this, Tamila and Yulia fell to their knees and began to bow to the floor, laughing uncontrollably.

"What is wrong with you?" the boys shouted from below.

Miia waved her hands to signal them to wait until her fit of laughter ended.

"Guys, none of you were hurt by those eggs? Are everyone's clothes clean?" Miia, calming down and wiping her tears, asked them.

"And what?"

"I suggest you be wise and forgive the naughty girls."

"How is that, just forgive?"

"Well, you guys are gentlemen. They have already repented, admitted their prank was stupid, made a thousand apologies, and promised never to do it again." Turning to the girls, she nodded at them. "They will say it themselves. Yes, girls?"

It was already apparent that the stones would not fly.

"Then let them talk."

"Guys, forgive us." Tamila was the first to run to the window, followed by Yulia and Tanya. "Forgive us. We don't know what has come over us."

"And what is your name?" one of the young men turned around, but the girls didn't know who it was.

"Who, exactly?"

"You!" he said, pointing his finger.

"Tamila," she waved at him.

"It's very nice, but not you."

Tamila decided to introduce everyone.

"Her name is Miia, and hers is Yulia, and we also have Tanya and Natalka. How about you?"

"My name is Kiril, and his is Illia. This is Maxim, girls; come out and let's get to know each other better."

"Yeah, we'll come, and you'll start beating us," Tamila said, taking the lead in the negotiations and successfully turning them into a humorous exchange.

"Girls, go downstairs and let's chat, because soon the others will start throwing eggs at us for staging such a riot here."

The girls shared glances. They believed nothing would threaten them as long as they kept talking on the sports field right below their windows.

"Bandits!" the guys exclaimed when they saw the girls

coming out of the dorm.

"Why the sudden bandits?" Tamila smiled sweetly at the guys. "You were the first to start calling us rustic halfwits."

"Was it really like that?" Miia asked, looking curious, first at Kiril, then at Illia.

"Well," the guy hesitated.

"People!" Miia addressed everyone in an authoritative voice. "I suggest you forget everything! First, no one was hurt. Second, the girls repented and apologized. And third," the guys understood that although we are village girls, we are not simple girls."

Fewer than ten minutes were remaining before the dormitory closed. The commandant was already standing on the threshold, loudly warning that all students should finish up dates.

"Miia, let's meet tomorrow," Kiril said. "If you don't have a boyfriend."

The girl thought to herself, "I still don't have enough happiness."

"How old are you?"

"I'll be seventeen. In October."

"Are you still in school?"

"Yes."

"I'm so sorry," Miia interrupted him, remembering Ivan, "I have a boyfriend."

"Did you make it up? Is he your local?"

"He is your local." Miia didn't like the young man's self-confidence.

"And why wasn't he there today?" he asked, looking curiously into Miia's eyes.

"He was, before the eggs war started," she replied with a smile.

Then the commandant's voice was heard:

"The dates are over. The dorm is closing. Miia, what are you waiting for?"

"Do you hear? They're calling me already. Goodbye!" she said, running up to the commandant and dancing. "Vira Ivanivna, I'm already here."

"You're the final one."

As she opened the door, Miia heard Kiril's voice:

"You're very handsome," but the commandant, threatening the boy with his finger, quickly closed the door.

"Oh, these gentlemen. Borko."

"What?" Miia turned around and stopped.

"He's a schoolboy."

"Yes, I know. He won't come anymore," she answered, pleased with herself. After a short pause, she asked the commandant, "Do you know my last name?"

"Thanks to your game Panas, your water wars; you're riding on the tubs down the stairs; all the commandants know not only yours but also your parents' names."

"This is a mess." Smiling sweetly, she looked at Vira Ivanivna. "But what can you do? We were born like this."

"Run and go to bed, and be quiet there because I know you."

"I hope it will stay quiet. Good night."

"Good night to you, too, you little brats."

Returning to the room, Miia was surprised to see that the girls were already in their beds. However, she didn't dwell on it; she thought, "I've been laughing a lot these last few days. I hope I don't have to cry."

X

As usual on weekends, Miia went home, where it was surprisingly calm and peaceful. She was happy to see Zhanna. Feeling the comfort of home, the girl's evil thoughts faded away.

Together with her sister, they quickly cleaned the house and helped in the kitchen. It was evening. The neighbor girls, Tanya and Vika, came running, and together they started getting ready for the disco. They styled each other's hair, helped with makeup, and chose outfits.

"Miia, I'm the first," said Vika, sliding onto a chair closer to the light. "You are the best!" Miia had an extraordinary skill for drawing arrows around her eyes. Her talent for drawing was remarkably developed even in childhood.

"Yes," her sister picked up, "her drawings in the school wall newspapers were the best."

"Did I have at least one chance to refuse you, Zhanna? You were responsible for their design," the girls laughed, looking at each other.

"The caricature drawn on us, because of the broken mirror, is still before my eyes," Tanya laughed.

"Wait!" Zhanna and Vika exclaimed in unison, "Was that you?" Looking at each other, Miia and Tanya nodded their heads, laughing.

"Do you remember?" Tanya turned to Miia. "That evening, we went for a walk to the center so that we could return home with your mother at the same time."

"Yes," continued Miia, "there was still an hour left before the end of work. In the center, we met the Kotsyubayev brothers and Malachi Jr. We saw that the school was still lit, and for some reason, we went there."

"Why didn't you tell me?" my sister was surprised.

"Not everyone should find out about everything at once; everything has its time!" and with excitement in her voice, she continued to share the adventures of that evening. "Tanya and I went up to the second floor, where we sat on the side table with a mirror." In confirmation of what was said, Tanya nodded her head, smiling. "The guys started fooling around, telling funny stories. You know these clowns, right? And

79

then Malachi pushes Misha Kotsyubai. He, falling, pushes us onto the mirror, and it turns out to be not attached to that darn bedside table. And... how it will fly." The girl covered her head with her hands.

"The sound of broken glass rang throughout the school." Tanya picked up, "That evening, there was a pedagogical meeting. We heard the teachers, and we started to run away in fear. Until, suddenly, Miia shouts after us 'Stop. I can't do this. We're going back. We have to confess.' We stood for a while. We took a breath. And went to surrender." Tanya finished proudly.

"So Klaudiya Ivanivna and the other teachers knew it was you and didn't shame you at the school assembly?" Vika looked at the girls with wide eyes.

"Yes. Because we honestly confessed," Miia smiled.

"And what about those steppe eagles?" Zhanna already knew the answer.

"They got scared, and with the words. 'You've gone crazy!' They ran away."

"But we didn't surrender them." Miia declared. "That's why there were only two girls in the caricatures, me and Tanya."

Miia couldn't stop thinking about Mark. Neither the cheerful bustle of the girls nor the fuss with makeup, clothes, and hairstyles stopped her thoughts about him. She felt his presence in every cell of her body because it was this room that united them.

"What will this evening be like? Will we see each other tonight? How will I look him in the eye?" Holding her breath, the girl tried to find answers to these questions. Excitement took hold of her more and more. And the closer they got to the disco, the more she couldn't find answers.

But Mark wasn't at the disco. Mila wasn't there either. New questions began to arise... Miia was overcome with despair.

"Yes, let's go, your favorite lambada." The girls ran over and pulled her onto the dance floor.

Miia noticed that Timko kept looking at her. This had never happened before. The girl found it strange. She tried not to pretend that something was bothering her; she continued to joke, laugh, and dance. And only she knew how much her soul ached.

When the announcement of the last dance was made, Miia, Tanya, and Vika went to the exit. On the street, young men and women stood in groups. Some danced along. Some sang along. A fight had already broken out between some. Some were making plans to go to a neighboring village.

"They were healthy, girls!" Timko approached them.

Everyone greeted her in surprise.

"Miia, just a minute."

The girls moved away from them.

"What?" She tried her best to suppress her excitement.

"Mark asked me to convey his congratulations to you. It's too bad he couldn't come. There are still some things he didn't have time to finish. But next weekend, he will be here."

"How nice to hear that." This gave her hope and calmed her down. She smiled and was just about to answer when she saw that Nona was quickly approaching them. The girls greeted each other.

'What are you talking about?'

"About your own business," answered Timko and, grabbing her hand, turned to leave. But she stopped.

"Miia, you probably already know? Mark is going to marry Mila. She is pregnant," and, dragging Timko with her, left.

The ground disappeared from under her feet. Ice covered the girl's head. It all happened so instantly.

At that very moment, she wanted to die.

"What are you talking about, Nona?" Timko could be heard shouting at her.

On the way home, Vika and Tanya tried to find out what Timko wanted from her and why he was questioning Nona so much. 'He doesn't know yet? She will tell him herself.' The girls quoted the words of Marko's sister.

"Miia, what are you going to tell him?" they questioned their friend.

"Nothing."

Miia was silent all the way. Until, near the yard, she barely managed to squeeze out:

"It's all supposed to be like this! Goodbye, girls."

The night felt like an eternity. Despair turned into anger. Anger became disappointment. Wild pain ripped her soul apart. Thoughts intertwined and confused. Miia searched for

81

the strength to control the chaos that had overwhelmed her. She wanted to run to a distant field and scream. However, she stayed still in bed, gazing icily at the ceiling, which was black from the night. There were no tears. There was a desire to find an excuse for what had happened between her and Mark. Her thoughts contradicted each other. Inside, two different Miias were talking. One reproached the other for weakness, and the other, in response, reassured her, 'Better him than some scumbag.' One demanded a frank conversation with Mark; the other let him go because she didn't want him to abandon the pregnant Mila.

On the web of thoughts, Miia recalled a book in the dormitory that offered the necessary support. And she wanted it right then and there.

The night passed.

"Where are you going?" mama asked in a sleepy voice, surprised, entering the room. "Half past four in the morning. Are you leaving today?"

"Yes, mom, I'm leaving today. Right now. I need some quiet." Miia understood that mama would want a more convincing explanation for her daughter's unexpectedly quick preparations. "Do you remember? I mentioned to you a month ago that our class teacher had organized the purchase of a book by an American author for the entire group. A psychology book. I need it right now."

"Are you okay?" mama was worried.

"Yes, of course!" her daughter assured, smiling. She had such a fire burning in her for that book that mama could tell by her face that her daughter, maybe not, was not okay, but under control. "I'll tell you everything, but first I need to sort everything out myself."

"I'll quickly pack a bag of groceries for you, get dressed, and see you to the bus." As soon as my mother left the room, Miia put on her boots, grabbed her jacket and handbag, and ran out of the house.

"Mommy, don't worry. I don't want to be late for this bus. I love you!" She ran up to her mother, kissed her, and ran outside.

"You'll be hungry for a week," the girl heard behind her.

"But I'll be slimmer. And anyway, I live in a dorm, and there,

82

everyone is either hungry or not. "

"She'll never sit still." Looking after her daughter, her mother was sure her daughter would cope.

The three-hour trip flew by in an instant. Miia was mentally revisiting the wise advice she had managed to remember from reading the book.

And what a lightness took over her soul when she finally discovered in the book what was most fitting for her.

"It doesn't all depend on circumstances," she reread that phrase again and again, out loud. "My God! Thank you."

A week passed. According to tradition, to make the guy's time in the army easier, he was supposed to be entertained with music, songs, and dances.

Therefore, in the yard of Mark's parents, tables were generously covered with a wide variety of dishes. The musicians had nearly finished setting up their equipment, and the cheerful relatives, neighbors, friends, and acquaintances of the conscript were happily chatting, looking forward to an invitation to the table.

"Timko, let's go," Mark called his friend and went to the motorcycle.

"Where are you going?" Nona ran after them.

"Why are you always running after me like a tail?" Mark snapped at his sister. We'll go back now.

"Come back," she shouted demandingly after them.

But the boys no longer heard her.

Mila stood at the gate and just watched.

The motorcycle stopped near Miia's yard.

Miia's father came out to meet them. Mark went to talk to him. And when he returned, he silently looked at his friend with glassy, empty eyes.

"Dude, what happened?" Timko realized that something was wrong.

"She's not here. She called and warned that she wouldn't be there over the weekend." His voice trembled.

"I'll get behind the wheel." Timko felt his anger begin to boil. "Let's go; they're waiting for us."

Jumping off the motorcycle without stopping or saying a word, Mark grabbed Mila by the hand and pulled the girl

83

with him to the table. With the appearance of the conscript, together with the girl who had agreed to wait for him from the army, the musicians immediately played a banquet march, cheerfully inviting all the guests to pour glasses.

Timko remained by the motorcycle.

"Let's go," Nona called to him. The guy didn't even move. She approached him. "Why are you standing here? Let's go."

"Do you understand what you've done?" Timko's eyes burned with anger. "Do you understand?"

"Mila loves my brother. And I like her company," she answered calmly.

"Yeah… She does. You like it. And you asked him if he wanted this?" Timko did not calm down.

"Listen, Mark and Mila have been doing things like adults for a long time." Nona did not back down. "He likes it. And why are you so tense?"

"Is Mila pregnant?" The angry tone decreased.

"Later," a satisfied smile shone on her face.

"Stop! Did you lie to Miia?"

"Hmm."

"God! Mark is my best friend! Why did you do this?"

"I already answered you. And you'd better think about how to calm your friend down." Her eyes shone with demand, "Do it for me."

"Oh, sit down; your seats are here. Timko, I had to drink without you while you were cooing with my sister."

Mark quickly began to get drunk and did not appear to be a loving gentleman at all. Timko, still sober, glanced at Mila. And the young man did not understand whether she truly loved him or was merely afraid of shame.

"Listen, my friend, don't offend my sister." Drinking his third glass of vodka, Mark snapped at his friend, "She is the only one I have."

"I should have told him everything. But… Nona…" thought Timko. He felt evil and disgusting in his soul.

"What, Mark, is a penalty?" He took the glass, poured vodka to the top, and drank it without stopping.

And before the hangover had yet to take hold of him, he whispered in Nona's ear:

"You'd better think about how to fix everything and not

break their lives."

Meanwhile, the only thing Miia wanted was a book. She didn't just read it; she became familiar with every part of each story the author used as an example. Most of all, she longed for her thoughts to take her somewhere far away, to the edge of the world, or even beyond it, just away from that evening when she felt happy. And no matter how hard she tried to find a wise excuse for how it all ended, she felt, with growing fury, the pain of losing both herself and Mark ripping through her soul. She couldn't find any excuses.

XI

The following school week brought the biggest surprise. Sergiy Vasylyovich was invited to their group for an after-school session. Miia, Natalka, and Vova were so happy to see him walk into the classroom. They couldn't wait to hear how Lida and Lora's story would end. They asked about it openly because, although they didn't know the sources, the entire technical school was discussing this story. The secret was out.

"The culmination of the story, which you have witnessed, has a tragic and bitter prehistory," he began. "The first two wives of Olexiy and the first wife of Mikhail committed suicide."

These words left all the students in a daze, so none could speak. Miia and Natalka looked at each other, their faces full of horror and despair in their eyes.

"Did they kill them?" someone finally dared to ask, breaking the complete silence.

"Inducing suicide. One of the articles they are accused of. Rape, corruption of minors, distribution of pornographic photos, and drugs."

"Will they be put in prison?"

"Moreover, for a long time."

"Oh, and it won't be easy for them to sit there," one of the guys roared. "They'll do the same to them under such articles."

"And how do you know what's going on there?"

"My neighbor's brother got out of prison, he told me."

"And what are they doing with them there?" The audience erupted in a roar.

"The same thing they were imprisoned for."

"What future awaits Lida and Lora?" Sergiy Vasilyovich indicated he had an answer, causing Natalka to stop her question.

"The investigation into Lida has also been closed. She is suspected of the same crimes as everyone else, except for sexual assault. Lora was not the only person Lida led to these criminals. She has known Olexiy for a long time."

"Now it's clear why she pounced on us like a viper... And

86

how long will they be imprisoned for?" Miia finally spoke, recovering from the shock.

"As for the main suspects, the prosecutor will demand fifteen years. And for the others, for some ten, for some from five to seven years."

"But they must be shot!" There was a commotion in the audience.

"Unfortunately, we have abolished the death penalty," the investigator shrugged his shoulders.

"For such crimes, no father's hand would tremble," Tamila exclaimed excitedly.

"Of course, not all people remain as humans. There are enough human-like creatures in society. But humanity, with its laws, is not ready to lose what makes us truly human," Sergiy Vasilyovich said without letting her finish.

"Tell me, what do we usually do with the weeds that overgrow our gardens or flower beds? We don't transplant them into separate plots and then tend to them. We destroy them mercilessly. So, what about the weeds of human form; can't we do the same?" Looking back at her classmates, the girl added, "I'm not calling for cruelty, but where is the justice?" Bowing her head, she remembered her conversation with Olexiy in the store, as well as their quarrels in the room. "God, thank you! You saved me!"

After finishing, Miia, Natalka, and Vova went over to Sergiy Vasilyovich. They had questions they didn't want to ask in front of everyone.

"When I went to that house with your colleagues, I overheard that this gang had been hunted for over a year," Vova began. "Why didn't they take them that same night?"

"There are two main reasons for this. First, I realized they were the same scumbags only after I got their passports. Second, we needed to track down their photo studio."

"And what if they hadn't come for the passports?" asked Natalka.

They didn't realize I was an investigator. They were confident I was a teacher from a technical school and that I wouldn't pose a threat to them.

"And in addition to the passports, they also had to take the girls. And these are two reasons that made them show up at the dormitory." Miia reasoned. "Yes, and what about Olexiy's parents?"

"They tried to buy their way out. But they don't care anymore. Other institutions have taken over the factory's affairs. The father was also arrested. And the mother can't handle such a global issue without him."

"And did everyone from their gang manage to get arrested?" asked Vova.

"Yes. Eleven people. Well, including Lida." Sergiy Vasylyovich scrutinized everyone. "I need to tell you. As witnesses, you will be summoned to court. When exactly is your school management informed, and each of you?"

"Wow," all three said in unison.

"Don't worry. You weren't worried when you talked to them in person, were you?"

We didn't realize at the time that they were capable of such horrible crimes," answered Miia.

Judging by your last conversation in the room, Miia wasn't afraid of him," Sergiy Vasilyovich said with a smile. "You hit him, didn't you?"

"How do you know?" the girl asked, surprised.

"Miia," Natalka leaned closer to her friend. "A pillow."

Students from another group began entering the auditorium.

"Oh, we need to vacate the premises. And I have to go too," said Sergiy Vasilyovich.

Approximately a month and a half later, the director of the technical school summoned all three students and, in front of the class teacher, informed them of the court summons. To ensure they did not go alone, it was decided that Tetyana Andriyivna, the deputy for educational work and a freelance employee of the internal affairs bodies, would accompany them.

"Now, the puzzles are complete." Leaving the director, they looked at each other, then Miia turned to Natalka.

Silence settled among the students. Each of their roles in this terrible story became crucial in exposing the gang of criminals. The lesson from this event pushed everyone to draw conclusions and rethink their attitudes toward frivolity, greed, honor, honesty, and humanity. And these three could be proud – they did not lose their dignity. Despite the wishes of those around them, none of the students heard a single word from them about the reasons for Lida and Lora's disappearance that September day. Miia and Natalka expressed solidarity with Lora as a victim of deception and violence. Vovchyk was ashamed of people like Olexiy and Mikhail. But all three shared a single, open desire: fair punishment.

XII

Almost two years have passed. During this time, all the love worries, anxieties, disappointments, and despairs faded away. Endless sleepless nights became a thing of the past. Peace returned to Miia, and she no longer asked herself questions to which she would never find answers. There were rumors that shortly after Mark left for service, Mila had a miscarriage. They said that she and Nona shared such a close friendship that every time her parents visited Mark in the military, they always took Mila with them.

They also started discussing Nona and Timko's wedding, which they would celebrate right after Mark's return. And he was supposed to come back in a few weeks.

"You know, there's a belief that a younger sister shouldn't get married before her older brother," the girls muttered. " It takes away his fate."

"So maybe they'll be celebrating two weddings at the same time," Miia said indifferently.

"Oh, and stupid Timko."

"Why?"

"Nona, she's such a bitch."

"Does he have a way out if she's pregnant?"

"You know, girls," Miia intervened, "I respect him for not abandoning her."

Tanya handed the girls some seeds.

"Well, she's like Olesya Sokolets," Tanya began pitifully.

"What about her?" Miia asked in surprise.

"They came here four or five times. There were even rumors about a wedding because Olesya was supposedly expecting a child."

"Her parents began preparing, especially Uncle Myron, who dreamed of celebrating all Ukrainian traditions. And that scoundrel turned out to be married."

"Oh my God."

"When she started coming alone," Vika continued, "Her parents asked, 'Where had Artur gone?' The belly is growing."

"Listen, there was such a commotion here!" Tanya interrupted the conversation. "Uncle Miron shouted: 'What a shame, a bastard in my yard… Mother, this is your doing. She raised a princess who never refused anything. It's good that at least she taught me how to cook."

"All of this, of course, is creepy. Has Olesya given birth yet?" Miia expressed her empathy openly.

She is due to give birth soon, and the quarrel happened two months ago.

"You missed everything while you were sitting at your practice in the city," she scolded her friend Vika with a smile. "Studying. Then continue, Tanya".

"Myroslava cries, but in response, she shouts at him, 'Come to your senses, old man! You called your daughter's child a scumbag. She is our only one.' And he roared again: 'If she had been a boy, he would not have brought such shame on his father.' And she continued, 'I will shoot myself.' After these words, an even greater uproar arose."

"Such details." Miia glanced at the girls.

"We hid quietly under your cherry tree." The friends laughed almost in unison. "Then continue, Vika; you're doing better."

"Miroslava runs out of the yard holding a gun and goes to Tanya's yard, then throws the gun over the fence."

"At my flowers," Tanya added.

"It's fortunate it wasn't loaded."

The girls, one after the other, rushed to share how it all turned out.

"Well, a miracle happened," Tanya said.

"Wow. What? Artur got divorced?" Miia's eyes widened in surprise.

"At the other end of the village lives Grandma Melina. You must remember her. We helped her when we were schoolchildren. So, she has a grandson named Andriy. He is much older than we are. He has two sons, aged 10 and 6. His wife died giving birth to their second boy, so he is raising them alone. A month and a half ago, he came to their house and asked Myron and Miroslava to marry Olesya to him."

"Wow." Surprise freezes on Miia's face.

"They say Myron looked at him carefully and said just one word, 'I bless!'. That same day, Olesya left with him. And Uncle Myron went to your dad with a bottle of moonshine, which was made for the wedding, and some sausage."

"He knew who to go to. Yes, Miron doesn't drink," Miia interjected.

"Yes." Vika smiled. "They got drunk, and cried, and sang."

"I'm walking somehow, and they, hugging each other, can barely stand on their feet. And your father: 'And I have two girls,' and how he started crying. Miron follows him. Yes, and again, start, 'Oh, what are you, Kalina, didn't you save the girl?'"

"Moonshine cried in them," said Miia, smiling. "And what about Olesya?"

"Olesya and Andriy celebrated their wedding with a small group. Here, they gathered neighbors; it's nice to sit, though, without the newlyweds," concluded Tanya.

"They showed everyone a photo. Olesya is wearing a white dress, not a wedding dress, but it is very stylish, with a living white lily in her hair. Andriy, although he is 14 years older than her, is so handsome." Vika smiled slyly. "I would marry him myself."

The girls were laughing.

"You see, fairy tales have a happy ending."

Each of them was thinking about her fairy tale at that moment.

"You hear, Miia! And what went wrong with you and Mark?" Vika's question stunned her.

"Did you come to think I should be involved with him?"

"He liked you, right? Everyone saw that." Vika looked intently at her friend. "And that evening by the river? He used to come to you then."

"Everything is over." Miia felt a twinge in her soul but kept smiling. "Now tell me about yourself."

"The last time they went to see him, he refused to marry Mila again." Vika didn't stop. "He said, later."

"He's right." Miia was happy to hear that. "And why again?"

"Because he's constantly being pushed to do it. They want Mila as their daughter-in-law."

Miia was so surprised that she couldn't say a word.

"I'm in chaos," Miia began emotionally. "He's in the army. They're taking her to him in the hope of marrying her off. He refuses. Over and over again. Mila is an idiot! She doesn't respect herself."

Miia had a real pun in mind.

92

"Maybe he's waiting for you?" Vika hesitated.

"Oh my God, I feel sorry for Mila," Miia said, looking at the girls worriedly. "Mila is my classmate. We got along very well when we were kids."

She was disgusted by the situation that had developed for Mark in his family. And at that moment, as if she had a flash of insight, intrigues became an obstacle on her way with him. The complete unknown that awaited Mark and Mila was even more intriguing. But she did not want to discuss it with the girls. It was her secret. And the girl preferred to enjoy it alone.

"Let's close this topic. Will it be your turn to tell stories about yourself, partisans?" Miia turned her demanding gaze on her friends.

"I have nothing to tell," Tanya hurried. "I am free as a bird."

"I have no news," Vika became visibly nervous.

"Just wait, he'll come running again. It always happens to you," her friend said, taking a handful of seeds in her hand.

"Tell me," Miia smiled.

"They've broken up ten times and met again just as many times." Tanya nudged her friend with her elbow.

"So, what's going on with you and Artem?" Miia looked at her friend closely. Vika stayed silent.

"You know, we have quarrels out of nowhere. 'Why are you late?', 'Why are you early?', 'Why are you walking?'. Or he to me: 'Why without me?', 'Why didn't you warn me?', Vika said thoughtfully.

"Maybe it's better this way than living and guessing who has what thoughts?" commented Miia, "The truth is born in the argument. So, you are given time to understand whether you can be together in life."

"Miia, is it true that you started dating Anton Kulishchenko?"

"Something like that."

"What is he like? We don't know him very well."

"Kind. Sensitive. It seems practical. But life will show. Hey, have they switched to me again?"

"But there isn't much about him."

"What else can we say?" My mother married a handsome man with golden hands, so what? I pray to God that I never live with a man the way she does."

93

"That's why? Why do they start drinking, fighting, cheating, and hanging around?' The girls sat in silence for a moment. "But not everyone is like that. For example, Andriy. He's a real man." Mia picked up the guitar: "I learned a new song for the upcoming concert."
Song after song until the clock showed 2:30 a.m.

XIII

"Good morning, Maria Markivna!" Miia greeted with a smile, briskly walking past the commandant.

"Oh, Borko, you're staying for the weekend? Good morning to you, too! He was interested in you today."

"Who?" The girl was surprised, stopping.

"At 6:30 in the morning, Stefan called. 'Tell me, please, is Miia Borko from room 403 staying for the weekend?' I looked, and there were no keys in the place. I saw your girls yesterday. So, I told him that you were here. What was wrong?" she was worried.

"We don't know each other. Well, I bumped into him a couple of times in the corridor while we were playing the game Panas's," Miia tried to understand what his call was about.

"Oh, you and that game, 'Opa Panas', you're turning the whole dorm upside down."

"Only half of the fourth floor," the girl corrected herself, laughing.

"Half of the fourth floor. And who is that, with a loud rumble, coming down the stairs from the fourth floor in the bathing troughs?" Maria Markovna seemed stern, but her eyes were smiling.

"Everyone talks about it. Well, we're just like that." A childish playfulness flickered across Miia's face.

"Okay. If you're in a hurry, run."

"I'm heading to the store. I'll return shortly, and I'll have the key with me."

Miia hurried to meet Anton, who was already waiting for her near the college. After the store, they went to the dorm. At that moment, the commandant was not there. Miia wanted to find her to inform her, as the rules required, that a guest had arrived and would be staying until the next day.

"Miia, my dear," he leaned toward her, smiling softly, and said, "Let's go quickly. That's how it should be. Let my presence stay a little secret."

"I have to tell her. These are the rules," but he grabbed her hand and pulled her toward the stairs.

"Rules exist to be broken." An arrogant smile never left his face.

As she entered the room, Miia started unpacking the products.

"That's all." He moved closer to the girl, hugged her tightly, and started to kiss her. "No one sees us here anymore... I missed you very much."

"I missed you, too. But..." pushing him away, "Let me go and say that I have you. She should write you down in the guest book. I don't want to get in trouble."

"Yeah, we're not going anywhere, and she won't know I'm here," he said, taking off his sneakers.

Mia stepped back from him and looked at him with a curious and displeased expression on her face.

"We agreed that we would go for a walk around the city: to the park, to the embankment. Look how wonderful the weather is."

"Why do I need that park if you're with me?" he started hugging her again.

"Anton, are you serious?" Miia asked him flatly, with a hint of indignation. "Are you suggesting that we stay in the dorm all day?"

And what's wrong with that? We celebrated the birthday with the guys. I got up early because I was going to see you. So, let's rest."

Miia looked at him in surprise.

"In that case, we both had to go home. You would rest peacefully, and in the evening, we would meet."

"In the evening. We will be together here all day and night." Having understood where her bed was, he sat down on it. "You'd better go to my place."

"I'll go prepare breakfast. I don't know how you are, but I'm hungry," and after gathering the necessary ingredients and dishes, she headed out of the room.

"Don't be mad. Why are you acting like this?"

"How?" Stopping at the door, she looked at him with displeasure. "How come? What did we agree on? I could go home. This is the second weekend I haven't gone home."

"And why didn't you go with the last ones?"

"I told you this week is a week of tests for us. All my girls stayed because they were getting ready. Only Lusi went to

96

see the child. I don`t understand why you're not listening to what I'm telling you at all?" and she left the room.

There was no one in the kitchen. Quiet, empty, calm. Only it was not cleaned. Miia's mood was ruined. She was openly angry with Anton. "How is this possible? He suggested that we come and walk around the city... And you, you fool, believed it," she said to herself.

She had no desire to go back to her room. After inspecting the kitchen, she decided to clean it thoroughly.

"Now I'll make breakfast and do something more useful than sitting and entertaining that selfish person," and went to check the kitchen cabinets for detergents and utensils. She didn't know where they were stored yet because the kitchen duty hadn't reached their room yet. Having found everything she needed, she was satisfied and began cooking breakfast.

When she entered the room with the hot sandwiches and tea, she saw that Anton was sound asleep. She was even more overwhelmed with despair and anger.

"Why the hell did you come here at all?" But she realized she only had herself to blame. "Then why are you so naive?" she scolded her. After breakfast, she grabbed the tape recorder and headed to clean the kitchen.

The appearance of Stefan's friend in the kitchen reminded Mia of her morning conversation with Maria Makarivna.

A wild excitement gripped the girl. To calm down, Miia began washing the windows intensively.

"Hi, little one!" he said, turning to her. "And what is it that you clean for everyone yourself?"

"I have the desire, and I clean. This is not a violation."

"Of course."

Miia felt awkward around him, but she knew he was meeting with a girl from the parallel group, Irina.

Following him, Irina also stepped into the kitchen. The girls greeted each other warmly.

"Miia, we're going to the movies today. Come along with us." Such an invitation was so unexpected that Miia was speechless. Before, with Irina, they had only exchanged greetings. But it was hard to imagine any other kind of interaction. And now, such an invitation. Noticing her

97

confusion, Irina moved closer to the girl and said, "Stefan will be with us. You've seen him. You don't know each other, but he'd like to meet you."

Miia didn't know what to say. These guys were already twenty-five years old. They had served in the army, graduated from college, and worked in the police force. That was all Miia knew about them. They were different from the troublemakers Miia had dealt with earlier that year. Stefan was very handsome, with a reserved way of speaking and a calm demeanor. Summoning her courage, she finally responded.

"Ira, I am very pleased, and I admit that I am..."

But she cut her off:

"He is reliable. With him, you will feel like you're behind a stone wall. He liked you." Her smile was sweet, and Miia had no doubts about the sincerity of her words. As she left the kitchen, Irina added, "Think."

Miia stood confused. She remembered how, without looking ahead, she ran away from the game Panas and collided with Stefan, who was thrown against the wall, and she fell to the floor. He approached her and, asking, 'Are you not hurt?' offered her his hand. After moving away from the girls who continued the game, he stopped and watched for a while as the players, fleeing from the game Panas, fell again.

The second round was even more epic. This time, she was in the same game. Blindfolded, with her arms outstretched, she tried to catch one of the girls. At one point, it seemed like the wind had moved through the fingers of one hand. Turning sharply, she lost her footing and was carried away, knocking someone over. Deciding that it was one of her girls, she grabbed her elbow. Laughing, the girls loudly exclaimed, "Don't take off the blindfold; guess first." And Miia began, laughing, to run both hands over the jacket. The girls laughed even louder. Miia thought she had caught Vova. Until she felt her blindfold being removed. Stefan stood in front of her, smiling sweetly. There was so much tenderness in his eyes that she felt faint, and shyly she barely managed to say, 'Again, you?' He took her hand, 'If you catch me, don't let go anymore.' Miia didn't know what to say to him. She only apologized. But she couldn't play anymore.

98

Natalka ran after her: "You don't want to anymore?"

"His look seemed very strange to me." She looked thoughtfully at her friend.

"It seemed that way to me as well. Since he doesn't meet anyone here, he'll go to Irina's, have a cup of tea, and then leave." Miia knew that Natalka and Irina studied in parallel classes at school and had a good, friendly relationship. Irina praised him a lot, saying the owner was both intelligent and decent. Toma wanted him, but he told her not to get her hopes up. Miia looked sadly down the corridor where Irina's room was. Natalka noticed the sadness in Miia's eyes. "Listen, isn't it because of you that he comes here? Do you like him?"

"Is there something about him... Honestly? Yes."

Remembering those moments, the girl couldn't figure out what that look was concealing. Only the fire that had engulfed her then whispered with its hot tongues what she had heard from Irina today. She felt hurt and sad. She caught herself thinking that she regretted Anton's arrival. But she quickly pushed that thought away, considering herself a traitor.

"Yes, Miia. Come to your senses. Who is Stefan?" she said to herself. "What do you know about him? What if this is some game?" She remembered Lida and Lora. "God forbids! Finish cleaning and go to the room. Maybe Anton's arrival is your protection against temptation?"

Having quickly finished cleaning, she managed to prepare dinner, take a shower, and when she returned, Anton had already woken up.

"You slept all day. It's already almost six o'clock," she said with a smile. "Time for dinner."

"And what do we have?"

"Home-made potatoes, baked meat in the oven, vegetable salad, and for dessert, we have ice cream."

"Delicious!" he said as he came up and hugged Miia. "I'm going to shower."

"On the right, the last door. Today, freer than ever." She grabbed a towel and shampoo, then handed them to the young man. "For you."

Meanwhile, she dried her hair with a hairdryer, styled it into a cute hairstyle, put on her favorite dress, and started setting the table. When he returned to the room, Anton approached Miia and hugged her.

"Wow, how delicious."

"I'm setting the table," she playfully tried to break free from his embrace.

"Okay, honey! I won't bother you!" he said as he moved away, took his guitar, and sat down in a chair to play the strings.

He asked, 'How do you play it?' as if surprised and dissatisfied.

"I'll show you," she came up and showed him

"But I don't want to. I don't understand at all; why do you need it?"

"How, why? For myself. For development. It's so wonderful."

Taking the guitar from him, she began to play.

Just then, there was a soft knock on the door.

"It's open!"

Without entering the room, Stefan lingered on Anton with a look. Then he calmly asked Miia:

"Can you come out? Please."

She left the room and headed to the hall. Approaching the window, Miia silently watched the children playing on the sports field. Her excitement knew no bounds. All her thoughts vanished. She had no idea what to say. Stefan slowly approached her, so close she could feel his breath. With a gentle movement, the young man turned her toward him. The girl stood with her head down, afraid to even look at him. For a while, they were silent.

"You shouldn't be afraid of me."

"I'm not afraid," she proudly raised her head.

"Finally," he smiled. "Do you play the guitar?"

"A little." Trying to calm her excitement, she answered in a quiet voice.

"That's wonderful. It means you have a strong character and a high sense of beauty if you learned to play the guitar. I'm sure you draw well. And your culinary abilities, judging by the smells, everyone can envy."

"A psychologist?"

"I had to study," he answered calmly.

"Are you practicing your knowledge on me?"

"I don't need it anymore. I know a lot about you. Where do you live? Who are your parents? The only thing I don't know is who this guy is. He stared at her intently. "The commandant just told me that you are alone. There is no one recorded in the guest book. Is this your brother? A boyfriend?" Miia tried to turn away to the window, but Stefan stopped her. "You're silent... I understand. Are you okay with him?"

"If he is here," she tried to demonstrate confidence, but he interrupted her.

"The fact that he is here doesn't say anything. You didn't answer. Are you okay with him?"

The last time she experienced confusion mixed with submission was that evening with Mark. She also sensed an unfamiliar calm and a charming warmth coming from Stefan – wonderful and pleasant feelings. In six months with Anton, she had never experienced anything like this, not once.

"Okay." Finally, she squeezed out.

"I don't believe you. I can see in your eyes that you are not happy with him." He adjusted her hair. "How soft and fragrant."

At that moment, the door to the room opened, and footsteps could be heard in the corridor. Before entering the hall, Anton stopped in the corridor.

"Honey, are you okay?" There was an evil tone in his voice.

"Of course. I will come right away."

"Exactly. Are you okay?" he asked again.

"I will be right back," she answered, her voice trembling. He stayed there for a moment before walking away.

"Do you want me to talk to him right now, and he will leave and never come near you again?"

"Why do you need this?" She began to feel irritated.

"I want you to be happy." He took her hands. "With me. I never just come to anyone."

"You shouldn't think that I'm not happy. I'm fine." She tried to leave, but he grabbed her other hand.

"Your lips say that, but your eyes say the opposite." He started to warm her hands with his breath. "Why are they so cold?"

"Stefan, I have to go." She tried to free her hands and looked directly into his eyes. Her soul burned with the ache of a

101

secret desire she already felt, and a wave of excitement swept through her body. His intense gaze moved over her face, hair, and shoulders, seducing her with its fiery honesty. "You didn't answer." He leaned toward her, gripping her hand tightly, and whispered.

A little more, and she would have burst into tears, but her cold mind wouldn't let her. "I'm sorry!"

Realizing that she and Anton had to report his presence without stopping near the room, Miia ran down to the first floor.

"Vera Andriyivna, write in the guest book, Kulishchenko, Anton. He will leave tomorrow," she said quickly, and turning around, she headed for the stairwell.

Hearing footsteps on the stairs, she quickly ran into the open pantry. She knew it was Stefan. She couldn't face him again because she felt it would end badly.

Passing by the commandant, saying goodbye, he added: "I will be back."

Miia couldn't hold back; she broke down in tears. Her inner voice urged her to give herself a chance with Stefan. Her thoughts kept drifting back to memories of Lida and Lora. She was scared of making a mistake. She knew Anton well. Additionally, she also knew his family. Her parents considered him a son. And she sobbed out of helplessness, pain, and rage.

"Where have you been for so long?" he asked her firmly.

"I came here to ask you to write your name in the guest book," she answered calmly.

"Who was it?"

"An acquaintance."

"What did he want from you?"

"The more important thing is that he doesn't want anything anymore."

"I didn't come here to..."

"I see, have you already had dinner?" Looking at him, she was surprised that he hadn't waited for her. However, she had been absent for no more than fifteen minutes. "It's good that you're not hungry."

"You're already cleaning everything up. What won't you eat?" he was surprised.

"I don't want."

"I want it," and with intense passion, he quickly approached her, hugging and kissing her. She tried to stop him, but she couldn't do anything against the strength of his hands and body.

"No… Wait… Stop…"

Their approach became so quick that Miia didn't have time to realize it could be like that.

"Why?" she almost cried. "I can get pregnant."

"Then, you definitely won't get away from me anywhere." Still holding her tight, he refused to let go.

"My God. Why?" She didn't understand whether Anton's determination was a blessing or a curse.

There was no room for two on the narrow bed. Anton was already asleep, but she couldn't fall asleep. That's why she moved to Natalya's bed. The feelings that overwhelmed her in Stefan's presence were the same as they once were in Mark's presence. 'Why do they have such an effect on me?' she wondered. She could easily refuse the boys' requests to meet or get to know her better. But with these two, she lost both her peace and her balance.

XIV

Friendly, youthful hugs radiated with the joy of reunion.

"Welcome back, friend."

The guys got on their motorcycles and, as is tradition, sped through the streets with cheerful songs and the noise of good news. People smiled at them and rejoiced with them, and back at home, the family's friends were waiting eagerly. A gentle breeze spreads delightful aromas. Women were setting the tables, and men were chatting lively, waiting for the first glass.

From somewhere in the distance, blending with cheerful singing, the roar of a motorcycle started to be heard, getting closer and closer...

And here is the yard.

"Mark."

"Look at him, a real handsome man."

"A handsome Cossack!"

"And the uniform fits."

Mark, with his natural sense of humor, kept everyone entertained with stories about the hardships of service, including vivid anecdotes from his own experiences and everyday tales. But no one tried to uncover the truth. Instead, they lively added their own stories to them.

"Mila, child, you seem a little sad," Mark's mother said, hugging her. "He is already home, so everything will be fine."

"I think so too," she said, tears welling up in her eyes.

"What is this? Calm down; you have no reason to cry. Let's go; we need to replenish the table with food," she said and headed to the kitchen.

At the table, Mark chose a seat among the neighboring uncles and paid no attention to Mila. Nona occasionally looked demandingly at Timko, and he understood why. When it was time to take a break from the table, Mark, grabbing cigarettes, put his hand on Timko's shoulder and led him out into the yard.

"You don't smoke," the guys shouted after him.

"And I'll try."

And they went to sit on the riverbank, which was gurgling

nearby.

"She didn't answer any of my letters," Mark began, lighting a cigarette. "I didn't know what to think. But there were no answers. Half a year was like being in a fog. In our unit, one shot himself. His parents came and said that his girlfriend had gotten married." Looking into the distance, Mark asked his friend, "How is she?"

Timko can`t collect his thoughts. He knew the actual reason behind what had happened two years ago, but he understood that dwelling on it now could lead to unpredictable outcomes. Over these two years, he had already calmed himself. Miia was not alone, which is why his conscience no longer troubled him.

"Listen," he finally dared, "Start your life with Mila, not just physically. Look, she is kind and hardworking. She loves you, fool." There was no response from Mark. "What did you promise her parents? Remember?"

What if I am wrong?

"You will make a mistake if you do not keep your word to her parents."

"You did not answer; how is she?"

"Alive and well." Timko's voice playfully brightened.

"My friend, if I hadn't screwed your sister, then I would have screwed Mila."

Mark looked at him sternly and wasn't impressed by what he heard.

"Yes, why didn't you screw her?"

"You beat me to it," he said with a smile, nudging him with his elbow.

"Now have the courage to say that you regret meeting my sister, and not her best friend."

"What are you talking about?" Timko instantly realized that he had blurted out something wrong: "I'll rip anyone's head off for your sister."

Nona watched them. Of course, she didn't hear what they were saying, but she knew her future husband would find the right words.

Returning to the table, Mark sat down at his usual spot, now with Mila.

"He asked about Miia?" Nona asked quietly.

105

"Yes."

"What did you answer?"

"What's the difference? There's the result," he nodded toward Mark, who, hugging Mila, kept telling his funny stories.

And everything seemed to be fine, but still, a sense of guilt tormented Timko's soul.

That same evening, Miia didn't feel very well. But the girls came running, chatted, and convinced them to go to a disco. Their gatherings, as always, were noisy and full of play.

"Mark came back from the army. Do you already know?" Having said this, Vika realized that the cheerfulness in her voice was unnecessary.

"The time had come, so he returned," Mia replied, maintaining her composure.

"Do you care?"

"I don't care anymore." Getting up from the chair, she quickly went to the bed and lay down. "Tanya, bring me some water."

Miia lay there thinking that in the past three weeks, this was the fourth time she had experienced this.

"Drink," Tanya said as she handed her some water.

"Do you care so much? My friend! That's how the news affected you," the girls smiled.

"I'm dieting," she quickly answered.

"Will Anton come for you?"

"No. We agreed to meet at the disco if I decide to come. If I don't go, he will come to me," she told the girls. "So, are you ready? Let's go, beauties."

As they approached the community center, they saw Mark with his friends, who were excitedly talking and laughing loudly. Miia looked around at everyone on the street but didn't see Anton among them. When she reached the stairs, she made eye contact with Mark. He suddenly went silent and looked at her. He wanted to move, but Timko held him back.

Miia didn't feel like dancing, so she sat down and calmly watched the lively dances of the young people and her girls, who cheerfully demonstrated exercises. After a while, they

106

ran up to Miia and suggested they go outside into the fresh air.

"I don't want to. You go," she answered them, smiling.

The music blared as the colorful bunnies danced to the rhythm. At some point, Miia started to regret coming here. She wanted to sleep. Tilting her head, she counted the multicolored musical bunnies at her feet – first green, then blue, then red.

Until…

Raising her head, she saw Mark. He stopped in front of her and stared at her intently without saying a word. His inquisitive gaze was full of anger and sadness at the same time. He didn't even notice that Nona and Mila were sitting three chairs away. Miia didn't understand what was wrong with him. And she couldn't look away either. Where had the noisy music, the bustling disco, and everyone around gone? Only they. Eyes locked. Reproach. Anger. Sadness.

This picture was interrupted when Anton appeared, approached Miia, and, grabbing her hand, pulled her toward the exit.

"What are you doing?" she tries pulling her hand away.

"We're going home." His agitated state indicated that something had happened in her absence. Looking back at Mark, she saw that he had stayed near the spot where she was sitting. "Oh God." Seeing the bruises on her boyfriend's face, Miia yelled, "Are you with him…?"

"I shouldn't have anything to do with you," Anton said sharply, his voice not sparing.

"Why?" This time, anger gripped her. She saw Mark approaching them quickly, followed by Nona.

"No. Mark, stop." She tried to stand in front of Anton when he pushed her away.

"Go! You've done your job." His eyes looked like those of an angry bull.

"Go to hell, both of you," she snapped, then turned and ran out into the street, hearing a quarrel behind her between Anton and Mark, with Nona jumping into the fight.

"Miia, wait." Vika and Tanya ran after her.

"So, listen to how it all happened. Anton approached the building. Mark went to him without hesitation. Someone told him about you and him," the girls said, panting almost simultaneously.

"A village. What did you want?" Miia expressed her emotions openly.

"Stepchuk and Yarik started to block Anton, while Timko and Ilya were pulling Mark away. It was so funny."

"Maybe we should wait for Anton," Tanya barely kept up with Miia."

"Sparks are flying from my eyes right now," Miia growled. "Damn gladiators."

"Miia, they started fighting when Anton began, well… How to put it properly…" Vika hesitated, "To bully. And then he shouted that you were pregnant, and Mark hit him."

"What did Anton say?" she asked, stopping suddenly, surprised, and turning to Tanya. "That I'm pregnant?"

"Is it true?" Vika grabbed her friend's hand.

"I don't know," Miia said slowly. "Two weeks late. And I've been feeling bad lately."

"I can see that something's wrong with you." Vika looked closely at her friend.

"But I didn't tell Anton about it." She looked thoughtfully at her friends. "He wanted to lie to Mark… God, how low of him."

Tanya tried to cheer her up, saying, "He loves you and is doing everything not to lose you."

"Mark wouldn't take me away. He has a much more powerful competitor." Miia smiled.

"What?" The girls, pleasantly surprised, started bombarding Miia with questions. "Why were you silent? Why didn't you tell? And who is he? Where did you meet?"

"Let's go inside because it's cool outside," Miia suggested to her friends. "I'll tell you."

With tenderness, she began to tell the girls about Stefan. Her soul seemed to bloom, her heart sang, and sweet memories floated through her thoughts. The girls listened to this story as if enchanted. Their eyes sparkled. Of course, the ending saddened them.

"You can only see this in the movies," Tanya said sadly. "He said he would come back. To you. And what if you…" She hesitated, not daring to go on.

"I don't know." Miia couldn't help but cry. "But something is somehow complicated with Anton. I catch myself thinking that we shouldn't rush into a future together with him."

Vika looked intently at her friend: "If it turns out that you will have a child, it will be good if Stefan becomes the second Andriy and your story becomes as happy as Olesya's. And if not? Don't rush to conclusions about Anton."

"Girls, I might have a change in my cycle." Miia tried to reassure herself more than the girls.

"Go to the doctor." Only the girls said this when a soft knock was heard on the window. There was silence; the girls looked at each other with smiles. The knock was repeated.

"Yes, girls, whoever it is, let's sit quietly," Miia whispered. "The light is not on in the room, so I'm already asleep. Soon, they heard footsteps and soft voices behind the fence."

"I can't see anything. Who exactly could it be?" Opening the curtains, Vika tried to make out the visitors, but the night was so dark that she couldn't even see their silhouettes.

The next day, Anton showed up, looking very irritated and unfriendly. Their talk started with an argument.

"You left yesterday; you didn't even want to wait for me."

"To stand and watch you, like two rascals, punch each other in the face?"

"According to others, you have no idea what a laughingstock I looked like."

"Sorry, if you had used your brains, you wouldn't have gotten into a fight the second time."

"Great! I'm to blame."

"You also embarrassed yourself by yelling about my supposed pregnancy in front of everyone. Why?"

"Did these two gossips tell you?"

"Firstly, they are no longer gossiping because they did not slander you but told the truth about your words. And you don't turn the tables, but be a man. Give me an answer."

"No, tell me what went down between you and him."

"Anton, did you come to interrogate me? I will disappoint you; it won't work. And do you know why? Because I have no desire to satisfy your selfishness."

"Yeah, my selfishness... No, my dear, listen to me. I leave my affairs behind to come to your dorm, and what do I see? Miia,

109

cooing affectionately with someone, says, 'I don't know...'
It's a good thing you didn't hug or kiss him."
"Think whatever you want. But you'd better learn to control
your jealousy; it's disgusting."
"Jealousy?" he was shaken. "And why are you turning
away?"
"I will at least put on a gas mask."
"Oh, I was so angry with you yesterday that the guys and I
just went out drinking. I asked what you had to do with it
and who was in the dormitory."
"It was easier for you to go and get drunk instead of coming
and talking to me," Miia said this to try to understand if he
had been knocking on the window at night.
"I came now, but I never got an answer."
"And I didn't get one either; why did you shout about my
pregnancy to half the town? Only I have the right to discuss
such matters. And you made it up. You just lied in front
of everyone," she got angry. "You did everything so that I
wouldn't want to see you anymore... Go." She just wanted
to turn around and leave, but he grabbed her hand so tightly
that she couldn't break free.
"Are you kidding me?" There was open anger on his face.
"Do you want to learn more about me? Alright! Come on, I'll
start telling you everything, starting from the moment I was
born. Listen, I was born..."
"No! That's not what I asked you."
"Why, no? I'm sure you need to know more about me.
Maybe you'll remember at least something from my life and
figure out how you should behave around me and how,
categorically, no," she looked at him demandingly. "I'll tell
you more. Remember the danger. And now you're standing
half a step away from that very danger." She pointed to her
hand, which was starting to turn blue; he was holding it so
tightly. "Let go and walk away. And don't come near me
again."
He shoved her aside and walked off without saying anything.
"Is he really that inadequate in life?" she asked yourself.

110

XV

Another week went by, but the delay persisted. Miia started to worry. She was feeling sick more often, and her body was demanding more food.

"You ate almost all the canned food," Lusi said with a sweet smile. "I had the same thing with Taras." Miia silently looked at her with excited eyes.

"I'm already three weeks behind."

"I've noticed from you that you've changed lately." Lusi hugged Miia. "We'll go to my place on Thursday, and will go to my doctor on Friday. Then everything will be known. And if the pregnancy is confirmed, you'll have to tell your parents. Is Anton the father of the child?"

"Oh, Lusi," sighed Miia. And she began to tell her the story about Stefan, which happened precisely on the day Anton came to her.

"Anton deliberately didn't protect you back then. He was jealous."

"Do we still have any cucumbers?" Miia asked, biting her lips and smiling.

"We still have two jars of cucumbers and three tomatoes."

"Eureka! I'm saved!"

All doubts were confirmed. Miia was truly six weeks pregnant.

"You'll be babysitting." Lusi started talking on the way home from the hospital. "And as a mother, I congratulate you."

"Your Taras, such a smart boy. He shares a lot of information and is genuinely interested in everyone. A sweet child."

"You know that Viktor is not the father of my son. His father left us when I was five months pregnant. He admitted that he wasn't ready to be a father."

"What a scumbag! I'm sorry about that."

"Don't apologize; that's just how it is."

"And how did you and Viktor get along?"

"He often visited the store, always friendly and cheerful. Before I gave birth, we regularly took walks with him. He knew I was pregnant. The one time he visited, I was already in the maternity hospital. It was a miracle for me to see him carrying a huge bouquet of roses. That same day, he told my parents that he wanted to be Tarasyk's father. So, they listed him as the father on the birth certificate."

But initially, everything was fine for about a year. Then, he started accusing me of raising someone else's child, not his own. He also accused me of taking birth control pills, but I know for sure I don't take anything. I barely convinced Viktor to get tested, and now he's undergoing treatment to have children. Still, I don't want to live with him anymore.

"Is everything that serious?"

"In fits of anger, he doesn't control himself. And the scariest thing, he yells at Taras."

"You said that when you are studying, the child is with your parents. Do you live in his apartment?"

"Yes. Just don't think I'm ungrateful."

"Well, why should I think that?"

"My best friend recently told me, 'Victor is such a gentleman; he picked you up with the child, brought you to his apartment, provided for you, and you're so ungrateful that you didn't give him a child.' Hearing that from her, I realized that I no longer have a friend."

"Is she married?"

"No. And what?"

"Maybe she has her eye on Viktor?"

"And you know, anything is possible."

"And your parents know about your problems."

"Mom does."

"And dad?"

"If he found out, then Taras and I would live together."

"Do you love him?"

"How can I tell you? I have never felt such a passionate desire for him. And lately, he has been telling me about it all the time."

"Your parents supported you through the hardest times. So why don't you divorce him? Are you waiting for him to start hitting the little one?" Lusi looked at her in fear. "There are different situations. And there are cases where parents abuse their children. My father beat my sister like that... I remember it with horror. And if you say that, he screams and is already swinging. I think you have something to think about."

"But I also thought about all of this. And I haven't figured

112

out how to tell him about the divorce yet."

"Tell your friend that you've started thinking about divorce. Just be sure to tell her that you'd feel calmer if he were to want it first. You'll see, your Nyura will do everything for this."

"And that's the idea."

"The main thing is that you don't regret it later."

Dinner was already ready at home. The cabbage soup with smoked ribs that Father had made was better than any other cabbage soup Miia had ever tasted. And my mother's pancakes with cheese and herbs became love at first bite. Miia was surprised, but Taras, only four years old, enjoyed the food without asking for candy in return.

After cleaning up the kitchen after a delicious dinner, Lusi and Miia stayed to continue their conversation. Grandfather and grandson went outside for a walk.

"Girls, it's none of my business, but can I ask?"

"Mom, of course," Lusi answered, smiling.

"You must understand that, as an adult and much older than you, I notice everything you're trying to hide." The girls looked at each other. "Miia, I hope you won't consider an abortion."

"Mom."

"Lusi," she interrupted her daughter, "do you remember your despair when your scoundrel left? What were you screaming then? My father and I prayed to God that you wouldn't take your life."

"Yes. There was something like that." Lucy looked at Miia.

"God forbids!" Miia barely spoke.

"Okay. I'll tell you and go outside to see grandfather with Taras," she said, sitting down next to the girls. "Miia, can you imagine if we hadn't supported Lusi during that difficult time for her, what would have been left for us and my grandfather? Trouble, grief, and a lonely old age." She took Miia by the hand. "I don't know how your parents will react to the news. But promise me, if you face difficulties that try to overwhelm you, you will come to us, and we will all find a way out together. Promise me that you won't do anything reckless. Just look at our boy. This is our life, our joy, our happiness, our little angel. You are a future mother.

113

For every woman, this is the most precious gift from God."
She got up and left.

The girls were silent for a while.

"Olena Maksimivna, my mother's friend from school." Lusi broke the silence. "I guess they had time to chat about you while they were walking home."

"I had such thoughts."

"My mother was four months pregnant. At that time, it wasn't even obvious from her that she was pregnant. Her parents were strict. Therefore, to tell them such news about a rebellious daughter, she was both ashamed and afraid and decided to get rid of the child. She began to look for someone who would help her with this. For more than a month, there were no results. In despair, she started to think about suicide.

"And where was the child's father?"

"They had known each other for a long time. He kept running to her to confess his love. Mom trusted him. She was nineteen at the time. When he found out about the pregnancy, he quickly decided to go north to earn money for the family. That's what he said. He promised to take her too. But a month later, mom received a letter in which he wrote that he didn't recognize the child and also accused her of cheating."

"What a disgusting scumbag." Miia grimaced.

"There was a doctor who agreed to induce labor at her home. She worked at the women's clinic attached to the factory where her mom worked. In the evening, they administered the necessary injections, and by morning, the process was complete. But mom started bleeding heavily, so they had to call an ambulance. She was in serious condition when she was taken to the hospital unconscious. They saved her. When her parents found out about the pregnancy and the artificial birth, they cried so much and apologized to their daughter for their harshness, which the whole hospital could hear. And you know, even at that time, no one present condemned the mother for the pregnancy. On the contrary, they discussed that parental harshness should not be fatal for the child, for the sake of people's opinions."

"And what about that doctor? She was not imprisoned?"

"No. Mom said that she bought those drugs on the black

114

market herself, injected them herself, and came to her when it all started."

"A sad story," Miia said thoughtfully.

"My mother gave birth to me when she was twenty-nine. She didn't trust men. My father followed her for two years. He called her to marry him, but she didn't want to. She was afraid that history would repeat itself. Yes, one day her father came to her with his parents, the matchmakers, and a wedding ring, a wedding dress, a veil, and a luxurious bouquet of white gladioli. His aunt worked at the registry office, and they were married the next day."

"And I can see from him that he is a real hero for your mother."

"Yes. He blows the dust off her. He's a wonderful father and husband. Honestly, there are very few like him. One in a thousand men."

"Did he know about your mother's first pregnancy?"

"Yes. My mother told him about it herself when she finally decided to push him away from her. But in return, she received a wedding ring and a stamp on her passport."

"Wow... I am delighted with your father. A real man."

"And you can see that you can't call him handsome." Lusi smiled.

"But it's not about beauty. It's about the soul of a person."

"True. In the general photos, my mother showed me Ivan. A rascal. But what a piece of shit."

"And where is he now?"

"He returned from the north five years later, married and with two young children. She's from somewhere near Chernihiv. And she met him there, in the north. Here he worked as a driver. He started drinking and fighting. So, she took the children and went to her parents. He wanted to catch up to them. He took a factory car, but he couldn't manage the steering and went off the road.

"Was he driving drunk?"

"Yes. They couldn't give him anything because of the high alcohol content in his blood. Two days later, he died in the hospital."

"That's his fate."

"So, listen to my mother; she knows what she's talking about.

115

Don't listen to those who can condemn you. And listen to those who support you."

"That's how it is. The life of each of us, except for ourselves, no one lives for us."

XVI

Returning to the dormitory, Miia was met with the news that Stefan had come to see her on Saturday. He also promised to return the following day. She was not pleased about this at all. In fact, she agreed with the girls that she would not be in her room in the evenings, and when he arrived, they would tell him that she had gone to her aunt's and would stay there for the night. Such a plan was unnecessary because the surprise caught up with her a few days later, after he visited the college for a lesson in commodity science. The door opened, and the teacher went to speak to someone.

"Miia Borko, come out! But don't be late; today's topic is important."

Miia's surprise knew no bounds. Stefan stood with a rose in his hand.

"What are you doing here?"

"This is for you!" he greeted her, handing her the flower.

She hesitated to take the rose, feeling confused and unsure of what to say. The director of the technical school stepped out of one of the classrooms.

"Take it because he'll think the girl gave me a flower," he whispered, leaning toward her. Miia felt amused by the young man's humor and accepted the rose.

"Thank you!" she said, turning around to greet the director, who was walking past them, smiling and pointing his finger at the young man.

"During classes."

"So, this is the only place where I can catch her," he answered, smiling.

"What, is she running away?"

"She's both fleeing and hiding. I want to ask why."

"You need a frank answer," he said, and then went up the stairs.

"Miia, did you hear what he wished me?" He took her hand and looked at her closely. "Is it just me, or are you pale?"

"Stefan, I won't say that I don't enjoy spending time with you. But you don't need that. Because our paths in life are different."

"Why do you say that? Is it because we didn't communicate

117

much? It's easy to fix."

"Unfortunately, there's nothing you can fix."

"Be honest."

"I'm pregnant."

There was silence.

"The father of the child, that guest?"

"Yes."

"Are you getting married?"

Miia was silent. She probably should have answered yes, but she didn't want to lie.

"We fought."

"He knows you're expecting his child?"

"No."

"Your relationship is a total mess." He kept looking at her without taking his eyes off her.

"I have to go. And don't waste your time either," she said, but he held her hand without letting go.

"Listen, maybe it's better that he doesn't find out. Don't tell him. The thing is, I need to get married as soon as possible. And I want you to be my wife." Seeing her face flush with embarrassment, he quickly added, "And the pregnancy, that's even better. Please don't rush to answer. Tomorrow I'm going on a business trip; I'll be back next Wednesday. I'll come to you on Thursday; we'll find a quiet place, sit down, and talk. All I ask is, don't hide from me. Do we have an agreement?"

Miia was at a loss for words when talking to him.

"I won't hide."

"Great!" He hugged her gently and released her.

Natalka was eagerly waiting for her friend to return to the audience.

"Was that Stefan?"

"Yes, him." The girls started to pretend they were paying attention to the lesson explanation while they chattered about their own topic.

"He's stubborn. What did he want?"

"He asked to get married. However, it all feels somewhat strange. Some of us are already married. We saw how it all ended for them."

"No. He isn't like that. He and Viktor came to our town

together. He behaved calmly. The girls clung to him, but he responded appropriately. Then he saw Toma off and went home to Viktor."

"Here are the details."

"Listen, Viktor and Irina submitted their applications to the registry office. They will sign papers in two weeks, and the wedding is in a month and a half."

Miia looked at her friend in surprise.

"I'll talk to Irina; maybe I'll find out something."

All the girls decided to leave for the weekend. Miia didn't want to stay in the dorm alone. She wasn't sure if she would have the courage to confess, at least to her mother.

The mother met her daughter coming from the bus and, on the way home, told her that her father had been taken by pancreatitis, so he hadn't had vodka for over ten days.

"So, there's peace at home." With these words, the mother finished her story, realizing how much it mattered to her daughters.

"Mommy, it's a sin to say this, but for peace, does the family have to rejoice in their father's illness?"

"Oh, I'm so tired of everything. I'm glad that you and Zhanna are doing well."

And then Miia realized that now was the wrong time to talk about her misfortune.

"The girls were interested in you."

"Oh, I don't want to go anywhere. I want to get some sleep," Miia said with a smile.

"Anton went to the store and asked about you."

"We fought with him the weekend before last."

"Ulyana told me. Mark, despite Mila's presence, fought with Anton because of you."

"I don't know how my life will turn out for me, but I feel sorry for Mila."

At home, both her father and grandmother were happy about the arrival of their daughter and granddaughter. Grandma had already prepared dinner, and there was nothing more comforting for Miia than family togetherness. She disappointed the girls with her lack of enthusiasm for going out that evening. Additionally, a series she really enjoyed was airing again on television. But half an hour

119

after it started, the girl went to bed because that's all she was dreaming of.

The morning brought sad news. In the evening, a fierce fight broke out in the village center between Anton's cousin's husband and her ex-boyfriend. Polya had gotten married while Boris was in the army. When he returned, he found out about it and got into a fight, during which his sister's husband was struck on the head and died before reaching the hospital.

"A horror." Miia broke down in tears when Anton told her all the details. She knew Nikita well as a sensitive and kind man. "And where were you all at that time?"

"No one thought that everything could end like this," Anton said with sadness.

"I am shocked by your frivolity, even irresponsibility," she cried, unable to stop herself. "Why are you so brazenly callous toward these most important aspects of life? It's just jealousy. Where is the sense? You are constantly trying to prove your importance to each other, especially when a girl or woman has made her choice, period! Because it is her choice! My God. What now? Polya is pregnant."

"Giving birth in three months."

"A horror! It's unbearable. One is in the ground. The other is in prison. And what about her now?" she almost shouted at him. "Do you know why I left when you and Mark got into a fight? My presence would have only stirred you up more. That's why I left. I also believed you'd be smarter than him and follow me. Not a follower, but a responsible man."

"Miia, forgive me, please," he muttered.

"What did you do instead?" she interrupted him. "You left and got drunk. Your drinking buddies became more important to you than me."

"I was so touched when he threw himself at me. I couldn't help myself." In despair, she looked at him silently. "I think about you all the time. Please don't leave me. If you do this, I'll drown, poison myself, or hang myself."

"Are you crazy?" In anger, she grabbed his jacket with both hands. "Don't manipulate. Do you want to keep me by blackmailing me?"

"No, he got down on his knees. "I love you and ask you to

forgive me. I understand everything, and I admit that it was, as you said, disgusting of me to shout about your pregnancy. I'm sorry!" She saw tears in his eyes.

She was silent. As she looked at him, it seemed to her that he was being honest at that moment. Sitting down next to him, her attentive gaze started to bring the young man back to his senses.

"Please don't manipulate me. Never."

"Are we together?" His pleading gaze unsettled her. "Please don't be silent. Have you forgiven me?"

"I'll just say one thing: everything has its time."

"Don't leave me."

"Let's begin communicating calmly."

"Why don't you want to answer me?"

"My answer is, let's start communicating calmly."

"That's all?"

"Yes. From the situation that has plunged us into negative emotions, there is, for now, only one way out: the reproduction of calm and balanced communication. Negative emotions still possess us, and negative thoughts still rage in our minds. We need to cope with them; only then will reconciliation, desire, and dreams for the future come."

"Are you ready to dream of a future with me?"

"I won't say I won't think about it"

"You're intriguing."

"I'm capable of that," she smiled.

"Almost a threat." Throughout the entire conversation, he also smiled for the first time.

"I told you that you don't really know me."

"I would like to learn more about you." Marry me.

It can't be said that Mia was surprised by this proposal. To some degree, she was prepared for the fact that this would happen sooner or later.

"Do you mean that you will listen more carefully to everything I say then?"

No, then I will be there, and I will see everything with my own eyes.

"Oh, now that it's coming from your lips, it sounds like a threat," she winked at him.

"It sounds like a desire to be with you!" he hugged her. "I

have to go. All the organizational aspects of the funeral."

"Yes. Can I be of any use?"

"You don't need it. My family is doing well, and we'll handle things."

"Thank you! I don't imagine myself being of any use in such an event."

"And I'm talking about. You didn't answer me. Do you agree to be my wife?"

She understood that now was not the right time to say 'yes' while the family was in such grief. She didn't want to rush. There was still a question left. Although deep down, she felt that Anton's marriage proposal brought some peace, on the one hand, she was disappointed by the need to give an answer she wasn't yet ready to give.

Again, two versions of Miia argued within her. The first was eager to avoid the shame linked to her pregnancy. Anton is the father of the child, but Miia felt no affection or desire for him. The second made her hesitate, not wanting to rush into happiness because it reminded her of the passionate seduction and longing for Stefan, who, knowing about her condition, was ready to discuss their future. It seemed she should agree with the first Miia; she had a rational, sensible point that obligation came first, but without feelings. The second Miia couldn't imagine life without feelings between two loving people. She couldn't picture happy souls without mutual support. She couldn't imagine the divine pleasures of two bodies united by love. 'I will not think about it now. Time will tell which of my two will win and which side my mind will take,' she thought, and, turning to Anton, repeated:

"You need to go now. You have more important things to handle that will require emotional peace. We'll still have plenty of time to talk."

"Promise?"

"We are not in kindergarten." She hugged him, kissed him on the cheek, and they headed to the car.

Outside the yard, she saw Vika, who was waiting for Anton to leave.

"I'm already frozen and just waiting, my friend."

"Do you already know what happened?" Miia asked her.

"Yes! It is terrible. I will say that Boris was not drunk."

122

"That shows what the absence of common sense proves."

"Why are you so harsh?"

"Have you forgotten how Anton and Mark fought two weeks ago? It is good that everything ended well."

"I agree. That is how it is. Have you made up?"

"Yes."

"And what is your problem with it?"

"Everything is fine. There was a delay," Miia confidently replied, smiling. "Can you forget everything and stop imagining nonsense? Don't you have anyone else to think about besides me?"

"I have. About Artem."

"Are you all right?"

"I'll admit it. I have a delay."

Miia looked at her, her expression a mix of surprise and fear.

"How long?"

"Eight weeks."

"Does he know?"

"No. I haven't told him yet."

"Say it!"

"I'm afraid."

"When did you last see each other?"

"Three weeks ago."

"Is he in the village now?"

"Yes."

"And he doesn't come to you?"

"We fought."

"Who's to blame?"

"Me."

"You're the same as always. How do you plan to act?"

"I don't know."

"Let's go to the disco today if they don't cancel."

"Are you serious?"

"Absolutely."

"And what about Anton?"

"And what about Anton? Listen, for me, I'm the boss, and I don't have to ask anyone for permission. So, let's get ready."

In the evening, the girls gathered as usual, lively and excited. After last night's events, the disco was canceled. Almost no young people were in town. A group of people stood on the

123

steps of the community center. Some were near the store at the main intersection. On the kindergarten grounds, Miia and Vika recognized familiar voices.

"Just look at the people!" Sasha exclaimed loudly, watching the girls.

"I think Vika agrees with me; we are also happy to see you," Miia replied cheerfully. "Sasha, the whole village can hear your jokes."

Everyone greeted each other warmly.

"Dear neighbors, you have lost a lot," Kostya chirped to the girls.

Then, not for service, but for friendship. Vika wants to sit down, but there are no seats on the swing. Which of you is a gentleman?" But without waiting for an answer, "Artem, all hopes are on you."

"Miia, sit down too." Sergiy got up with Artem.

"Sergey, I don't doubt your gentlemanliness, but thank you; I'll stand for now." At that moment, as Vika was busy climbing onto the swing between the guys, Miia, almost accidentally stepping on Artem's leg, causing him to fall, quickly managed to whisper:

"Let's make peace with Vika today! You have something to discuss and plan," and cheerfully shared her anecdote, turning to everyone else.

Finally, settling the matter of reconciling Vika with Artem was quick and smooth when, on the way home, Miia grabbed Sasha and Sergey by the arms and pushed Vika toward Artem.

XVII

On the way to the city, Natalka told Miia about the reasons for Viktora and Iryna's upcoming marriage.

"At work, they are making lists of young professionals who will be provided with service apartments. However, young families and those with children tend to get them first. Now I understand Stefan's proposal to marry you."

"He wasn't even embarrassed by my pregnancy."

Natalka looked at her friend with wide eyes.

"You told him about it, and he..."

"Yes. He said it was even better. But it doesn't flatter me at all."

"Why? He is sensible and, I am sure, he is responsible for his words."

"We will wait until Thursday, then we will understand."

"Does Anton know?"

"No. I didn't tell him."

"Have you made up?"

"Yes. But for now, we are just communicating. Now is not the time for love," she said, and she talked about the tragedy that happened to Anton's cousin. "Honestly, I like Stefan. Very much. And I would like to be with him. But it would not be fair to Anton. He is the father of the child, and he should know about it."

"You should have told him about the child. Maybe he doesn't want children."

"Natalka, he is calling me to marry him. However, I would like to have a conversation with Stefan first. What role has life assigned to him in my destiny? I will soon find out and understand how I should act."

Miia spent four days as if in a dream. Different thoughts flowed one after another, contradictory yet not completely. Some sparked wild excitement, others brought fairy dreams. Some nurtured responsibility, while others longed for happiness. While some sowed frivolity, others nurtured hope. Holding her breath, she waited for Thursday. And it arrived. Stefan came, just as he had promised. Seeing him in the doorway, Luci looked at Miia in surprise.

He shared his plans to provide housing for young families

125

and openly admitted that he dreams of settling down happily with Miia.

Her pregnancy did not scare him. On the contrary, a desire grew in him to protect her from Anton. According to his assessment, when he saw him in the dormitory that evening, he realized that Miia was not that important to her boyfriend. He explained why he had drawn such conclusions. That evening, he still planned to talk to Anton when she ran downstairs. But when he opened the door to the room and saw him alone at dinner, he wished him a delicious meal, closed the door, and left, knowing he would return. He also shared about his family. His mother raised him and his sister alone. His father died when Stefan was twelve, and his sister was only three. He shared how he had worked hard since he was fourteen, unloading cars to help his mother, and how he had mastered cooking and household chores. He talked about spending a lot of his time playing and studying with his younger sister, and how he arranged for her to give him lessons. His stories were full of funny examples. No sadness or hurt showed in his voice, facial expression, or gestures.

For the first time, Miia felt comfortable opening up about her childhood memories to him without hiding her father's struggles with alcohol. Stefan listened to her with genuine interest.

Under the guise of cleaning the rooms, Natalka and Tamila walked down the corridor six times, taking turns with Yulia and Olena. Their pretend busyness was accompanied by loud coughing just as the girls passed the guest hall. Their playful discussion of the work plan brought smiles not only to Miia and Stefan but also to themselves.

"You have fun friends," Stefan said, taking Miia's hand. "I watched your game, "Opa Panas", with pleasure. It's good when girls don't pretend to be grown-ups and aren't ashamed to be children. That says a lot."

"About what?"

"About the naturalness. About the lack of hypocrisy, cunning, or meanness. People who allow themselves such fun, who aren't afraid to show their bruised knees..."

"Ha, bruised knees..." Miia laughed.

"I remember them." Winking and smiling, he stroked her

knees with his free hand. "Well, such people are reliable because they openly show their ability to be different from others and not follow standards or patterns."

"Yes, it is we," she told him warmly, sharing a charming story about how they were the only ones in the group to fall asleep under an apple tree while doing fieldwork. When they were caught during a quiet moment and woke up, they managed to go beyond what was planned, turning a minor mishap into a memorable experience.

"I felt you before you knocked me off my feet for the first time." He looked into her eyes. "Can you guess when?"

"Yes." She looked at him shyly.

"I was scared when I saw you on the windowsill. At that moment, I thought, "God, save her!" and our eyes met. After that, you, in your short dress, jumped off him so awkwardly..."

"... and started running away from Natalka on my knees... I noticed that fear on your face; that's why I jumped down, because it also crossed my mind that I could fall from the fourth floor." Miia added with excitement in her voice, laughing.

They gazed into each other's eyes, their faces radiating kindness and warmth.

"Do you believe in my honesty?" Taking her other hand, he asked her.

"It's strange, but I believe you."

"Why is it strange?"

"And it would be strange if I weren't surprised."

They laughed.

"And you also have a good sense of humor and a sharp mind. You will never be bored with yourself." He winked at her.

The commandant's voice was heard on the floor, calling out the names of Stefan and Viktor and calling them to leave.

"Oh, what time is it?" Miia was confused.

"Half past nine." Smiling, she looked at her watch. "Now we, with Viktor, are the violators. Probably the only ones left."

They got up and walked to the exit on the floor.

"Thanks for the nice conversation, Stefan!"

"Thank you, Miia!" He stopped her. "I'm going on another business trip the day after tomorrow. This is an internship.

127

I'll be gone for two weeks. Let's agree that when I get back, I'll introduce you to my mother and sister. I told them about you. You'll like each other."

"Did you tell them about…?"

"Don't worry, please," he interrupted her. "You confessed, and I had time to think it over. I was the only man left for my mother and sister when I was twelve years old. I wasn't scared. And you want to scare me by becoming a mother?"

"Someone else's…"

"Shh," he put his hands to her lips. "Everything is yours; it can't belong to anyone else for me." He gazed deeply into her eyes, where tears had begun to form. "You mustn't cry. You don't have to. I'll be eagerly looking forward to our meeting when I get back. Promise me you won't worry. In your situation, it's harmful."

Victor and Irina were approaching them. Looking at each other, they smiled sweetly.

"Hey, Miia! "They turned to her almost in unison.

"Hey!" she replied, shyly hiding her gaze.

"I wanted to say…" Victor had just begun.

"Yes, Victor, let's go. Let's not bother you." Smiling, Irina showed him to the door.

"Okay, I'm going… I wanted to say that they're a nice couple. Goodbye, Miia!" I heard Irina's friend's farewell words on the stairs.

"It's a pity that time flew by so quickly."

"Yes. Me too. But I'll be back soon, and we'll have plenty of time to chat." He hugged her gently. "Wait for me!"

Returning to the room, Miia was ablaze with a fire that was impossible to miss. The girls weren't asleep; they were waiting for her.

"Well, what? How is he?" Natalka ran up first.

"Oh… girls…" She couldn't find the words to answer. She'd rather not share the flame that had consumed every corner of her soul and thoughts.

"Miia, watch out; don't get burned." Surprisingly, Lucy's voice was icy.

"Don't start. Everything will be fine with them." Natalka thundered, turning to her. "Everyone in life goes their way."

"Girls, time for bed. It's getting late, especially because

there's a test tomorrow," Miia suggested softly. Mostly, she just wanted to lie down and turn her face to the wall. She tried to remember every moment that linked her to Stefan, from the first glance at their meeting to the scent of his breath that stayed when they hugged goodbye that evening. The girls had no choice but to accept her offer because they understood – there would be no more conversations.

XVIII

It cannot be said that two weeks passed quickly. Having occupied herself with preparing for the final exams, Miia decided not to go home on weekends. First, she would rather not see Anton. Second, she was afraid to look her mother in the eye. But a call from Zhanna forced Miia to go because her mother was in the hospital. The girl had to miss the entire school week. 'Stefan, you back already... The girls will tell you that my mother is in the hospital. We'll see each other soon...' She was filled with worries about her mother and Stefan. Anton hung around her every weekend when she was at home. She tried to keep him at a distance, but she was not cold to him either. Peace came when her mother returned home from the hospital.

When Miia went back to college, the girls said Stefan hadn't arrived.

"Maybe he hasn't come back yet." She looked at Lusi with a sad look.

Various thoughts swirled in her mind, but she had no one to turn to. Irina wasn't there that week – she and Viktor had just gotten married, so she was at home. But Natalka said Stefan wasn't at the wedding. Miia tried to stay cheerful, forcing herself not to focus on the negative. Still, her soul felt restless and unsettled.

Another week went by. The excitement was burning inside her like acid, and she began to feel that all her reasons for peace were melting away like snow in the sun.

"Miia, come on, is waiting for you." Elena ran into the kitchen and called out loudly.

"Is that..."

This road from one end of the corridor felt impossibly long to her. Her hands trembled, and her soul lit up with a bright light.

She stood at the door, catching her breath before quietly entering the room.

A speechless scene.

Miia didn't understand anything.

She tried to gather at least some explanation for his arrival.

Lusi was sitting at the table in the room, enjoying a pleasant

130

chat with Anton.

"Oh, my dear," he said as he stood up from the table and went to hug her, "I have come such a long way."

Lusi left the room at that moment, which seemed very strange to Miia.

"Do you know her?" Her thoughtful gaze lingers on the cake and cups of tea.

"Why didn't you ask that...?"

"What didn't I ask?" She looked at Anton demandingly.

"I know everything. And your parents, and mine, already know too."

"What does everyone know?"

"Yes, Miia, I think it would be better if we went home now, and tomorrow we will go to the registry office and file an application."

"No. Which registry office?" Her confusion quickly shifted to anger. Her breath caught, and she felt a wave of dizziness wash over her. But she knew she shouldn't show her emotions so openly in front of Anton, so she forced a smile and said, "Wait, I'll be right back," then immediately left the room.

Hearing Lusi's voice in the hall, she ran toward her.

"How do you know him, that you communicate so kindly? You treat him to tea." Her eyes burned with anger.

"Trust me, it will be better for you this way."

Before she could finish, Miia grabbed her hand and pulled her into Tamila's room, where their whole girl group was gathered.

"What is better for me? Give me the answer." Miia shouted at her.

"Do you want to repeat my fate with Viktor?"

"What?" Miia's angry gaze tore Lusi in half. "Are you crazy? Who are you to decide my fate?"

"I want the best."

"What did you do? Answer me!"

"I only wrote to Anton. For your sake."

"For my sake, don't get into my life!"

"You don't understand that it's better for you this way. You're so young."

"What a scumbag you are, Lusi. And where did you get the address?"

"It doesn't matter."

"Did Stefan come when I wasn't there?" Lusi's eyes are running. "Did he come?"

"I didn't see him here."

"I think you're lying," Miia whispered, moving closer and leaning towards her face. "Do you realize what you've done, Lusi?" Having gone to the door, she turned to Natalka. "I can find out..." and she ran out of the room. Natalka followed after her.

"Are you to the commandant?" Natalka asked, catching up with her.

"Yes."

Breathing heavily from running, the girl stubbornly gazed at the commandant.

"Maria Markivna, my dear, please check the guest book. Has Stefan Boychenkov stopped by in the past two weeks?"

"We'll see now," and taking the book, she started to flip through it. "And what happened? I see you're excited."

"Is Lusi such a disgusting creature?" whispered Natalka.

"You heard. The conclusions are unambiguous!"

"Yes, he came on November nineteenth at eighteen twenty." Tears began to appear in the girl's eyes. "And is there a record of when he left?"

"It's written that in ten minutes."

"Thank you!"

"Are you all right, Miia?" Looking out the window, she asked her.

"I think not..." Miia answered, but the commandant could no longer hear her. "Natalka, I don't know what's going on." Tears were streaming down her face.

"Maybe Lusi told him something?"

"Possibly. And Ira is here?"

"Yes, she was. I saw her."

"I'm heading to her place, and you'd better watch out so my guest doesn't look for me. Go and keep him in the room," she hugged her friend.

After going upstairs, the girls checked to see if Anton was in the corridor. They ran in different directions along the hall. Running up to Irina's door, Miia knocked softly.

"Ira, please open it; it's Miia!"

Irina quickly opened the door. She and Viktor were alone in the room. After greeting them, Miia burst into tears.

"We agreed that once Stefan returned from his two-week business trip, he would come. It was during that time that my mother was hospitalized. I was away for a week. He came, as we had agreed, and left ten minutes later. That's what's written in the journal," she said through tears, swallowing her words. "I don't understand what happened."

Irina and Viktor looked at each other.

"To be honest," Viktor began, "up until this moment, I thought everyone understood everything. But now I'm not sure."

"Stefan, is he okay?" she asked, looking at Viktor, who was unnervingly silent with fear. "What's wrong with him? Please tell me."

"He's already far away," Ira said softly. "Your note..."

"What's my note?" Miia interrupted her.

"The one you left for him before you left," Viktor answered.

"I didn't write any notes."

"I read it."

"What was written in it?"

"I'm sorry, but I'm marrying the child's father."

Miia's surprise knew no bounds. She looked from Viktor to Iryna.

"Where is Stefan? You said he was far away. Is there any way to contact him?"

"He quit and left, but he didn't say where. He promised to tell later."

"That can't be happening! Miia burst into tears bitterly. I didn't write him anything. I was waiting for him. My God..."

"Let's calm down first and think." Ira sat down next to her.

"You're friends." Miia looked at Viktor. "He didn't say where he was going?"

"If I knew where he was now, I would have crashed, and I would have brought him back here."

"We don't know." Irina was also crying. "Who arranged such a vile thing?"

"I know. Ira, please give me a piece of paper and a pen." Having received them, Miia wrote her name and last name. "Here is my handwriting." She handed the paper to Viktor.

133

"Beautiful handwriting. In a note, scribbles were on it."

"What should I do?"

"Wait a couple of days. I'll go to Alla Sergiyivna and ask; maybe she knows where he will stop. Then…"

Miia was looking at the wall with misty eyes. There was a soft knock on the door, and Natalka entered the room.

"Your guest is asking about you."

"Who?" Irina asked.

"Guest of Miia. Lusi wrote to him that Miia was pregnant and was afraid to tell him."

"What?" Victor jumped out of bed and started walking around the room. "Lusi, that slob who lives in the same room as you?"

"Yes, she is. I would strangle her." Natalka answered angrily. "What are we going to do, Victor? We need to go to Alla Sergiyivna."

"I'll go tomorrow."

But she didn't enter the room; instead, she sat on the stairs. Natalka joined her. They sat silently, leaning on the balustrades.

"What are you going to do?"

"I don't know yet."

"Are you going home with him today?"

"No. Let him stay at his aunt's overnight. I'll come over on the weekend; we'll figure it out."

"So, how are we going to live in the same room with Lusi now?"

"I don't know. Unfortunately, there are no free rooms."

"Or maybe we can agree with someone to swap?"

"Natalka, there are two months of internship and graduation."

"Maybe let her look for a room of her own?"

"If someone wants to take her in."

Returning to the room, Anton began to scold Miia

"Where have you been for so long? We didn't make it to the night bus."

"Listen, spend the night at your aunt's."

"Are you kicking me out? Do you even understand what kind of situation you're in now?"

"My situation is my business. So, don't speculate on what this bitch wrote to you?" She nodded towards Lucy.

134

"Miia, I did it for the sake of..."

"Shut up, I'm not talking to you," she interrupted angrily. "In general, such situations are resolved with one doctor's appointment."

"Are you hinting at an abortion?" He smiled sarcastically.

"Don't even think about it. Remember, I warned you that I was ready for anything if you left me."

"Leave this blackmail. Go to your aunt."

"I stay with you..."

"No, of course. This is not a hotel but a women's hostel."

"Let's go to her together. We'll talk at the same time."

"I'm tired and want to rest. And there's still a lot of time for talking ahead."

"Miia." He approached her. "I understand that you planned to tell me about your pregnancy in your own way, and everything should have happened differently. However, you would have told me that you were expecting a child anyway."

"And if I haven't made up my mind yet, would I want to tell you about it? After all, you did your part. Now I have to decide how to live my life."

"Promise me you won't do anything stupid." He went up to hug her.

"Stupidity is your thing." Avoiding the hug, she continued. "And who told my parents?"

"I said."

"When did you manage to do it?"

"I was home yesterday. I told my family and then went to yours. Please don't be upset. I promise everything will be fine with us. I understand that you are in a state where women usually get nervous."

"You can't understand anything, so that's enough!" She interrupted him. "You need to go. Goodbye."

"We will overcome everything," he said and left the room.

Miia was overwhelmed with pain. She realized that Stefan shouldn't have taken on someone else's child. However, she gave him a sincere and open confession. She couldn't even imagine that afterward, he would follow through with the decision he expressed. As she thought about it, she wondered if she would agree to raise his child if he had one, like it had

135

happened with Lesi. Andriy has two boys. Miia admired how gently and warmly Andriy and Lesya interacted with each other. How tenderly he treats the girl who isn't his biological child. But he became her father. Seeing this family, Miia started to believe more in the sincerity of Stefan's intentions. Lucy went back into the room.

"Luci, I feel sorry for you," Miia said coldly. "You are not afraid of God's punishment for meanness."

"Miia, you will still thank me."

"Oh, so you don't have enough of the word 'thank you' in your life? I think you lack intelligence."

"Is this such gratitude for my help with the doctor?"

They say the truth: 'If I had known where I would have fallen, I would have sent straw.' So, do I. Now I understand your Viktor. I'm sure he saw through your rotten nature."

"Why are you insulting me?"

"Are you really that stupid?" Miia's surprise knew no bounds. "You told Anton because you decided it was better that way." Getting out of bed, Miia walked over to Lucy and, locking eyes with her, continued. "Well, tell me, why did you write a lying note to Stefan, and with your scribbles? Just look me in the eyes."

"I have nothing to justify myself for," she said, turning to the wall.

"Live in peace. I forgive you for your wickedness. It's not for me to judge, and she left the room, taking her bed linen."

"Miia, wait." Natalka jumped out of bed and quickly gathered her things. "They have another free bed. I'm with you," she said, turning to Lucy. "Your act is disgusting, and I'm sure it will catch up with you soon.

Two days later, Irina talked about Viktor's meeting with Stefan's mother.

"She said that he packed up and left quickly, without explaining where. During this time, he called only once. He said that he had sent letters, but there was nowhere to write to him. Viktor asked her to tell him that a terrible, vile deception had occurred."

I know I'm about to say something painful, but you should be aware of it. Steph would never hurt you or the child. You resemble his mother a lot. When he first saw you, he came

in and sat on the bed – right where you're sitting – looked at me, and then said, 'I want to know everything about her.' A kind smile appeared on her face. "Viktor and I didn't understand anything. We started asking who he wanted to know everything about. And he led us into the hall, where you were playing the game "Opa Panas."
"After that, your Viktor was constantly checking our room."
"Stefan didn't dare to come up to you. He said that for now, it was enough for him to see you. I'm so sorry that everything turned out this way. I want to believe that..." She took Miia's hands. "That everything will work out."
There was silence.
Ira looked silently at Miia.
Having dared, she continued:
"He signed a contract as a long-distance sailor. He has already started his voyage."
"God… The length of such voyages can last six or even seven months."
"I am so sorry…" Tears appeared in Irina's eyes.
"This is the end." Covering her face with her palms, Miia burst into tears.
Viktor stepped into the room, and Miia knew she had to leave.
"Wait a minute, I will calm down…" she said quietly and calmly, looking at Viktor. "I know that eventually you will meet. Tell him that in my almost twenty years, Stefan Boychenko is the best that destiny has given," she added, moving to the door. "I will always remember him."
"Miia, wait," Viktor said as he approached her. "Promise that you won't hurt yourself."
Looking closely into Viktor's eyes, she replied with a smile:
"I promise, because I wonder what will happen next."

137

XIX

Thinking about her married life, Miia went to the bed where Anton and Niki were sleeping peacefully, and kissed them tenderly.

"Together we will move mountains! We will melt glaciers! We will reach our stars, with or without dad."

Hearing a knock on the door, she quickly left the children's room.

"My God, Zlata, what happened?" – she looked in shock at the battered hands of her friend, who was barely holding her nine-month-old daughter in her arms.

"Give me the bike. Anton hasn't come home yet either?"

"No. And the godson with them?"

"With them."

"Do you know where they are?"

"They are with the chief mechanic. They are getting drunk."

"They don't need to go home after fishing," Miia growled. "You didn't answer. What happened?"

"It's time to look after the livestock. I'm gone. The child was next to me in the cart. I had milked one cow. I stood up to go to the other. Suddenly, the horse broke free and jumped towards us. I suspect he was scared of a rat. He kicked me with his hoof. Then he pushed me. I fell and injured my leg, side, and head. I miraculously managed to grab the child and run outside." Not finding words, through tears, in anger, she continued. "Look at the legs and back..."

"My God! He almost killed you." Horror filled Miia's eyes.

"I'll go. Rest assured, I'll have the nerve to arrange a "fun life" for an alcoholic. God help me!"

Seeing the director's and chief engineer's cars in the yard, Miia realized that in the presence of the state farm management, she needed to behave more restrainedly than she would have liked. So, gathering her thoughts, she went into the house. A group of men was sitting at a table, discussing something loudly. Among them, leaning on the table, sat her seven-year-old godson. When Miia saw, everyone fell silent.

"Hello, everybody!" she said calmly and turned to Zlata's husband. "At your house, a horse almost killed your wife and child. They need you now." Then, looking at Anton with a wistful expression, she added, "Thank Goodness we don't have a horse."

Returning home, Miia made herself some tea and sat down to drink it in the kitchen. Anton burst into the house, slamming the door loudly.

"Who are you to humiliate me in front of men?" he roared, rushing at her.

"If you've forgotten who I am, look in your passport. That's the first thing. Second, in front of men, I thanked you for not having a horse." Her tone was so even that he was furious at this.

"Oh, you..." And swinging, he hit her in the face.

Miia's reaction was immediate. She threw her hot tea in his face.

"Remember! If you hit me again, I will kill you. And this is not a threat. This is a promise. I will make sure that no pathologist finds out the real cause of your death," her eyes burned with ruthless fury. "I am tired of your antics with drinking and parties with pussies. You constantly recommend that I look at myself in the mirror more often, assuring me that no one needs me. You consider yourself a hero who saved me from shame. So, here is my advice to you: look at yourself in the mirror and ask yourself, 'Who am I to you?' Are you truly worthy of me? Who do you need more in your life – a wife with children or a bitch with drinking buddies? By the way, one of your bitches came running here just a couple of days ago. They're not ashamed anymore..." Miia approached him, gazing into his eyes. "Doesn't it bother you that all the work at home falls on me? Two small children. Cattle, pigs, and poultry require twice-daily feeding and weekly cleaning. The house is so big. The yard is so vast. And everything is clean and tidy. Have you ever wondered how I manage all this alone?" she asked, moving toward the door with a sly smile. "Don't wake the beast in me! I'm a Taurus by horoscope!"

She turned around and went to sleep in the children's room. Time passed. Anton was three and a half years old, so his in-laws increasingly took him with them to work or to relatives. The girl, two years and two months old, was her mother's daughter – they were always together.

"Niki, my little girl, let's go for a walk. Dinner is ready, the

139

house is cleaned, clothes are washed, the pigs and poultry are fed, and the cows are milked," Miia said softly as she dressed the child. "While Antosha is working with his grandfather and grandmother, you and I will go meet dad at work."

Set amidst lush evergreen thujas and towering blue spruces, the trees bathed in a glorious burst of autumn orange-red, creating a truly breathtaking view. The charming honeysuckle's white blossoms brought a delightful zesty touch to the scene, beautifully enhanced by their divine fragrance. As the yellow-pink sun slowly dipped toward the western horizon, its last warm rays seemed to hum a gentle lullaby, wishing everything on Earth a peaceful and restful night.

And it would be necessary to admire this beauty, but Miia did not notice it, just as she once did in childhood when she grazed geese. Over the past year and a half, her soul has begun to erode from the blackness of disappointments. Yet another unjust, humiliating insult completely knocked her off the path of a peaceful life. "How many tears have already been shed? And how many more will there be? And is there even a glimpse of change for the better?" No answers came. She felt that the edge of the abyss she was walking along was endless. And there was no hope of finding a way to the other side – the side of dreams, mental stability, and life's comfort.

A dozen yards away, Margo and her daughter, the daughter-in-law of the director of their state farm, waved to them. The young mothers became such close friends that their families celebrated all the holidays together for two years. What united them was not only the desire to share recipes for cakes or pastries but also honest conversations about their struggles.

Miia admired her daughter's small steps, which slowly brought them closer to Margo.

"Aren't we the only ones going to Ira's with sweets?" Seeing how the director's car stopped next to her friend and immediately drove away, Miia took her daughter in her arms. The director was driving.

"Hi, beauties!" He smiled and greeted.

"Good evening, Andriy Gavrilovich!" In his presence, Miia was always overcome by an unprecedented feeling of shyness.

"And where is your Cossack?" and he looked at Nika sweetly.

"He manages the grandmother's work."

"Oh, there is someone to manage there. Now I will help him. His smile, as always, was sincere and beautiful – I am told a lot about your problems in relations with Anton." The smile disappeared from his face. He looked deeply into Miia's eyes. She was confused and unsure of what to say because she couldn't immediately understand why he, the household director, was talking to her about this. She lowered her eyes and stayed silent. "I understand your silence. You left him twice. With two children in your arms, you are brave."

She could not say a word, and tears welled up in her eyes. He continued, "In my life, I have seen twice as much of you because I am twice as old as you. I know that without support and help, you cannot do it. Therefore, please don't hesitate to contact us. We will not leave you to your fate. Always remember this!"

Miia looked at him with surprised eyes.

"I don't know." She was gathering her thoughts, but couldn't say anything.

"Don't be shy to ask. Did we agree?" he said in a cheerful voice. "Now, smile and promise!"

"I promise." She smiled and, in confirmation, nodded her head.

He started the car and drove off.

Margo and Ira were walking toward them. The mothers warmly greeted each other, and the girls hugged and kissed each other playfully.

"Two babies! My soul rejoices to look at them."

Miia felt how powerfully these two minutes of communication with the director had filled her heart with hope.

"Do you remember that Taras has a birthday on Saturday? We are waiting for you and Anton."

"I haven't forgotten," she replied with a wink. "We will come."

"Oh, and Andriy Gavrylovich gave Oksana and me a spanking a couple of days ago."

"For what?"

Over the past week, Oksana and I haven't done any work at

home. We didn't clean, didn't cook, and we didn't even have time – we were watching the series." Margo began her story laughing. "Usually, Andriy has lunch in the dining room. Suddenly, he comes home for dinner, and we lie by the TV. Oksana is on one sofa; I'm on the other. We don't notice him, and then he stands and watches us. And afterward, he asks, 'What will feed me, girls?' We almost fell off the sofa.

"When was that?" Miia asked with a smile. "Four days ago."

"I understood that you didn't feed him at home?"

"No, of course," she replied, laughing. "We were "glued" to the TV."

"That day, I was cooking dinner at my in-laws' house because they were waiting for Polay to arrive. I tried really hard and made borscht, baked pork with homemade sausage, and mashed potatoes. I also managed to make two pans of eclairs. Then, my mother-in-law walks into the kitchen, followed by Andriy Gavrylovich..."

"Listen, your eclairs are divine," Margo interrupted her. "When he came back from you, he scolded us and made an example of you: 'The Kulishchenko has a daughter-in-law like a bee. She manages to do everything. She cooks deliciously. Everything in the house and the surrounding area is tidy. Two little kids, and she even manages to take care of herself. And you? Look at yourself.' But how it turns out..." Margo said, shaking her head excitedly. "He said we were lazy and reproached himself for being to blame because we live on everything ready-made."

"How am I supposed to go to your party now and face Oksana?"

"Don't even worry. She wants you to show me how you make your eclairs."

"That's a twist." Miia was pleasantly surprised.

"When will you have time to cook together?"

"Let's meet on Friday, in the afternoon, if it's convenient for you."

"We agreed. What ingredients should we buy? You tell me."

"I'll write it down and bring you a list tomorrow. We have to go. Anton will be brought soon."

"Which one? The older one or the younger one?"

"They will bring the younger one. However, I'm not sure

142

about the older one. If he can't crawl on his own, they will probably bring him. You can't even imagine how exhausted I am."

"You know, we often talk about you at home. One time, Andriy was silent for a long moment, then he said, 'I don't understand what she saw in him. She looks like a queen next to him. A wonderful hostess.' You probably don't know."

"About what exactly?"

"The second time you left Anton, he called him to his house for a talk. He reminded him that the company offers housing assistance, not to leave a woman with two children homeless or let an alcoholic husband continue to control the mansions they had built for you."

"Wow, I didn't know. Now I understand where he got the phrase 'house for a family' from.

"From that conversation."

"See you soon." The young mothers hugged their daughters and said goodbye, then went home.

Miia was mistaken about older Anton – that night, he didn't come home at all. The next evening, when he returned, he explained that he had a lot of work, and he and his partner decided to stay and finish it by morning. Of course, these stories didn't affect his wife at all. Smiling, she only brushed a few red hairs from his clothing and said, "Tell your partner to dye his hair." Miia noticed how his eyes looked puffy and how his voice trembled, searching for words to justify himself. His actions and behavior as a husband, father, and master were more expressive, in a figurative sense. She calmly noted in her diary: one more, penultimate, minus, which brought her one step closer to the final decision of divorce. After rereading her diary, Miia thought,

"The vast majority of minuses..."

"Do you remember that your parents are going to a sanatorium for two weeks?"

"Well, I remember."

"And you understand that their farm is entrusted to us."

"Why are you starting this conversation?"

"I want you to understand that I can't afford two more cows, four bulls, two calves, fifteen pigs, and poultry, considering the size of our farm."

143

"Grandma will come to help with the children."

"I didn't tell you about the children."

"If I have to stay at work…"

"Then you will come, take care of your parents' affairs," she interrupted him, "and you will be free as the wind."

"Do you want to fight?" He looked at her carefully.

"No. I want you to become more responsible for your parents during these two weeks."

"Don't worry. Everything will be fine."

"Taras Merkovets has a birthday on Saturday. We're invited."

"Yes, he told me." By the way, he was also with us yesterday and stayed almost until the morning," he added with a smile.

"Anton, it doesn't mean anything to me. The only thing I know for sure is that everything will not just be fine, but even better!" Looking at him carefully, she added. "For each of us."

XX

"Miia, why are you so dressed up?" her husband asked her in surprise as he entered the room.

"It's so that I don't forget that I'm not some village girl who only knows cows, pigs, and bulls," Miia answered with a reproachful tone, but as she looked into the mirror and smiled, she added, "And you know, I'm happy because I see that I haven't changed much, despite having given birth to two children. As beautiful as ever."

"Oh, praise yourself." He teased her sarcastically. "You've got a hang of lying to yourself."

"Are you serious?" She turned around and looked at him carefully. "When was the last time you said something nice to me? A compliment? A thank you?"

"Do you think you deserve this?" He said it entirely seriously. "I would rather not spoil my mood. So, say whatever you want."

The Merkovets hosted about twenty guests, including friends and colleagues. Also among them were people who had come from Kyiv to see the director on business. The celebration was building up momentum. The amusing stories of Andriy Gavrylovich and his guests made everyone laugh a great deal. Each new adventure lifted their spirits more and more. At those moments, it seemed to Miia that she had nothing to fear from changes in her future – strange imaginations opened up unknown, mysterious horizons before her. The fun alternated between dancing and songs played on the guitar. As it turned out, not only was Miia playing in this company, but also one of the Kyiv guests, Artur.

Going outside to get some fresh air, Miia saw a car from Kyiv – an expensive black SUV. 'People know how to make money,' she thought without any envy. In the yard, there was a commotion of guests leaving the house, who began demanding cheerful dance music from the birthday boy. It turned out that Andriy Gavrilovich could dance as well as speak elegantly and tell jokes. At his wife's request, they started to perform a waltz. It was impossible to take your eyes off them.

"Anton, let's dance!" Margo suggested approaching him.

Almost at the exact moment, Arthur approached Miia, circling, bowing his head, and extending his hand with a sweet smile, and with the same circling movements, pulled her into the dance.

"Oh, charming lady, accept the compliment – you are lovely and bright. You not only know how to play the guitar well and make delicious eclairs – I couldn't resist and grabbed one but you also dance wonderfully. Where did you study?

"At school."

"Do you have children?"

"Yes. A son and a daughter."

"How old are they?"

"The boy, who is three and a half years old. The girl is two years and two months old."

"Another compliment to you. How did you manage to keep your figure?"

"I'm working on myself."

"Incredible! And who are your children with now?"

"With cousin."

"But it seems to me that things aren't so good between you and your husband."

"Arthur, we are fine," she interrupted him. At that moment, he wanted to add something, but then Oksana pulled him away, and Miia found herself paired with Andriy Gavrilovich. With one hand, he tightly hugged her waist, and the sweet mystery in his gaze reminded Miia of that conversation and his proposal.

"You dance so charmingly." Miia, having dared, said.

"I am trying harder than ever."

After a few minutes of waltzing, Miia received compliments from two respectable, intelligent, and successful men, which boosted her confidence.

It seemed that the waltz would never end. Circle after circle, they danced, unaware that their couple was the only one on the floor, while others who had not gone to smoke watched the beautiful waltz performance. Andriy Gavrilovich, with his skillful and gentle movements, supported his partner's fragile and supple body. It was clear that he did not want to stop.

However, Anton, who was very drunk, did not share Miia's

partner's desires in the waltz. Unable to resist, he stopped them and shouted:

"I will have a different conversation with you at home." And turning around, he left the yard.

"Now I have also become a witness to his rudeness." Noticing Miia's excitement, Andriy Gavrilovich looked closely into her eyes. "Is he always like this with you?"

A dull sound was heard. Looking around, Miia asked, "What is this?"

Anton came back, moved closer, and, grabbing Miia's hand, yelled:

"We are going home. The dance is over."

Andriy Gavrilovich took a step towards him, but Miia stopped him.

"Tomorrow, he will ask for forgiveness." Nodding towards Anton, she smiled and left.

At home, Anton started a claim. Miia didn't say anything to him. She didn't even look his way. A beautiful melody played in her mind, and she kept sinking into the depths of the waltz.

Not even ten minutes had passed when someone's voices were heard in the yard. Miia went to the yard, where the Mercedes was parked, and next to it was Artur with Andriy Gavrilovich.

"Go admire what your husband did to the car," Oksana growled.

"What happened?" she asked softly while inspecting the car in the dark of night.

"Do you remember that sound?" the director calmly asked her. "Look at the rear window."

"My God..." Her voice shook as she saw the completely broken window.

"They told me that he was inadequate. But to such an extent." Andriy Gavrilovich said quietly.

At that moment, Anton stepped out of the yard and started chasing everyone away. Miia immediately went to him, grabbed his sleeve, and pulled him toward the car.

"Your job?" she asked sternly, but kept her emotions and voice in check.

"It's your fault," he replied insolently, pulling his hand

147

away. "You've behaved like a whore..." With these words, Artur ran up to him.

"Shut up, boy. Your wife is a decent woman. You should be ashamed of yourself for using such dirty words."

"How much will it cost to replace the glass on your car?" She understood that they would have to pay, and the cost would be significant.

"If I were a criminal," said Arthur, "I would take him to the forest belt for re-education."

"Anton! At 9:00 a.m., I will wait for you in my office. I recommend that you sleep well and come in sober, without being late," Andriy Gavrilovich said sternly. "And don't you dare insult her. A husband can only dream of such a wife. And you're a fool to despise her so much," he paused before adding, "Do you know why? Because you know you're not worth her." Then they got into the car and drove off.

That night, Miia didn't sleep.

In the morning, Anton went to the directors. When he returned, Miia had finished doing the housework at her parents' house. Without saying a word to her, he went inside the house and came out with a two-liter bottle of whiskey.

"Why did you take this whiskey? It's a gift for mom for her anniversary. Is everything so bad?" She looked at him and added excitedly, "How much?"

"You did your job!" he shouted at her. "How much?"

"You have nothing to blame me for. Absolutely! Your jealousy conflicts with your attitude towards me. What is it with you? Egoism. Narcissism. Stupidity. What?" she said calmly to him. "How much?"

Having uncorked the bottle, Anton began to drink directly from it. A motorcycle drove up to the yard.

"I'm surprised I didn't catch you in the barn with the director."

"What are you talking about?"

"What? You didn't see yourself from the outside. My wife, a whore!"

At these words, Miia could not stand it.

Approaching him, she looked him sternly in the eyes. "My body is clear before you. However, you don't deserve this. Do you think I don't know about your Tatyana from Kakhovka?

Some people told me about your trips to Zoi." She turned around and went into the house to call the director.

The amount she heard scared her. She had no idea how to get the money she needed to spend within two days. At that moment, she was overwhelmed with anxiety, worried that Anton might harm himself while drunk. She also feared what would happen when her in-laws came back. At that moment, Anton's grandmother, who came every morning and evening to look after the children while Miia did the housework, entered the yard. Without saying hello, her first question was about the news that had spread throughout the village.

"They say that you danced not quite decently with the director, which made Anton jealous."

"Honestly, I don't care what anyone says," Miia interrupted her sharply. "It's impossible to dance indecently in front of the director's wife and my husband. Your grandson has one problem – he thinks of me as his equal. But I didn't cheat on him, unlike him doing."

"He is a man, and men do have this..."

"It happens." She interrupted her again. So, do you consider adultery to be a normal phenomenon?"

"You are still so young and don't realize that families depend on the patience of wives, who, for the sake of the children, must either forgive or pretend not to see anything. And you have two little kids. I have three daughters. They all went through this with their husbands. And they endured, and forgave, and didn't pay attention, because..."

"I don't have time for this pointless talk. I will share my view on adultery, but only after we pay for the broken car window. I've already done the housework. I have something to attend to. And you look after the children, please. I have to go." She grabbed her bicycle and left the yard.

Miia spent half the day with Yegor trying to find money. She approached everyone she thought might lend her at least some amount. But she had no success.

"Yegor, I am in despair and don't know what to do. My in-laws will return; how can I explain it to them? You won't believe how exhausted I am from their accusations. Always, I am the only one to blame for everything. Anton constantly

149

complains to them about everything."

"Complain about you?" he said, surprised. "I've told him more than once that he's mistaken about you. And not just me – everyone in our guy group told him the same."

"All his relatives know what is in my refrigerator, they know what I have or haven't done, and they know everything we are talking about." With tears in her eyes, she kept going.

"He is a fool. Have you tried to break up with him yet?"

"Twice. The third time will be final."

"He needs to change. Maybe talk to him again. I want to believe he'll come to his senses. After all, he has two children. Miia stayed silent, her eyes fixed on the clear sky.

"Thanks, Yegor, for dedicating your time to our family matters."

"I'll take you home."

"Take me to the garage. There's a bike there."

Miia had barely entered her in-laws' yard when she heard the phone ring. She immediately ran to answer it.

"Miia, good afternoon. The director's reception!"

"Good afternoon!"

"Andriy Gavrilovich asks you to come right away."

Miia instantly grabbed her bike and rode off. She went up to the second floor to the reception and met Yegor at the entrance, who had just left the director's office.

"Sorry, but I told everything." He said to her and headed for the exit. Surprised, Miia watched him go.

At this time, the secretary called on the internal phone:

"Andriy Gavrilovich, Miia is at the reception." Hearing an affirmative response, Maria Olexandrivna hung up the phone and invited Miia to come in.

"Good afternoon, Andriy Gavrilovich!"

"Good afternoon, Miia! Sit down." After pausing to look her over carefully, he continued. "Yegor told me that you were asking for money to give to Arthur. Why did you do it?"

"I was afraid Anton might hurt himself."

"This was his idea?" The director's voice was stern.

"Mine." This answer was firm.

"Yeah, yours. And where is he now?" His meticulous gaze pierced Miia sharply. "Why are you silent? Don't you know where he is?" Miia lowered her eyes and stayed silent. "I'll tell you where he is. He calmly left this office this morning and went to drink vodka."

"Calmly?" She was embarrassed.

"Yes, calmly. Now imagine – they give you one and a half thousand dollars. They lend it not to him, but to you. How much time do you have to pay back the money? A month. And in a month, where will you get this money? Your in-laws will again create such living conditions for you that you will file for divorce. And you have two children and a debt that your in-laws will refuse to repay."

"Well." Miia was already beginning to understand the meaning of the questions the director had started to ask her. "We would have to sell our livestock." Her answer sounded uncertain.

"Are you sure that you would be allowed to sell the livestock?" He looked at her intently. "Are you sure that you have this month in this family? Are you sure that when your in-laws return from the sanatorium, they will not kick you out of the house?" Miia didn't say a word, but she agreed with everything that was said. "People will come to you because they gave you the money."

Miia was silent. She would rather not cry. She started planning her actions for the upcoming week and month. It was then that she realized what had become the "control shot" in her marriage. She stopped fearing what her in-laws, relatives, or Anton would say to her. An unprecedented ease and peace washed over her because a thirst for the unknown replaced these fears.

"You are right!" she said confidently and firmly. "You are one hundred percent right. Thank you, Andriy Gavrilovich!"

"Thank the people you turned to for money, and that they did not give it to you."

"That is so," she laughed.

"And for Anton, don't even worry. He won't do anything to himself. He knows that his parents have money and that he will bring it tomorrow morning." Noticing the frank surprise on Miia's face, he continued. "Given the position that your mother-in-law holds and the affairs that she is engaged in, I know that they have money. Well, let their beloved son blink his eyes in front of them and explain why he is such an idiot."

"I will be to blame for everything. Don't doubt it."

"I'm not sure. They won't dare to disgrace me and my guests. The question is in justice, which they will have to accept."

"Thank you! I hope it will be so." Having gone to the door, Miia stopped and turned around, adding, "Andriy Gavrilovich! I already know what to do with my life. Thank you."

On her way home, Miia enjoyed the warm, gentle breeze that softly brushed her face. A special feeling of peace inspired her to explore unknown paths of destiny.

Four days later, Miia left Anton and left a note: 'I'm getting a divorce.'

XXI

Looking at her sweetly sleeping children, she once again remembered how, on the very day of the wedding, Anton got drunk to the point of insanity and, brandishing a bottle of vodka, began to boast to the guests about his heroic deed: 'I saved her from disgrace!' She was told more than once that if it weren't for the pregnancy, they would never have allowed Anton to get married to her. They suggested having an abortion.

One day, Miia couldn't take it and reminded them that it was not her, but their son, who insisted on getting married, driven by the selfish logic of 'So that no one else gets it.' During that quarrel, she also admitted that they would never have known about their grandson's existence if it weren't for Lusi's disgusting prank.

"Stefan... In bitter moments, I often imagine what kind of father and husband you could have been. All my inner voices tell me that you would be caring, kind, and loving. It's a pity, this was not destined to be."

"Granddaughter, come on," her grandmother called softly. "I don't know what he wants."

Miia was seized by wild excitement, and she jumped up, her heart pounding and her hands trembling.

"Who?" She closed the door of the children's room and went out to her grandmother. "Anton?"

"No," she quickly tried to remember.

"My God!" Miia said, seeing the uninvited guest.

"What kind of wind carried you away?"

"Hi!"

"Are you on foot?" she asked, looking around; the motorcycle was nowhere in sight.

"Yes," he approached her.

Miia turned to the yard, where the grandmother, having dropped all her affairs, was looking in their direction.

"You will now continue the conversation with my grandmother. Therefore, it is better to stand where you were standing."

Looking into the yard, he stepped back half a step.

"How are you?"

153

"Are you interested in something specific?" she smiled.

"What is the matter with you and Anton?"

"The same goes for you and Mila," she replied, not hiding her irritation.

"Well, yes." His tongue began to tangle and become confused.

"You also believe that a woman should be raised?" Now she approached him. "And you not only believe it, but you also actively embody it in your life with Mila from time to time."

"He..."

"Does he beat me? Did you want to ask that?" she interrupted him and looked him in the eye. "No. Honestly? Once. But he got a hot tea in the face and an even hotter warning. So, you were luckier in life than he was."

Mark's thoughts took him back to that unforgettable evening, to her genuine smile, bashful eyes, and eager breathing. Nearly six years had gone by, and his memory kept every moment of every feeling alive.

"You have two children, and the same slender one, even more beautiful," he had just said when Miia interrupted him.

"Mark, why did you come?"

"I came for you, but you weren't at home. You didn't answer any of my letters," he said, staring into her eyes. "Why?"

Her surprised gaze froze on him.

"What letters?"

I wrote to you every two weeks for six months, and then.

"There were no letters." She looked at him with surprise.

"Why aren't you telling the truth?" He grabbed her by the shoulders.

"Why are you making it up?" She snapped back at him.

In each other's eyes, they were looking for an answer.

"I don't understand anything." Leaving her, he started to pace. "You didn't forgive me that evening. Right? Confess." He grabbed her by the shoulders again. "Could you confess? Could you write one word?"

"Mark, there weren't any letters."

They didn't know what to say to each other.

"Miia," Grandmother's voice was heard. "The children woke up."

"I'm going," she answered instantly.

"Miia, wait." He took her hands. "I didn't just come."

154

"I have to go." She tried to tear her hands away and looked around. "Listen, I don't want any more gossip to spread through the village." Miia noticed that her mother-in-law's colleague was watching them from the yard across. "Let go," but he held her tightly.

"I don't care." He cut her off. "Listen, let's leave the village now. Take the children and come with me to Zaporozhye. We'll stay with my uncle for a while. And then..."

"Are you crazy?"

"I'm serious," he said, standing in her way. "I've wanted children for a long time."

"Do you need other people's children? What are you talking about?" She looked intently into his eyes. You and Mila are young; there will be children. Just don't hit her, she said gently, and added, "I need to go. Good luck to you."

"We haven't finished," he shouted after her.

The grandmother approached the gate with the demeanor of a loyal guard.

"Oh, go on, young man. Leave her alone. Go with God." She closed the gate and went into the house with Miia and the children.

She gently stroked both children at the same time.

"Wake up, my little ones."

Grandma came in.

"A copy of the grandfather. And why did he come?" There was a demand in Grandma's voice.

"He says he was passing by, so he decided to visit," Miia answered indifferently. "My little darlings, sweeties, sweeties."

"He's married to your classmate, the Shepels' granddaughter, Mila."

"With her."

"I remember you used to hang out here all through your childhood, until her parents bought a house at the other end of the village. You got along well with her."

"Oh, we can remember so much," Miia laughed. "Like in eighth grade, when we celebrated her birthday together. Her grandmother treated us to plum liqueur. She kept laughing, and we said, 'How sweet it is; pour more.' And Grandmother poured and said, 'Enough, girl.' What is enough? And we

155

started singing songs to the whole street." Grandmother laughed.

"The father sits on the threshold of the house, listens, listens, and then asks: 'Who is that singing so merrily there?'"

"Oh, in the cherry orchard, there the nightingale sang.
"Yee-yeee-yeee, tooh-tooh-tooh, ah-a-a, oh-ho-ho."
There the nightingale sang."

Dressing the children, Miia sang merrily.

'Yee-yeee-yeee, tooh, tooh-tooh!' Shall we eat, my nightingales? Let's go, my sweet one. The grandmother took the boy's small hand and started to list what he was ready to eat: "A loaf of bread just out of the oven, fresh borscht, potatoes with meat, and cheesecakes with fruit compote. What would you like, Anton?"

"Meat," he grumbled in a still sleepy voice, yawning.

"Oh, like a man smiling, the grandmother turned to the girl, whom Miia was holding in her arms. "And what will eat Niki?"

"Niki will be bread, borscht, and potatoes with meat, and then cheesecakes with compote," Miia kissed her daughter.

Grandma cut off a piece of freshly baked bread and poured some compote.

"I was at the mill, and there the women were talking about how this Mark had beaten Mila again and badly. Olga and Vasyl came to pick her up, but she didn't go. Grandma washed down the bread with some compote. The aroma of fresh bread filled the kitchen.

"It smells so delicious," she continued, taking a deep breath.

"I don't understand how she can endure it. For what?" Miia grabbed her head. "Eat, my little ones."

"That's how his grandfather was – stupid. As long as I can remember, Dunyasha has always walked around with bruises."

"God forbids!" Miia said, looking at her grandmother. She continued, "That's also how it's not fun at our house."

"Yes, but not like that. It happens when Father drinks too much and fights, you know, very rarely. He just grinds his teeth when he's drunk," Miia closed her eyes, shook her head, and spoke.

"Mark almost doesn't drink, but he constantly beats Mila. And why didn't Dunyasha divorce Grandfather Danil?"

"There was nowhere to go. Her parents died. The old grandmother stayed. Danil did all the work for her in the house and in the yard. And who would feed six children? Two died. Dunyasha seldom worked." It felt as though the grandmother, telling the story, had returned to her youth. "He kept blaming her for not saving the youngest. Oh, and he beat her then. If the neighbors hadn't come running, would she have stayed alive?"

"It is horror." Ants ran over her skin from these stories. "And what about the youngest?"

"He was five years old. They went swimming. She stayed at home. Ten minutes later, the children came running. 'Mom, there's Mikolka under the water,' the grandma sighed deeply.

"A disaster."

"The men who were fishing nearby, hearing that the children had started to make noise, ran to them. But the little one was no longer visible. They found him, and he was already dead."

"Oh my God..."

"Why do you think I always ran after you with Zhanna when you went to the river?"

Miia silently fed the children.

"And another child?"

"The girl died a couple of weeks after birth." Grandma put cheesecakes with sour cream on the table.

"And why aren't you eating?" Grandma asked her granddaughter.

"I'll eat after the children," she answered with a smile.

"Oh my God, eat; look how you've lost weight."

"I've gotten slimmer." Miia gave Grandma, who was getting ready to continue her story.

"Keep listening. He loved Varvarka very much. She loved him, too. And Danil's mother wanted Dunyasha to be her daughter-in-law. So, she went to Varvara and told her that Dunyasha was expecting a child from him."

Miia looked at her grandmother with wide eyes.

"Stories repeat themselves. What next?"

157

"Varvara vanished. The entire village searched for her. Three days later, her body was found. She drowned."

"Why did she do it? She would have gone somewhere to sit."

"Oh, child," the grandmother sighed heavily. "Do you think it was like now? In those days, we peasants could not go anywhere outside our collective farms. We were serfs of the Soviet era. You did not teach this in history lessons."

Seeing the sadness in her grandmother's eyes, Miia decided not to ask why.

"Yes, but was Dunyasha pregnant?"

"No. So the mother just told Varvara that. And a couple of weeks later, she took Dunyasha to live with her and told him, 'Now you don't have to run anywhere.' – Listening to this story, Miia couldn't believe that fate had repeated itself with her grandson Danil. 'Thank you, God, for the character that I inherited.' Meanwhile, the grandmother continued. "He walked like that all his life. He would take the accordion and go around the village with his friends. And she sat with the children beaten." The grandmother paused and looked at her granddaughter intently.

Miia's gaze was fixed on the icon with the image of Saint Nicholas, which hung in the corner.

"Oh, look, child. Mark is the grandson of his grandfather. When he was a guy, he used to run to her, then to you. You remember that on your wedding day, he beat her two weeks before their wedding." Shaking her head, she sighed heavily also. "She will be beaten today, too."

"I would not have endured such a mockery."

Without taking her eyes off the holy image, Miia felt relief start to wrap her in its quiet, steady embrace. A light, like fluff and divine feeling, drifted over her universe of future hopes, smiling sweetly at the cold wind of past suffering – memories flashed by – the horrors of childhood, the betrayal of youth. A sense of thankfulness began to fill her at that moment.

"Merciful God, thank You for Your love for me! You have given me strength and wisdom, which have again and again lifted my spirit during the most difficult times." "Crossing herself, Miia looked at her grandmother." Surprisingly, his parents cannot do anything with him.

"And what will you do? 'You have crippled my life.' Danil kept reproaching his mother."

"All this is disgusting." Miia again looked at the icon, the holy image that was watching her closely. She stood up and moved closer to it.

Eyes to eyes. Her soul was filled with peace and tranquility. The grandmother silently watched her granddaughter.

"Thank you, Saint Nicholas! How old is this icon?"

"One hundred and fifty years old. Maybe more." The grandmother stood beside her granddaughter and crossed herself three times.

"And how old is the icon of the mother of God with the little Jesus?"

"The older one. She's two hundred years old. They used to bless my great-great-grandmother with her."

"How much they've seen in human life, and how much they keep in their majestic silence?"

Loud children's arguments echoed from the street, and this brought Miia to her senses, prompting her to go to them quickly.

"Anton! Nika! What didn't you share?" After gathering the scattered toys, she sat down beside them. The children looked at each other. "You need to make peace! You're not some robbers. Play peacefully."

Struck by her grandmother's story, she started to think she wouldn't have a peaceful life in the village.

What lies ahead with Anton? It's already apparent. Trust in Mark is foolish. Her inner voice told her that life would reveal the right paths, and no matter how thick the thorns were, she would have enough strength to get through them. Miia looked tenderly at the children. And what overwhelmed her at that moment was not the fear of being left alone with the unknown, but the desire to touch it.

"It's my turn to make my new lemonade." She remembered another phrase from a book she had almost memorized: "I choose the unknown! God will help!"

Inspired by a fierce determination, the first thing that came to her was that she needed to change the situation. Exhale. Gather her thoughts. What are the next steps she should take into the unknown? She stood. She thought.

159

"Grandma, look after the little ones." Looking around the yard, she called out, "I'll be back right away," and ran to her bicycle.

"Hey, where are you going?"

At that time, only people connected to the local government had landlines in the entire village. So she had to drive to the end of a nearby street.

"Nadyusha, congratulations! Does the phone work?"

"Yes."

"I'll call Zhanna."

A few minutes later, Miia came back. Her face shone with incredible joy. Nadya approached her, carrying a bag of candy, cookies, and pies.

"Here, for the babies. I haven't seen you so happy in a long time. What happened?

Miia was beaming."

"I don't know yet. But I promise to tell you when I figure it out," she answered briskly. "Thank you." She got on her bicycle and immediately headed out. Stopping near the yard where the Meskhetian Turks lived, she saw that the children were playing there and asked them to call their father.

"Hello, Madat," she said, greeting him, and noticed that there were traces of cement mortar on his hands. "Are you busy now?"

"Hi! I've already finished. You came for a reason," he smiled.

"I have a request and a million, but a million not now."

"Better not now than never." He was in complete order with his sense of humor. "Speak."

"I have to leave today for Zhanna. I can't stay in the village. I'll fill up the car. Please."

His wife came up to them. Miia greeted her.

"Hi. How are you? We only talk about you."

"Why about me?"

"Why did you marry him?"

"It's time to fix everything." Miia smiled, and her heart ached. "I ask Madat to take me to Zhanna. Today. Now."

"Madat! Why are you standing there? Without delay, she snapped at her husband. "We remember the kindness of your family, who were the first to help us when we arrived in the village. Uncle Vlad did all the electrical work in the

160

house. Then, they helped repair the fence and sheds. Every day, your mother and grandmother brought bread, then eggs, then oil, flour, and vegetables." She stopped when she heard the car start. A kind smile of gratitude was on her face. "It couldn't be otherwise."

"And who babysat our children? The smile never left her face." Please always contact me when you need assistance.

"Faride, thank you. Thank you very much."

"Madat is leaving. Run. My greetings to Zhanna."

"I'll pass it on, thank you." She quickly left.

In the yard, the grandmother and the children were busy with the geese.

"I'm going to Zhanna's with the children." Miia ran past them and into the house.

"What's so fast?" the grandmother exclaimed in surprise.

"Give me time to gather the gifts for Pavlik."

"Don't worry. I assure you; everything is fine! It's just that I won't survive another meeting today. You'd better help the children go to the car; Madat is already waiting. "With hastily gathered things and toys, she took the boy in her arms, and the girl, the grandmother."

"When will you be back?"

"I don't know."

"Well, really, maybe it's better that way." The grandmother's voice was already calmer.

They hugged. Grandma hugged and kissed the children.

"Tell your parents that everything is fine. I love you all."

"Kiss from us for Pavlunia, Zhanna, and Bohdan," and turning to Madat, she continued, "Young man, be careful on the road."

"Don't worry! I've been in this car from Samarkand."

Grandma crossed herself as the car drove away, getting farther and farther, and she wholeheartedly kept asking for God's mercy for her granddaughter.

And the granddaughter, admiring the purity of the boundless horizons, felt the presence of her grandmother's prayers with all her heart.

"God will help! He is merciful." Grandma said to herself and went to drive the geese to the pasture."

When she hears the dog barking, she sees Anton standing in

161

the yard.

"Good evening," he greeted, looking around the yard.

"And you." Her voice was not entirely gentle.

"I can sense that you are not happy to see me. Grandma, where is Miia?"

"Why do you need her?"

"I want to talk."

"Have you said a lot to her in four years?" Grandma's tone became harsher.

"Where is she?" He began to get annoyed.

Looking at him closely, she realized that he was drunk.

"Listen, Anton, can you ever be sober? My God, you are so young. What a beautiful and modest wife he has. What smart and pretty children, and you? Grandma spoke calmly but sternly: "You have joined forces with the lazy; all you know is how to get drunk and drive around the village. What have you come for now?" Seeing a motorcycle near the yard, on which his friends were riding, Grandma started up. "Who are you trading your family for? My God."

"I don't hit her," he interrupted, but didn't have time to continue.

"He doesn't hit her." Here, the grandmother couldn't stand it. "Get out of the yard. He doesn't hit her. Hero." The grandmother swung her wand at him.

"Why are you acting like this? I wanted to apologize." He stepped back and started to ramble.

"He doesn't hit her. You're hurting her with your words. Get out of the yard. She'll decide when to talk to you," and she pushed him with her wand until he was forced out of the yard.

XXII

Zhanna was happy about her sister and nephews' arrival. Their house was both spacious and cozy, making it perfect for hosting guests. Because of Zhanna's busy work schedule, Miia started helping her sister with housework, cooking, and gardening right from the start.

"Listen, sister, look how beautifully the children are playing," Miia said, looking out the window."

Breaking away from shaping cookies, Zhanna moved to the window. Her son, Pavlik, was only six months older than Antonchyk, which is why they played skillfully and got along well with Nika. In the yard, besides them, four other neighbor kids were playing. Surprisingly, there were no disputes over toys or other issues that often come up during children's games.

"Have you finally decided to divorce?"

"Yes. Finally."

"Two children." Zhanna looked at her sister cautiously. "Aren't you afraid of being left alone?"

"Something else is scarier." Miia's gaze froze, taking her back to her memories.

"Wha"

"I had a moment when I lost faith in life itself."

The sister looked at Miia in surprise.

"Just don't say what you wanted..."

Without rushing to reply, Miia looked at the children playing peacefully in the yard. Zhanna was waiting.

"That morning, mom should have been at work. The summer kitchen had not yet been completed, and the ceiling had not been hemmed with boards. The beams are strong..."

"Oh, God! No." Zhanna interrupted her. "When was that?"

"Two weeks ago. Once again, Anton's family took turns giving me educational lessons." Watching the playful children, she smiled. "The children were also playing quietly in the yard. But my mind was so clouded that I lost sight of my responsibilities to them. What would happen to them? How would they grow up? I didn't care."

"You're crazy!" Zhanna said as she approached her sister and grabbed her hand.

163

"At that moment, it was just like that," Miia answered her calmly. "But my mind immediately turned on when I heard my mom's voice in the yard. I rushed to pull the belt from my robe off the beam, but from my tearful face, she understood. 'I didn't give birth to you and raise you to lose you because of these people. Pack your things and go home,' she said. I admit that I felt ashamed in front of her for my weakness. Her words, 'It's not any calmer here, but no one will bring you to suicide,' were decisive. That same day, I gave her some of my clothes. For the next three days, so as not to be noticed, I began to transport my own and the children's things to my parents."

"Well, you had to do it because the first time you left Anton, you didn't return your clothes. They also made you give up the gold jewelry."

"Oh! They almost robbed me of the gold jewelry. And so, they wouldn't rip me off alive, I had to take it off myself. They demanded my wedding ring, too." Hearing the roar of the car, the children ran out into the yard. "Bogdan has arrived."

While setting the table, the sisters heard a loud childish cry. Not understanding what had happened, the young mothers rushed out of the house. In the yard, the kids tried to say something, one after the other.

"Mom," Pavlik shouted, holding Nika's doll and a bag of sweets in his hands. "Uncle Anton and Grandpa just took away Anton and Nika."

Miia ran out into the yard, but all she saw was a column of smoke from a car. Zhanna and Bogdan ran up to her, followed by Pavlik and the other children.

Bogdan ran into the yard, saying, "I'll catch up with them now."

"Pavlik, were they the ones?" Zhanna asked as she sat down next to the child.

"Well, of course. Grandpa was driving, and Uncle Anton was sitting next to him."

"When the car stopped, and they called Anton and Nika, they happily ran to the car," interrupted the neighbor boy.

"Uncle Anton got out of the car, handed us a bag of sweets, opened the back door, and put Anton and Nika in the car.

Nika dropped the doll then."

"I asked him to run and pick it up, but Uncle Anton said they were rushing and wouldn't let me," Pavlik continued, clutching the doll tightly and choking with excitement. "Nika was crying so much."

Bogdan drove out of the yard.

"Miia, get in, let's go."

Looking into the distance where only a dust cloud from the car was visible, Miia shook her head. The neighbors hurried over and started asking questions.

"Miia's husband and his father, and their children have just been kidnapped," Zhanna answered in an icy voice.

"How so?"

"Without informing you, Miia?"

"We need to make a quick decision."

"Maybe call the police?"

They were talking. They felt surprised. And everyone wanted to do something to help.

"No police are needed," Miia said quietly in a trembling voice. She tried with all her might not to lose her composure. "They are with their father."

"Yes, but what should we do?" Pavlik's godmother asked eagerly.

"I'll think about it," Miia said and then went to the yard. Zhanna hurried after her.

During dinner, everyone focused on the incident that had happened. They discussed different plans for what to do next. After a long talk, Miia suddenly announced.

"I won't talk to them. It's not for nothing that I've heard threats from them lately to take away my maternal rights. What happened today wouldn't have helped me if I had set a chase." Her voice suddenly shifted from panic to a confident firmness. "I need a consultation."

At nine in the morning, Miia was already in the reception area of the district prosecutor's office. She was worried because she knew that anything she reported could cause serious problems for her mother-in-law, which Miia definitely wanted to avoid. Still, her maternal instincts gave her the resolve she needed. She kept repeating to herself, "Oh, this is not my way." Her racing thoughts were suddenly

165

interrupted by a loud male voice.

"Good morning, are you here for me?"

"Good morning! If you are a prosecutor."

Raising her head, Miia saw a young man in front of her. The first thought that came to her cheered her up. "If all men were this tall, I could wear heels without any shame."

"What brought you to me?" the prosecutor asked in the office.

I'm Miia. In January, it will be four years since I got married. However, I'm filing for divorce. We have two children. The boy is three and a half years old; the daughter is two years and two months old. I wouldn't have come to you, but my husband and his parents have recently started to threaten me with their plans to strip me of my maternal rights. Of course, I'm not going to sit idly by and wait for my mother-in-law to join this effort, along with some of her friends." The young man listened carefully to her calm and sensible story, not even trying to interrupt. This surprised him. Miia noticed this and spoke with more confidence. "I know some things about my mother-in-law's work. And I, without hesitation, am ready to report it to the prosecutor's office if I feel a real threat to myself."

There was silence in the office. For a moment, it seemed to Miia that the "good deeds" of her mother-in-law extended to the prosecutor's office as well. She looked intently into her interlocutor's eyes. Her gaze was full of determination and courage.

"Are you ready to confirm in writing about your mother-in-law's deeds?"

Miia didn't quite like that his first question was exactly that. "I'm ready. In case I have to defend my reputation." Miia caught a light and sly smile on the face of the man, who was in such a strict profession. "Unfortunately, before that happens, my conscience won't allow me to do that. Do you understand?"

"Hmm. I know." The cunning on his face was replaced by seriousness. He got up from the table and moved to the shelf that held rows of law books. Picking one, he began to flip through the pages quickly. Stopping somewhere in the middle, he handed it to Miia.

166

"Read. It clearly states what, according to the law, can lead to the deprivation of maternal rights."

Miia started reading. She had to read the same article several times to understand it at least a little.

"My God! Where did my intelligence go? With domestic chores, diapers, cows, and pigs, my brain has become covered with mold. This is some horror," she said aloud, smiling as she turned the pages.

Looking at you, Miia, I don't see a drug addict, a drunkard, or a woman of loose morals. And therefore, you are not a candidate who should be stripped of maternal rights," the prosecutor said in a gentle tone. "So, calm down first. And explain to your husband and his parents that not all issues can be resolved through connections. I'm sure you'll have enough courage.

"Thank you, Mikhail Viktorovich!" Noticing the surprise at the address, Miia pointed to the door with a smile. "A sign."

"And what town are you from?" he asked her.

"It doesn't matter." Miia didn't want to respond to this question. "If something goes against me, you'll have an answer." Having said goodbye, she left the office.

At home, she shared the meeting's results with Zhanna. There was no despair or confusion in her soul. A plan for future actions, discussions, and conversations was forming in her mind.

"There are two days left until the weekend. We'll take you home. At the same time, we're visiting our parents."

"I want to call and ask how the children are."

"Are you sure?"

"Yes."

The mother-in-law picked up the phone.

"Mom, good evening! How are the children?"

"They're having dinner now."

"We need to discuss everything. But not over the phone.

"I don't know what you're up to, but you need to come to your senses."

"I'll be back on Saturday. I'll come and talk to you. Hug the little ones for me."

"What are you doing?"

"Not now. Good night!"

167

The beeps rang in response.

Sister saw tears in Miia's eyes.

"Zhanna, I miss the children. I know they're safe, but I miss them so much."

Returning to the village, Miia attempted several times to speak with her in-laws. However, she was denied permission rudely. She was also not allowed to see the children. Miia didn't want to start fights on the street because she realized that any such antics would only disgrace her. And she couldn't afford to let that happen.

Almost two months passed in this manner. During this period, she did not see the children. They weren't taken to kindergarten because the father-in-law and mother-in-law took turns being on vacation.

Various gossip spread throughout the village. Some people condemned Miia for her alleged affair with the director. Others, however, defended her, citing Anton's constant drunkenness and his shameful attitude toward the family.

Initially, Miia painfully reacted to the downright absurd judgments of her fellow villagers about her. She was even afraid to go outside. It seemed to her that everyone was condemning her – some for marital infidelity, some for indecent treatment of her in-laws as respected people in the village, and some for Anton's "spoiled" life.

But her confusion was short-lived. After deep reflection, guided by thoughts of salvation, she asked herself, "What will lemonade from this lemon taste like?" Smiling to herself in response, Miia, inspired by the stars of the screen, started gossiping about herself with everyone she talked to.

One day in the store, amid several women squinting in her direction with disapproval, Miia, without hesitation, smiled sweetly and turned to face them.

"What a joy it is to feel like a local Hollywood star. Can I leave my autograph for you?"

And the stars must have heard her. As soon as she left the store, the director stopped beside her.

"Congratulations! Have you really decided to get a divorce?" he asked her in a calm and steady voice.

Having greeted her in return, she nodded.

The women from the store, passing by, tried to catch

something interesting in Miia's communication with Andriy Gavrilovich. Noticing their curiosity, the director winked at Miia and, turning his gaze to the women, greeted them in a flattering manner.

"It will be something for them to do." He followed them with his gaze before turning to Miia.

"I just told them in the store that I feel like a Hollywood star." At this phrase, Andrey Gavrylovych laughed out loud.

"Did you say that?"

"And I offered an autograph." A playful smile appeared on her face. "Well, I'm a star!"

"You deserve to shine." Miia was puzzled by these words. But the director quickly went on. "I'll go to Kyiv. Our young people, Margo and Taras, are coming with me. A few days of rest in the capital will do you good." Miia looked at him with eyes wide with surprise.

"I suggest you come with us."

"Your offer is so tempting, but..." Miia was confused. Your wife must have heard the gossip going around the village about," she didn't dare to continue.

"About us," he continued. "You have no reason to worry, because Oksana's brother and his wife are also going. So, agree.

"When?"

"The day after tomorrow. I will have to stay for two weeks. Our young people will also stay with me."

"I have to return earlier. How?"

"By train."

"I have never been to Kyiv." Miia felt a surge of excitement. Andriy Gavrylovych noticed this.

"We will take you to the railway station. We will put you in a carriage. And how to get home from Kherson, you know. I remember you said that you studied in Kherson."

"Yes."

"The day after tomorrow, at six in the morning, we will pick you up. Smiling, he started the car and drove away.

These few minutes of communication passed like a healing experience.

"Is this possible?" Miia asked herself as she watched Andriy Gavrilovich's car drive away. While I was afraid of all the

169

gossip and tried to resist it, I felt invisible, as if I were nothing – a complete zero. Despair gnawed at my soul. And as soon as I helplessly accepted, with all my heart, mind, and soul, the dirty negativity of the rumors and gossip, strange things began to happen. Unbelievable!"

"Who are you talking to?" a neighbor's voice called out behind her.

"Oh," Miia smiled, coming to her senses, "I tell myself I want lemonade, but what a pity, our store doesn't sell it."

The trip to Kyiv was successful. On the way home, Miia met a young man in the compartment who, according to him, was an officer of the country's security service.

Miia briefly told him about the recent problems with her acquaintance, Andriy Gavrylovich. While in Kyiv, she learned that confident regional leaders planned to retaliate against him for exposing their corruption schemes, which aimed to destroy livestock in the area.

Even before this trip, events occurred in her village that terrified people. Almost all the livestock, mainly large cattle, was taken from two farms to a meat processing plant, leaving the workers at these farms unemployed. Then, two types of rumors spread through the village. Some accused the director of initiating the actions. Others, in his defense, claimed that he was following orders from both the district and regional leadership. At that point, people began discussing removing Andriy Gavrylovich from his position and opening a criminal case against him.

"These are the contacts of the most powerful international law firm that has not lost a single court case." Oleg handed over a piece of paper with the address and phone number written on it.

But Miia couldn't hand it over.

Immediately after returning from Kyiv, Andriy Gavrylovich resigned and, along with his family, traveled to Lviv.

170

XXIII

Meanwhile, the wedding season was starting in the village, and Miia's cousin kicked it off. While talking to one of the guests, Miia learned that her mother-in-law had begun complaining at work about how hard it was for her and her father-in-law to have children. Anton wasn't helping at all. After hearing this, all her worries about losing her maternal rights vanished. The next day, after gathering some courage, she went to her in-laws. When she saw her at the gate, the children happily ran to greet her.

"Grandma, open the gate; mom has come."

The mother-in-law was home alone. When she saw Miia, she started calling her children over, but they didn't listen.

"Don't tear the children's souls," Miia shouted. "You can't hide them from me forever. I've come to talk."

The mother-in-law had no choice, and the children's joy knew no bounds. Setting aside sentimentality, Miia acted decisively:

"I am filing for divorce. This is final."

The mother-in-law's gaze showed confusion.

Miia, you have no idea how hard life can be. How tough it is to work and make a living. And you have a house. By keeping the farm, we'll have food on the table. Anton has a job, which isn't great, but he has it.

"Excuse me, but that's the problem, which isn't good. So, what will happen next? Have you noticed how, over the past three years, it has gotten more difficult? First with jobs. I have no opportunities in the village. Think about it. To make money, you suggest that I keep three or four cows and sell dairy products at the market?" Miia hurried to add. "However, there are questions that scare me: What future awaits our children? That's the first. And the second is, I would rather not spend my life with cows, pigs, vegetable gardens, and markets."

"I repeat, don't you realize how hard everything is? You don't like cows here, and do you at least understand how you'll live?"

"I'll go to Kyiv."

"God, what have you thought of?" She clutched her head.

171

"Throw away these fantasies."

"When you were my age, you also didn't see all the life opportunities and prospects. Therefore, I have twenty years to spare. Let's evaluate my decisions today in twenty years."

"We will not give you the children," she said sternly.

Here, Miia realized that this was undoubtedly the moment to put the information she had received at the wedding to use.

"The main thing is that you let me see them. It is enough for me if it's only on your territory."

Surprise took over the mother-in-law. A silent scene followed. She couldn't say a word. She stared with wide eyes at her daughter-in-law, who needed that kind of reaction.

The state district attorney greeted Miia with a gentle smile, witty remarks, and a preventive talk about the importance of family for society. Watching him, she tried to contain her emotions.

"My parents are your age." After listening to him, she started to speak. "When they were as old as I am now, the family was only important to society because that was the party's policy. I will not apologize for my negative attitude toward the CPSU. I am not here for that."

"Divorces were unacceptable." He put on his glasses, set the typewriter on the table, and, looking at Miia, began to type.

It took a little over an hour to print the three lawsuits. Holding them in her hands, Miia was surprised.

"That's all? Three lawsuits on three sheets of paper?" Surprise froze on her face.

"Two sheets are enough for divorce and alimony," the lawyer replied with a smile.

"What's wrong with the lawsuit about the division of property?" Miia's voice sounded demanding.

"To file it, you need to pay a court fee, which is quite a lot." She thought he smiled.

"What?" Her inquisitive look made him come to his senses.

"One percent of the amount of the lawsuit."

Miia thanked him and left the office. Stopping, she began to reread the lawsuit about the division of property. She felt doubts creeping up on her. "I don't like this toilet paper," she said quietly to herself, folded the sheet of paper in four,

172

and put it in her bag.

A month later, a court hearing was held on the two lawsuits. Alimony was ordered immediately. However, Mia was upset by the decision in the divorce lawsuit. But the judge reassured her. According to the law, you can't divorce immediately if the couple has children. The minimum period for reconciliation is six months. There was only one way out – to live, plan, dream, and wait.

Time passed quickly.

To earn a living, she had to work in the fields, which was becoming the most common way for most villagers to make money. At first, she was embarrassed. But there was no other way to earn money. A friendly group of fellow villagers gathered at these jobs. It was like a big family. No one was offended, humiliated, or ridiculed. At these jobs, everyone was equal.

It was necessary to wake up at four in the morning and spend the whole day under the scorching sun, clearing the pumpkin beds from weeds. And in the evening, barely reaching the bed, she quickly fell asleep. Gradually, the body adjusted to this, and Miia began to perceive this work as a form of physical exercise, considering the judgment amusing, joyful, and justifying it to herself.

The spring and summer months passed at this pace.

With the onset of autumn, Miia was increasingly overcome by sadness. She was afraid to think about the future and could not see it clearly.

"Miia, think," she said to herself, looking at her reflection in the mirror. "This is not the life you wanted. Pull yourself together. What is wrong with you? Where is your determination? Where are your dreams?" The answers were lost in the abyss of unknown fear and confusion. Leaning her head against the mirror, she cried. Salty tears burned her face, falling to the floor, scattering like crystal beads. She raised her eyes and stared into their green-gray distance. Surprisingly, at that moment, she felt the craziest, most incredible, and most daring thoughts, which, like a flock of white swans, circled over her hopelessness. It was one of the most mysterious moments in her life. Wiping away her tears, she smiled at her reflection. "The calm before the storm," she

173

said quietly, then sighed heavily and continued: "Well, I'm ready!"

To the news. To the unknown.

The office of an international law firm was located in the very heart of Kyiv. The administrator told Miia that Pysarchuk Alex was responsible for housing issues and currently worked as an assistant to a member of parliament. Of course, Miia did not know that she needed to make an appointment with a lawyer in advance to avoid waiting. But she was used to waiting – sometimes an hour or two. She had learned a valuable life lesson long ago: patience, in God's eyes, is a sign of good luck.

As she waited, Miia looked at each visitor, imagining that one of them might be the lawyer she was preparing to meet, pondering her thoughts and rearranging sentences in her head. She had no experience dealing with people of such high status. The soothing music that played softly throughout the office made her feel sleepy. But with each loud phone call that broke the gentle silence, a sense of vigor appeared.

Five hours had passed. The workday was already over, but Miia stubbornly waited.

Then, the door opened, and a handsome man appeared in front of Miia. His stylish suit skillfully enhanced his tall, athletic build. His clean-shaven face was striking. The tired look in his eyes clearly showed how difficult his day had been.

Miia greeted him.

"Are you waiting for me?"

"If you are a family lawyer."

"Are you divorced?"

"We are already divorced. Division of property. I have a statement of claim with me, prepared by the district attorney."

At these words, his tired eyes smiled, causing Miia to fall into a trance. Noticing this, he turned around and asked.

"Would you like tea or coffee?"

"I don't know..." she began to stammer in response.

"What's your name?"

"Miia."

"That's a rare name," he said, picking up the phone and

174

dialing the number. "So, what would you like, Miia? Tea. Coffee."

"Tea," she answered quickly, realizing that refusing would be a sign of bad upbringing.

Having placed the order, Alex turned to Miia, who was reading the statement of claim she had brought with her. She looked up at him. As a sign of questioning, he silently nodded his head.

"And what's in there?"

"Here," Miia held the statement by the edge of the sheet with two fingers, "Toilet paper, not a lawsuit. Excuse me for the disparaging remark to…"

He smiled.

"What's wrong?"

"I can't go to the district court with this piece of paper. Not because there's anything wrong with it. In this form, this statement doesn't protect me before the judge. I need a document that the judge would hold with both hands and pray over."

"Should the claim look like this?" Alex handed Miia the specimen claim he had prepared on the company's letterhead. "Wow. Yes!" Miia exclaimed, cheering up. "Can you draw up my claim the same way?" She examined the letterhead, which featured its logo. The details were printed in two languages, Ukrainian and English, and looked very prestigious.

"Of course we can…" At that moment, there was a light knock on the door.

A minute later, fragrant tea with cakes decorated with cream flowers stood in front of Miia.

"How beautiful. Thank you. Miia beamed.

"We won't have long to have tea, because in an hour I have to run to the boss again. Usually, we work until late." Having finished his tea, the lawyer began to read Miia's lawsuit. Miia carefully watched the expression on his face.

"How much will I have to pay?"

"If you just reprint the text on our form, it's almost nothing. The cost of the paper and twenty minutes of work by my assistant. However, just reprinting won't work."

"Why?"

"Don't worry. It's a rural area. We need to consider the land

plot where the house is built, and... Are there children?"
"Yes. Two."
"Then the property must be divided, including the children. That is, demand three parts out of four, not half."
"This is how it should be according to the law?"
"Of course. Didn't the lawyer who prepared this application tell you that?"
"No." Miia smiled confusedly.
"Then you did the right thing by coming to us. I know that in remote areas of the country, laws are often ignored in favor of some, harming others. We will fix it."
Could you please provide me with an estimate of the cost?
"Miia, I haven't done anything yet. What's worse is that I don't even know where to find the time."
"Listen to me. I was always great at writing essays in school. I know it's not the same as writing a lawsuit, but we can do this: you give me the collections of codes and laws along with a list of the necessary articles." Mia's emotions overwhelmed her with every word. "Write me the sequence of the text of the lawsuit. I'll calculate the areas, write everything down, and then you'll need to check and make the necessary corrections. Please."
"How long do you plan to be in Kyiv?"
"A week."
"Then we will do that."
For two days, Miia felt like a respectable person, working on her lawsuit in the prestigious office of a well-known international law firm. And what surprised her even more was that communication with the employees did not contain any pathos or arrogance on their part. In the capital, people could afford it, at least regarding her. After all, Miia is a country girl, and she was seeing some things for the first time or only in Hollywood movies.
"Here you go! The original. Three copies," Alex proudly smiled, solemnly handing over each copy separately. "You did a fantastic job."
"You're kidding. Without you, I wouldn't have done anything."
"I only fixed a small part of what you wrote. Now, neither you nor I have much time."

"Oh, yes, I'm completely lost in time." Looking at the clock, Miia snapped back to reality as if she'd been burned with boiling water. "My God, my train leaves in half an hour."

"That's what I was talking about. "Quickly collecting the necessary papers in a folder, he called the office administrator. "Mari, call my driver; have him wait at the front door as soon as possible. Quickly." Miia stood confused, not understanding what to do. "We'll take you to the station, because if you take the subway, you'll be late. Is this your bag?" Already in the corridor, he asked.

"Yes." Miia almost ran after him.

"Let's go." Alex grabbed Miia's suitcase, and after saying goodbye to everyone in the office, they quickly headed to the car.

On the way, the lawyer advised Miia on her behavior in court and reassured her of his support.

"Leave the money to the children. I don't always accept money from my clients. Plus, you did all the work."

I just wanted to let you know that there was no time to argue. "The train was sent to the penultimate thirteenth track." Laughing, Miia tried to keep up with Alex. "I thought that this happened in the movies. I didn't even realize that I would personally experience something like this."

"Come on, hurry up. The conductors are already raising the upper steps."

And here was platform number 13. Miia and Alex had to run along it to get to the door of the nearest car.

There was a minute left before departure. The conductor quickly prepared the stairs to catch the passenger.

Mia, breathing out, handed the ticket to the conductor.

"I've never run after trains before."

At that moment, the train started moving.

"Remember, about support," he quickened his paces,

"Alex, I'm grateful to you," but he couldn't hear it anymore, because the train was going faster and faster.

177

XXIV

In the district court office, the secretary, holding the statement of claim, was stunned. She silently looked from Miia to the bundle of documents.

"Is something wrong?"

"The package of documents is complete. However," the secretary replied softly.

"What's wrong?" under her sweet smile, Miia's voice turned icy.

"I need to show your statement of claim to the judge. Perhaps she will have comments so that the court can consider the statement without delay."

"Listen," Miia interrupted her sternly and continued with a fake accent. "Do you think that in Kyiv, lawyers from an international law firm know less than the district judge? That's the first thing. And secondly, you are obliged to register the statement! And, assuming that some documents are missing, they can be added during the consideration of the case. Well, I don't need to explain that to you."

"No, no... You have everything in full set," she fussed. "I have to inform the judge about... Wait, please," and, jumping down from her seat, quickly walked to the door. Miia followed her.

"In general, you have no right to run around the corridors with an unregistered statement of claim. Maybe you have plans to destroy it?"

Having reached the judge's office, the secretary quietly asked Miia to wait in the corridor. However, Miia did not like this, and she went inside after her.

"I asked you."

"Good afternoon! I am not always obedient. So I took the liberty of coming in without an invitation. The district court secretary just broke the rules by refusing to register my statement of claim. Of course, I can guess why?". Miia looked sharply into the judge's eyes.

"Hello! Why?"

"The answer is in your hands."

The judge looked at the secretary in confusion, then took the lawsuit to read it.

"Irina, you can be free," and, turning her gaze to Miia, began to read the lawsuit. "I remember, in the first lawsuit, you asked for half of the property. In this lawsuit, you are demanding three-quarters. Why is that?"

Miia smiled.

"The Kyiv lawyers probably know the laws better. Everything is described there."

Mia was filled with immense pride in her determination. The fear she saw in the judge was directly related to the company's popularity, especially its founder's. Where had her arrogance and swagger gone, with which she had thrown Miia the first lawsuit? That time, she had been in control. That time. Not right now.

Looking at the judge, Miia could not help but feel amused.

"Will a lawyer be present?" she asked quietly, neatly placing the application on the table.

"If there is a need for it," was the confident answer.

On the way home, Miia briefly felt the bitterness of the situation.

"Life is cruel. But I have no right to lose the battles for myself!" She remembered the words from the fable about the hare, the wolf, and the lion.

However, concentrating as much as possible on her dreams, Miia began to get used to her plans for the future. Vasyl Ivanovich and Olesya Kirillovna were ready to accept her and let her live with them. She understood that she would not be left without a job in the capital, despite having only a vocational education. It was a little disconcerting that among her acquaintances in Kyiv, there were only Vasyl Ivanovich, Olesya Kirillovna, their neighbor, and lawyer Alex.

"For the capital, it's a good start."

Three weeks flew by like one day. A preliminary hearing was scheduled, and that day finally came. Miia was overwhelmed with nerves. Her whole body was tense and trembling. So, she first went to the pharmacy. "I need the most effective sedative. The most super."

"We have this. It doesn't make you sleepy and doesn't lead to loss of concentration or attention. You need to take two pills a day."

Having received the green pill, Miia immediately took one.

179

To avoid embarrassing the pharmacist, she took another one as she left the pharmacy.

There was still half an hour and three hundred meters left until the court hearing. The day was gloomy, with occasional rain. Miia liked this weather. She remembered a song about gloomy days and walked, humming it under her breath. She began to feel the effects of the sedatives. It was an unexpected phenomenon. Her nerves played music that was the opposite of excitement.

On the threshold of the courthouse, she saw her ex-husband with his parents and a private lawyer. They had gathered in a small group, animatedly discussing the court case. Miia greeted them. Only their lawyer answered. The young woman was not even embarrassed by the coldness of her former family. She and her parents had experienced many humiliations and insults. How many arguments and unfair disappointments had they caused? How many reproaches were expressed? But most of the negativity centered around money – what, in the husband's family's opinion, Miia's parents should have provided in the form of construction assistance, furniture assistance, or other support. Money seemed to be considered the highest good.

Miia knew that her parents lived honestly and did not have "left-wing" earnings. It was too dangerous to have them. The punishment was too severe for any fraud.

Miia was snapped out of her distant memories by the loud, cheerful voice of the state's district attorney, Korolenko.

"Oh, Borko." At that moment, Miia's opponents entered the room, whom he greeted with a smile, and, turning to Mia, he continued: "My statement did not suit you, so you went to the deputy speaker of parliament." The tone of his voice strongly emphasized the importance of the law firm.

"However, I will be frank, not with him directly, but with his first assistant," Miia answered him playfully.

"I have heard about him. An influential lawyer. He has not lost a single case." Korolenko sat down next to her, put his arm around her shoulders, and continued to speak clearly and loudly so that everyone in the corridor could hear. "Are you alone? There will be no lawyers?"

"Alone," and, leaning closer to his ear, Miia whispered:

"Would you like to meet Alex?"

In response, he laughed loudly.

"What are you saying? We are insignificant to them."

"Honestly, I did not feel it."

"If it is not a secret, how much did you pay for the services of their company?"

"According to the contract, the calculation will be made after the case is completed."

Of course, she made it up, thereby adding more weight and seriousness to her intentions.

"Hmm..." scratching his chin, the interlocutor looked around at the company with which Anton had arrived, continuing in a low voice. "Is this your husband with his parents?"

"Yes. Most likely, they took him with them, not the other way around," Miia replied, feeling completely calm.

"They were so worried about their property for their grandchildren that they even brought a private lawyer with them." He shook his head. "Well, what can I tell you? I'm not promising that the court will award three-quarters, but I guarantee half."

"I'll also tell you something. If the decision doesn't meet my expectations, there will be an appeal."

"Everything will be decided with your patrons today. What's more, you did a great job of stirring everyone up here."

At that moment, the assistant judge came out and called them into the courtroom.

"Thank you for the moral support."

He raised his fist in solidarity and added,

"My respect to you."

It was already dark outside when the hearing ended. There was no more transportation to the village. "Thank God that cousins live in the district center," Miia thought, and she slowly walked toward the main street. Suddenly, her in-laws' car stopped beside her.

"Miia, let's go," her mother-in-law called softly. "We'll talk everything over calmly at home."

Resisting was pointless. Miia knew today she would see her children, and that was all she truly wanted.

Incredible joy the children experienced when they saw their mother. Miia couldn't contain her tears, sweet hugs, and kisses for her little ones.

"Mommy, don't cry," Niki said, persuading her as she wiped her own eyes.

"You're going to live with us now, right?" Anton chirped. "We missed you very much."

Watching this scene, the mother-in-law could not stand it.

"Child, forgive us for allowing our anger to inflict such abuse on you and the children. And on herself." The mother-in-law burst into tears bitterly. "How painful it was for me to realize that all our efforts for you were in vain. I could not understand why you were forced to make such a difficult decision. Ignat and I have experienced so many quarrels, insults, and even betrayals. But for the sake of the children, preserving the family became the most important thing." Her confession was frank.

"Mom, don't cry. I beg you." Miia approached and hugged her. "That's how it should be. It's hard for me to explain. After all, life goes on."

Anton walked into the room, his father-in-law following behind him.

"Girls, stop crying. The most important thing is that everyone is safe and healthy. Better yet, let's get together and have dinner."

"For you, only to eat," the mother-in-law snapped grumpily.

"Well, what's the matter?" The conversation started to get humorous. "If you don't feed me, then who will do my work? You won't survive without me." Smiling, the father-in-law took the children by the hands and led them to the table. "Well, take your places."

The women quickly set the table. The mother-in-law knew that they would return late today, so she had prepared food in advance.

After dinner, Anton Sr. wanted to stay and have some tea together, but his mother-in-law asked him to take the children and go to the TV, where the evening fairy tale was about to start.

"Sorry, son, you did your job; you didn't save the family. "So, I don't see any reason to talk to you about your children's future right now. Go."

After these words, Anton left the room silently, following

the children.

"Right now, we don't have the money to pay you according to the settlement agreement." After waiting for the door to close, the father-in-law started. "But we will find it. However, I would like to understand what your plans are for the future."

"We hope you will stay in the village," his mother-in-law said to Miia. "You will have enough money to buy a house. The Kozachenkos are selling their two-room apartment."

"We are here to keep the children in our sight. My mother and I will help and support you."

Hearing such reasoning, Miia was filled with horror. She pictured her life in the village, a life she was desperately trying to escape. She already knew what it would be like, and that thought terrified her the most.

The unknown.

Only paths into the unknown.

She had no fear in front of this. Instead, she felt an insatiable urge to dive headlong into this.

Because it was the unknown that provided hope for the future.

"I don't know if I should stay in the village. I didn't think about it," Miia said quietly, breaking the silence. "And now we're all tired, and it's time to rest. You need to have the strength to discuss such issues. And I admit, I don't have that right now. Even talking about my future and the future of my children won't give me that strength now."

She didn't tell the truth because she wasn't tired. She was sure she wouldn't get support for her plans; she didn't want to say that she planned to leave for Kyiv to start a new life.

"I agree," the mother-in-law said after half a minute. "We will still have time to talk about it."

At that moment, the phone rang.

"Ignat, long-distance call. It's our Dmitry."

It was a call from my father-in-law's older brother. They didn't talk for long. When he returned, his father-in-law smiled contentedly.

"Polya, I can tell you, he will help us out, then, turning to Miia, he said, "In two weeks, we will pay you."

Miia was embarrassed by these words. At some point, she felt ashamed of herself. However, she quickly regained control of her emotions.

"I will use this money wisely" was the only thing she managed to say. "I will go; it's too late. Our need to rest."

Anton entered the room.

"Are the children asleep?" the mother-in-law asked as she got up from the table.

"Yes."

"I'll go and kiss them." Miia also got up and went into the room, where Anton and Nika were gently snuffling in a peaceful sleep. Admiring them, her mother felt an overwhelming sense of gratitude to fate for her two little angels.

"It's too late and cold." Anton's voice was heard near the door. "I'll take you."

No one said a word on the way. Miia felt relieved. She didn't know what kind of life awaited her, but she knew what kind of life she definitely wouldn't live.

She was the master of her future.

XXV

There was a lively atmosphere at the train station. Olesya Kyriylivna met Miia near the carriage. Watching each other through the window, they smiled and started to exchange gestures. Miia wasn't in a hurry to leave, because she had three large suitcases with her. And Nika. Olesya Kyriylivna and Vasily Ivanovich knew that Miia was planning to come with a child and had no objections.

"Now we won't be sad." Olesya Kyriylivna said happily when she saw the girl. "Call me Grandma. I'll be happy," and then, turning to Miia, she continued. "I'm almost sixty, but I don't have any grandchildren yet. And this will be both entertainment and worry for my grandfather and me."

On the way home, Olesya Kyriylivna told us about her sons, whose married lives also hadn't worked out. The guys were older than Miia, and they didn't have any children. And no one said any reason.

"Maybe if they had at least one child each, they wouldn't be talking about divorce," she sadly remarked. But Miia didn't answer her; instead, she thought, "If parents are indifferent to each other, children will not save the family."

Entering the apartment, Vasily Ivanovich welcomed the guests warmly. The table was already prepared for breakfast. Freshly baked pancakes with various fillings adorned the center of the table, paired with cheese canapés. The highlight of the table, however, was a porcelain saucepan painted with a regal design.

"Yes, girls, let's wash our hands and get to the table quickly. I would rather not eat cold food," Vasily Ivanovich ordered, opening the saucepan.

"Oh, an English breakfast." Miia smiled, helping the host. "Oatmeal, sir."

"Niki, where is your plate?" he asked politely, turning to the girl.

The child felt embarrassed and started to hide his face behind his mother.

"A day or two, and Nika will get used to us," Vasily Ivanovich said. "You'd better tell me how the trial went. How did it happen that one child is with you and the other with his

185

father?"

And long stories began.

"I agreed to the settlement only because I would rather not wait an unknown amount of time until our house is sold, from which I would receive three parts. Time is more valuable. Every day in the village is a real emotional ordeal. I wasn't afraid of working in the fields, but I was suffocated by the realization that I was trapped in a hopeless quagmire. I was suffocating from it. Around us are our magical southern steppes, and I don't have enough air to breathe freely. I don't have enough space. I feel like I'm in a cage where I can't even move. It's terrible.

"Did the boy stay with his father?"

"With grandparents."

"Does anyone live in your house now?"

"Yes. Anton." He was silent for a moment, then went on. "I withdrew the application for alimony."

"Why?" Olesya Kyriylivna asked in surprise. "He kept the house. All the furniture. The livestock."

"Antonchik stayed with his parents, and they will look after him. Niki is with me. It was our mutual decision. I understand perfectly well that going on principle and taking both children with you is almost suicide."

"But there is no need even to discuss this. You will find a job. It is good if it is nearby. And if…" Olesya Kyriylivna thought for a moment. "It is tough with two children alone. I know."

"In general," Vasily Ivanovich cheered up, "you did everything right. Have your relations with your in-laws improved?" Miia nodded. "Then there is nothing to worry about. The child will be cared for and fed. And we will look after the girl together here. You need to find a job. You will start interacting with people; maybe you will get married in Kyiv."

"Oh, no, no…" Miia interrupted him, "God help me. I was already married once. Enough."

"You know, it would be good if you took some courses."

"Accounting." Miia smiled. "After finishing school, I entered the institute in the Faculty of Economics. I passed all the entrance exams, but I didn't stand out from the competition. Half a point wasn't enough," she briefly recounted the

186

scandalous story, which ultimately led to such consequences.

"So, you have a specialty?" Vasily Ivanovich asked suspiciously, in a strange tone.

"Yes, I do. I followed in my mother's footsteps. I graduated from a cooperative technical school."

"What specialty?" Vasily Ivanovich asked, squinting.

"Commodity expert."

"Oh." Olesya Kyriylivna exclaimed. "Vasily Ivanovich also worked as a commodity analyst all his life."

"Is that so?" Miia exclaimed happily.

"We will have plenty of time now. I will tell you so much about Soviet trade – what was there not... And now I need to clear the table, and I am going to cook dinner."

"I will help."

"You don't need to help me. Put things away, and take a break from the road with the child."

Miia ignored the advice. She quickly gathered the dishes and took them to the kitchen.

"I will wash the dishes myself." Olesya Kirillovna shouted after her. "Guests are not supposed to do this."

Six months flew by quickly, but it had already made positive changes in people's lives.

Miia attended accounting courses. New acquaintances brought their advantages. New impressions quickly followed. The emergence of new hopes started to make sense.

"It seems very strange to me that Alik is always present on every walk you take with Yarina. The fact that she praises him to you, sorry, does not inspire confidence." Olesya Kyriylivna began, having listened to another story of Miia. But noticing the embarrassment on her face, she continued. "At my age, don't wear rose-colored glasses. First, they take you home, and then they drive on together. That's undoubtedly what's surprising."

"I understand what you are getting at," Miia answered after thinking a little. "But Alik is a member of their family. He knows Yarina's husband..."

"How long have you known them?"

"From the first days, as soon as I started the courses."

"Oh, remember how you met?"

"When Alik came at the end of classes. However, on several

187

occasions, he was with Yarina's daughter. He picked her up from kindergarten." Miia fell into thought.

"You understand, if Alik were interested in you, you would already know. You see him every day because you work in his store. As you say, he has been divorced for two years. He doesn't need either her or you. He has a close relationship with her, and even if she gets pregnant, he won't worry about it because she is married. And if he starts an affair with you, he will have to make serious choices. And what choices? He has a son from his first marriage, and you have two. He couldn't decide whom he liked more, her or you. It was clear from him when guests came to visit. And do you remember the first thing Vasyl said when your guests left?" A stubborn look pierced Miia. "Do you remember? He said, 'This sweet couple is not your friends.' Listen, child, I don't want you to be disappointed again."

"No, there will be no disappointment," Miia interrupted, waving her finger.

"You are all right. Alik is a smart, kind man, and you could even fight for his heart. But..." A mysterious, cunning smile appeared on her face.

"To be honest, I don't feel like adjusting to the moods of another mother-in-law again."

After this conversation, Miia's attitude toward Yarina started to shift. No matter how hard Yarina tried to act like a decent wife and friend, her falsehood was blatant. Miia was surprised that Vitalik didn't notice this. Her attitude toward Alik, who went along with Yarina almost professionally and pretended to be Vitalik's best friend, gradually began to shift as well.

One day, Alik's mother walked solemnly around the store, carefully examining the goods on display in the windows. She remarked to each salesperson about the layout and insisted on changing it immediately. When she approached Miia, her expression became gentle and mysterious.

"Miia, you work in the most pleasant department that exists in trade."

"Bread, butter, and sausage – aren't they important?" Miia smiled.

"Important. But it's better not to get carried away. You need

188

to eat natural products."

Miia was surprised. As a child, she was taught that bread is the most important thing. 'Isn't that what we were taught?' was the first thought that crossed her mind. When it came to sausage, Miia somewhat agreed. However, she kept her thoughts to herself.

"And I love bread with sausage, especially in hot sandwiches." Mariana, a saleswoman from the deli, defiantly shouted after hearing the conversation. "I'll make some for myself during the break."

"You need only to eat and drink water." Nila Abramivna addressed her with a teacher's intonation.

"My husband loves me like that." The answer was not long in coming.

"But is it really about your husband's love? You fool! What will happen to your health?" Then, waving her hand in her direction, she turned to Miia. "You're a smart girl. You take care of yourself. You're picky about food. Alik said that you have two children, and you have such a slim and fit body. The more I see you, the more I admire you. Mariana, learn from Miia," the saleswoman heard again.

Miia quickly glanced at her colleague with a smile and shook her head in disagreement.

When Nila Abramivna left, Miia quickly went to her colleague.

"She's right." Making sure no one could hear them, Mariana looked around and kept going. "Do you know how old she is?"

"No. I know that Alik is thirty-three."

"She gave birth to him at twenty-eight." Mariana stopped there, thereby allowing Miia to count.

"Sixty-one." Miia was so surprised that she lost all words.

"No. She looks forty-five, at most."

"That's what I'm talking about."

"And how old is Alik`s father?"

"Sixty-three."

"He also looks youthful." She was silent for half a minute; Miia nudged her colleague with her elbow. "So why are you protesting with your hot sandwiches?"

"Because I do love them. Although I repeat, she's right."

189

"Water should be your only food?" Miia laughed.

"What are you laughing at? Unless it's just for me. My "Yurko is five years younger than Alik, and his blood pressure is already giving him trouble. My mother is only forty-six, and she already walks around with diabetes."

"Wow. This is serious." Miia stated anxiously.

"Seriously. But, as she took out hard cheese and sausage from the refrigerator, she continued, we all love to eat deliciously. Girls, do you want to eat?"

"Mariana, maybe tea after all." Looking at her watch and realizing that it was already lunch break, Miia went to close the front door of the store.

"You drink the tea." Passing by the bread shelves, Mariana grabbed a whole sliced loaf. "So, you want me to make sandwiches for you?"

Miia and Taya refused.

"Are you even aware that Alik's mother is watching you?"

"In what sense does watching?" Taya's question surprised Miia deeply.

"She wants to know everything about you."

"It's clear why. I'm a new person on the team."

"Listen, I've worked in their store for four years, and she's never been interested in anyone the way she's interested in you."

"Why?"

You know, Nila Abramivna, she is not as strict as it might seem at first glance. And Maksym Fedorovych is a kind soul. You've already had time to notice it.

"I agree."

"You don't know why Alik got divorced, do you?"

"No, I don't know."

They discovered that the child wasn't his. He arrived in Kyiv before his parents. He met Ella. They got married. Stasyk was born. Nila and Maksym sold their apartment in Sochi and moved to Kyiv. When the boy was three years old, he urgently needed surgery and a blood transfusion. It then became clear that his Rh factor didn't match any of his parents' or grandparents' markers. A scandal ensued. Nila insisted on a DNA test. Later, Ella admitted that after meeting Alik, she continued to see both him and the child's

190

father, waiting to see who would marry her first. When she became pregnant, he left her. Alik got married.

"This is the story."

"Listen further. Nila and Maxim want grandchildren. However, they are against his relationship with Yarina because she is married."

"But Alik loves her. Well, it seems so to me."

"I don't know if he loves her, but she is driving him crazy – some devil. I know her as Alik and Vitalik; there's no difference. And the more of them there are, the more she'll see herself as a queen. Haven't you noticed? You're friends."

"You know, I try not to poke around in other people's personal lives. Of course, there were thoughts that I was there for her as a cover."

"As a cover, however, we all noticed that with your appearance, Alik changed. He became more cheerful, started dressing differently, and resumed his gym routine. Nila couldn't help but notice this."

Miia was silent.

A strange sadness gripped her.

Sadness and anxiety.

"I wish I hadn't heard this."

"Miia, they're a good family, trust me. Do you remember the earrings that Nila brought and tried on you? She said they were a wedding gift her grandmother left for Alik's wife."

"Oh my God."

"During Stasyk's treatment, it was revealed that Alik could not have his children."

"So why is it like this with Ella?"

"Calm down. They paid for the operation and rehabilitation in full. And later, Stas's father returned."

At that moment, Mariana's voice was heard, announcing that the kettle had boiled and the microwave was ready to heat lunch.

"Mariana, I'm not inspecting your mouth, but this mountain of sandwiches... Do we not know something?" Taya decided to joke. The answer surprised her.

"I'm eating for myself and for that man."

Alik's voice was heard saying, "Just don't say that the man is dieting."

191

"Or maybe for two guys," Mariana said, pulling the sandwiches closer as if she had overlooked the director's intervention in the conversation. A silent scene followed. Everyone looked at each other. "Why are you silent? If you all thought the same thing, then I can only confirm. Yes! The twins are confirmed."

Miia and Taya were so overwhelmed with happiness that they couldn't contain their emotions and started hugging and genuinely congratulating Mariana. She then turned her eyes to Alik and smiled.

"Mariana, you need to name one boy after the store director. When will you go on maternity leave?"

This day turned out to be overwhelmed with news and events that had a profound impact on Mia's future.

"Alik, I just had buyers." Miia showed the twenty dollars and the perfume.

"How did that happen?" The man looked at Miia in surprise. "There were three of them, dressed casually and in a humorous mood. While two of them were buying high-end alcohol, one approached my department. He asked for my name and said I reminded him of his mother when she was young. Then, he asked me which perfume I liked the most. I pointed to it. He took out dollars and explained he didn't have hryvnias. He handed me the money. I gave him a box of perfume. He looked at it and read the label. Then, he pulled out a business card. He took my hand and said, 'This is my gift to you,' before placing the box with the business card inside."

"Did the buyers leave both the money and the goods?"

Miia handed Alik a business card with 'Vice-President of the Ukrainian Farmers Association' engraved in sky-blue letters on a gilded background.

Having read everything written on the card, Alik twirled it in his hands and then placed it on the table. Miia reached for the card, smiled, and took it away.

"Excuse me, Mr. Director, but this is mine. And also, I don't need this perfume. During my time working for you, I bought the same one myself. I'm saving money so I can visit the children. I would be grateful if..."

"I understand. Keep these twenty dollars for yourself. You

could have said nothing at all. However, thank you for your honesty," and he looked her in the eyes so intently that her heart went cold.

For several days, Miia felt awkward after talking to Taya and meeting strange customers. And she increasingly began to think that Alik was not indifferent to her. His behavior raised specific questions, but the answers seemed to wander along the secret paths of circumstances invisible to the eye.

Every so often, he offers to take her home after work, and during the ride, he remains silent, only glancing at her sideways. Sometimes, for no apparent reason, he gives each salesperson a bouquet, even though two of them are identical, and Miia's is slightly larger and more attractive. He occasionally tries to observe her interactions with customers or coworkers secretly. Miia noticed that lately he has been repeatedly playing the same song, "My Distant Star." One day, without looking away from Miia, he openly said it was his favorite song. And only the words, "And the night is cold and dark when you're not with me," revealed the secrets his silence had been hiding.

And it seemed like everything was clear. However, Yarina's strange behavior kept Miia from feeling at ease. During their last meetings, she repeatedly complained about Vitalik's greed and his inattentiveness toward her. Then, she shifted her focus to Alik, who, it seems, also causes her stress and sparks family quarrels. She even openly suggested that Miia should be more proactive with her boss. When the three of them were together again, the same thing happened – the person being taken home first was always Miia. Alika's mother started coming to the store more often, talking kindly with everyone, and paying special attention to Miia.

Deja vu.

Someone has already experienced this in life.

"Bitter lemonade. Don't drink it; you'll get poisoned." Miia quit her job at the store.

The only thing that upset her in this entire situation was not having children with her. It happened that she had to ask her sister to let Niki stay with her. Without a Kyiv residence permit, finding a kindergarten was impossible. The work schedules were too busy. Miia saw the child in the morning

193

when she was still sleeping, or in the evening when she was already asleep. Even when Niki was sick, Miia couldn't be with her because she had to go to work. No one wanted to hire employees who had children, especially those as young as Niki.

However, despite these emotional struggles, patience and desire continue to drive Miia's life forward.

XXVI

"Isn't this what my childhood dreams were about? Bold and courageous enough to find the strength to come true."
Khreshchatyk.
Legendary.
For nearly a year, every day on her way to work, Miia admired the power of Khreshchatyk at the very heart of the city. She had already learned that life knows how to follow its mysterious paths. Things that once seemed complicated and unreachable turned out to be simple and unpretentious. She now knew that having the courage to face your fears is safer than running away from them.
During this time, Miia met many new acquaintances, including some important and famous people. Events occurred, both serious and funny, that will be remembered for a lifetime.
"I wasn't late." Miia was surprised, looking back at the men who burst out laughing.
Watching her colleagues, Miia started to laugh.
"Gentlemen."
Finally, taking a deep breath and slowly exhaling, Afanasy began.
"You were supposed to meet two guys from Poltava in the corridor just now. So, one of them was asking about you.
"He says he fell in love with you." Mykhailo Mykhailovych added hastily, still smiling.
"Vasyl asks me, 'Afanasiy, our Miia is so beautiful and smart. Is she married? I'm afraid to ask her,' I tell him that you're divorced. He continues, 'Why does she always go out with Konstantin? I thought he was her husband.' I tell him, she's his bodyguard. You say you're afraid of her. Konstantin himself is afraid of her. She has a black belt in taekwondo. So, guys, don't joke with her. She's cool!" Both colleagues start laughing again.
"What? A black belt in taekwondo? Now I understand why; after greeting me in the hallway, they walked past me so quietly, leaning against the wall." She also burst into passionate laughter.
About a week later, Miia was surprised by a call from the

195

sister of one of the organizers of the farm show. She noted that her brother liked Miia, that he was aware of her life situation, and even dreamed of getting to know her better. She said that he was a reasonably wealthy man, and Miia and the children would be well-off. Miia understood who her brother was. He visited the association's office twice a month. He openly communicates with the minister, has influential connections within the country's president's circle, and was at that time running for parliament from his district.

"What were you thinking about?" a colleague asked as they approached Miia's table. "Who was it?"

"Peter's sister. You remember him. Two brothers are coming to visit us."

"Are they the ones who always bring imported champagne and sweets?" Maria interrupted. Miia nodded in response. "What did she say to you?"

"I'm embarrassed." Her thoughtful gaze drifted to the distant expanses beyond the curtain. "She said that her brother liked me so much that he wouldn't hesitate to marry me."

"He is a good match! Smart, successful, purposeful, and well-mannered. And although he may not be Alain Delon in appearance, he is quite an attractive man. Is something bothering you?"

"I would rather not get married." Miia quickly and confidently turned her gaze to Maria and said, "I've already been there."

"Does he know that you have two children?"

"Yes. It turns out that he knows everything about me."

"Does this fact annoy you?"

"It annoys me. Do you know why?" Miia's gaze nervously swept around the office. "Because people I barely know, having learned some information about me, decided I was suitable for them. 'Miia, you will receive my brother's surname, and your children will receive both his surname and middle name. My brother is ready to give you this as protection.'" Miia repeated the phrase spoken by Peter's sister, and with each word, growing more emotional, she said, "Who did they decide to protect me from? From myself? Or my children from their father? Neither I nor my children need that! Listen, I've seen a lot of nerve, but this is the first

196

time I've encountered such foolish self-confidence."

"Calm down. Maybe you misunderstood her. She was probably referring to the prospects of a secure life. After all, Peter is a truly successful person."

"I have no objection to Peter's success. However, I don't need it! His success is his. I would prefer not to be just an ordinary part of his success, simply because he has realized that, to complete his status, he lacks a beautiful wife and even two children he can accept as his own – such a PR.

"Why do you say that? Just admit that you don't like Peter as a man. You are chasing after love."

"And you think it's normal just to accept the offer of the first man you meet, to save your life situation?" Maria winked, "For Peter's sake, you can step over your 'I' and agree to become an addition to his success for the sake of your secure future."

"Maria, what tree did you fall from as a child?" Miia laughed. "Losing your 'I' for someone else? That shouldn't happen. In my opinion."

"It seems to me that your opinion is selfish."

"Why is that?"

"A man who has achieved success through his mind and effort, offering a woman, along with his hand and heart, everything he has, has every right to the dominion of your 'I,' especially if the woman did not contribute to the formation of his 'I.'"

"And this gives him every right to push the woman far, far into the shadow of his 'I'. No, not from the very beginning of their relationship, but after the candy-bouquet period. And after the children are born, he will generally become the master not only of her 'I' but also of her entire alphabet. Yes, such a woman will have everything – material things. She will be a housewife with governesses for the children, visit beauty salons, and relax at the world's best resorts – a beautiful life. But without personal growth. She will always be in her husband's shadow.

"But, without needing anything."

"Material. Are you sure that material is the most important thing?"

"Still better than poverty. You look around, and you will

197

see how many women are unhappy because their husbands cannot provide for them."

I feel sorry for women who believe someone should always provide for them. Thank God, we don't live in the Middle Ages. Of course, when a woman takes care of children and is physically unable to work, it's the husband's duty, the father of the children, to support her. This is natural and should be this way. However, a woman shouldn't rely solely on her husband, his success, opportunities, or responsibilities. When a couple shares material possessions and maintains love and respect, that can be considered true happiness, regardless of wealth. Many families live this way.

Just like those women admiring their diamonds, they only mimic a happy life because they don't want anyone to realize how lonely they truly are. Yet, they quickly become accustomed to their situation. The presence of material wealth soon leads them to give up their ambitions. Some women still manage to succeed thanks to wealthy men. And believe me, I do not judge them for that in any way. On the contrary..." Miia fell silent. Her colleague stood with a thoughtful expression, showing slight confusion. "Well, Maria, every woman follows the path of her destiny."

"I hope you don't envy women who are married to rich men." Maria smiled condescendingly.

"Of course not. Otherwise, we wouldn't be discussing this topic now, and in a few months, you would have received an invitation to my wedding. However, I am not at all flattered by Peter's sister's confession. He will not be a good match for someone like me."

"And for whom?"

"For someone who needs to get married. I don't need to, because I've already been there. And I'm not looking for a new husband for myself or a new father for my children."

"Well..." her colleague interrupted, "It's hard to 'put' two children on their feet by myself."

"And I'll take the risk," Miia said with a sincere smile. "I believe in a fairy tale with a happy ending. Every time I look back on the difficult journey of my life, starting from childhood, I find myself increasingly trusting in my strength, will, and spirit. I keep building these qualities through diligent work on my knowledge, skills, and abilities. Then no one can reproach me for anything, and no one can take it away because everything I achieve will be mine to keep. That's what truly matters. And most importantly, I am responsible for my children. It's frightening to think that in my absence, someone might raise them with methods that aren't pedagogical. How many such cases are there?

"Peter is not one of those," Maria emphasized embarrassingly.

"And would you marry him? How do you like him?"

"Yes," Maria answered, not rushing to respond. "But he's interested in you."

"Not enough to dare to talk to me himself," she remained silent for a minute before continuing. "Do you want me to hint to him about you?" Smiling, Miia looked inquisitively at the young beauty. "I will do it qualitatively."

"Why do you need this?" Maria was surprised.

"You will be a good couple."

"And what will you tell him?" Simultaneous confusion and interest settled on Maria's face.

"I will suggest that he invite you to a restaurant. Who knows, maybe I am not a bad matchmaker." Miia's voice sounded cheerful.

Silence fell.

Outside the window, you could hear the bustling Khreshchatyk humming with everyday life. Occasionally, impatient drivers' signals sounded, and when the traffic light turned green, they couldn't wait through the delays caused by cars parked in front. Gusts of wind carried words like 'How can you not love me, my Kyiv?' or 'Because my godfather is Khreshchatyk.' The lively voices of ministry workers arriving at work echoed down the corridor.

"And, you know, I understand you," Maria broke the silence. "My brother and I have different fathers. My mother is now on her third husband. I don't condemn her for wanting to find her happiness. But I remember how my father didn't accept my older brother. It hurt me so much, but I couldn't do anything. When I complained to my mother, she didn't believe me. My father allowed himself to insult Slavik with bad words several times; he even hit him. And in the last year before the divorce, he no longer held back in front of my mother. When my mother met Oleksiy, my grandmother, my mother's mother, insisted that Slavik and I move in with her."

"Did he offend you?"

"She was sure that his kindness to me had nothing to do with parental feelings. And she was not wrong.

I was fourteen years old then. Slavik went to study at a vocational school after the ninth grade and lived in a dormitory. Mom worked two jobs, so she came home late. One day, Oleksiy came home from work early. I was in my room doing lessons. He said hello and asked if I was having any difficulties with my homework. I naively replied that I couldn't figure out the physics problems. He happily replied that he would come back and help, but first, he would take a shower. He came back, wrapped in something that wasn't even a bath towel. Sitting down next to me, you guessed it, you could see him, and he didn't even hide it. His voice changed, and his hands trembled, like a sick person's. I wanted to get up and leave the room, but he grabbed me by the neck so hard that I couldn't move from the pain. I was saved by the fact that at that moment, my grandmother came into the apartment. She had her keys. Seeing him, almost naked in my room, and me pale with fright, she gathered my things, and I went to her place. Since then, neither Slavik nor I have spent a single night at my mother's.

"Does Mom know about what happened?"

"She believes nothing happened. My stepfather reassured her that I was having teenage fantasies. In response to my grandmother's claim that she found him in my room wrapped in a towel, he said that I had called him to help, and he was rushing there, so he didn't have a chance to get dressed."

"And whose apartment?"

"Mom's."

"Is he registered there?"

"Yes. I guess what you're talking about. My brother and I don't claim anything." Then, glancing at the watch, she added: "It's almost ten o'clock. Where are all our team?"

"They're at a meeting with the minister. Then, at noon, they have a meeting at the American Grants Corporation. At three o'clock, Mikhail Mikhailovich and I are going to go on television. Today is the last rehearsal of our farm talk show. By the way, Petro will be there." Miia winked.

"I've completely fallen out of your schedule. Will you take me with you?"

"Do you already have a pass?"

"No."

"No pass." Miia shrugged.

At that moment, the deputy head of the Department of Agriculture and Plant Growing entered the office.

"Girls, I'm following you. Today is our Vasily Petrovich's birthday. Now we'll congratulate him on behalf of your department."

"Maxim, we are not from your department," Maria shouted. "And what kind of greeting is this if we don't even have a gift?"

"Oh, calm down, we have everything." The young man grabbed both colleagues by the hands and pulled them towards the door. "Only the girls are gone. Your presence is better than any gifts."

"Maxim, stop!" The young man paused, no longer holding Miia's hand. "Don't put us in a difficult situation. Our farmers work closely with Vasily Petrovich." Miia opened the safe, counted out some money, and solemnly continued: "We have a fund for such situations. Considering that our leadership is currently absent, we have every right to congratulate your leader on behalf of the country's farmers." She approached Maria and Maxim, smiling imperiously. "Let`s go! Today is a wonderful day."

Previously, Miia considered the people who work in ministerial offices to be extremely arrogant. When she met them in the corridors, they behaved almost like gods, as if the corridors of the ministry were Olympus itself.

The same Vasyl Petrovich, with whom Miia had had to communicate several times on issues related to farmers, was always strict and unbearably correct, which irritated Mia.

But today, this dispelled all Miia's thoughts about the superiority of these people. After the first glass, they became charming, humorous, cheerful people who shared numerous interesting stories, fables, and anecdotes.

"You and Maria, well done for going to congratulate Vasyl Petrovich," said Mikhail Mikhailovich, meeting near the television center.

"If it weren't for Maksym, we wouldn't know about birthdays. How did the meeting with the Americans go?"

"There is potential for cooperation. We have a lot of work ahead of us, because we need to prepare a business plan."

"A business plan for building a fruit and vegetable market?"

"Yes. By the way, you're in the working group."

"I'm not an expert in business planning."

"But you are an expert in trade."

"It's been a long time, but I agree."

"You're going to Poland with our delegation."

"Why me and not Konstantin?"

"He doesn't have a passport, and he won't have time to get one, because the trip is the day after tomorrow."

Approaching the entrance to the TV center, Miia paused to get a pass. As she looked on, she saw Mikhail Mikhailovich walk past the security guard without stopping, merely nodding his head in greeting. She was quite surprised by this.

"How did you manage to get through without a pass? Everything is so strict here."

"I have a protocol face," he replied with a smile.

"Well. That explains a lot."

Everyone in the studio was busy preparing. The talk show host, who skillfully gave advice and orders to everyone present, strictly adhered to the approved script. Meeting Peter's gaze, Miia smiled and went to him. She wanted to fulfill the promise she had made to Maria.

Miia's mind told her that this was a ridiculous idea. However, the situation became even more absurd after speaking with Peter's sister. And Miia wanted to put an end to it. She did not like certain temptations that kept her from living an independent life.

"Peter, your idea of tasting farm products in the studio is exciting, and most importantly, timely," Miia said boldly.

Without taking his eyes off her, he replied, "I hope the talk show host will allow this promotion."

"According to the channel's rules, advertising is paid.

202

Perhaps, in our case, these rules can be adjusted."

"Of course."

"Farm products can be provided as promotional samples."

"Farmers will sit in the front rows."

"Let's say, closer to their products."

"And the operators will do their job."

"They will do it professionally."

"And you and I, Miia, have a good understanding. With just half a word. Will it always be like this?"

"Only at work."

"Why is that?"

Not knowing how to respond politely, Miia took a lemon out of her purse.

"Can you eat it?"

"If it's sugar-free, I'll throw it away. Can you?"

"I make lemonade from lemons."

"Tasty?"

"Depending on the quality of the water and ingredients."

"Will you teach me how to make lemonade for you?"

"No."

"Why?"

"The lemonade my ex-husband made me still tastes bitter."

"Then, maybe we should try to drink some sweet wine? I'm a good winemaker, and I'll invite you to a tasting."

"Invite Maria. She likes sweet wines."

"Miia, why are you like this?"

"I'm worse than this lemon."

"Hmm…" he thought. "Was everything so complicated?"

"It's all over now."

"Very often people get burned by the hot, which they then blow on the cold."

"Invite Maria."

"Are you like this for everyone, or just for me?"

"For everyone."

"Well, that's selfish of me, but it's comforting." He stood opposite her and looked her in the eyes. "I want to remember you." Miia was silent. "You can see from your eyes that you're telling the truth. Thank you."

Watching Tamara, Miia reflected on how crucial every detail is for a talk show host's success. It was the final rehearsal for

203

the new format, and Tamara was putting everything she had into it.

"Your performance in three minutes, Peter." A satisfied, sweet smile lit up Miia's face – a smile of relief.

"I'm ready!" he answered, smoothing his hair. Then, looking at the smiling interlocutor, he said seductively, "And yet, I would try adding sugar or honey to your bitter lemonade. Think about it."

Miia didn't say anything. She felt he understood everything. And she also sensed that her proposal about Maria didn't leave him indifferent. As a result, she felt calmer.

XXVII

Miia accepted the offer to go to Poland instead of her boss as a given, without showing any surprise or embarrassment. She was even happy that Konstantin did not have a foreign passport. His colleagues mocked him, saying that he was behind the times. And rightly so.

As a passionate communist, he constantly spoke badly about Western countries, unfairly criticizing their capitalist development. His views often sparked heated debates in the office. Among the entire management team of the farmers' association, Miia's boss was the only supporter of the Soviet Union. Being in such a minority, he openly considered himself superior to others. Even the president of the farmers' association, waving his hand, gave way to Konstantin in discussions. However, Mykhailo Mykhailovych and Afanasy refuted his arguments in support of democracy, a market economy, and private property. When he ran out of arguments, he always turned to Miia with the boastful remark, 'We're from the south of the country; will you at least support me?' To which Miia, smiling every time, answered firmly, 'No!' and it greatly annoyed him.

"My director, he'll be so angry that I went instead of him," Miia said with a smile, waiting for the conductor to leave the compartment. "How did it happen that the decision to go to Poland was made so spontaneously?"

"The American grant company is interested in developing farming in Ukraine. They liked the concept we created for building a wholesale fruit and vegetable market."

"We worked so fruitfully on it. I remember."

"The Americans require this market to meet all technological standards. There is no example in Ukraine of how it should be. What heritage do we have? Soviet?"

"Poznan, did they advise us?"

"This is the closest market to us. We could consider visiting Germany or the Netherlands, but we don't have time, as we need to submit a business plan for approval at the next meeting. And that's in ten days."

"Wow, so soon," Miia exclaimed excitedly. "Then that explains everything."

"Don't forget that this Saturday we also have a recording of our TV show. The next ten days will be very stressful."

"We'll manage." Miia smiled.

"Honestly, I'm glad that Konstantin doesn't have a foreign passport and that you're going on this trip, not him."

"Honestly, I'm glad too. This is my first time going abroad."

"Never been anywhere?" A slight surprise flashed on Mikhail Mikhailovich's face, which instantly turned into thoughtfulness.

"And when would I have time? I was born and raised in a village among the Kherson steppes. I got married there. My children were born there. One of the reasons for the divorce was my desire to give my kids a better life than the declining village could provide. For this, my ex-husband constantly nagged me, "If you want stars from the sky, go and get them."

"And where is he now? Married?"

"Married. She is from the district center, and I'm glad he's not alone. The less he drinks, the fewer they'll curse at me. I believe his new wife will have enough strength to influence him."

Thinking, she remembered her acquaintance with her ex-husband's new wife.

Miia went home for Memorial Day.

"Listen to what she says about you: 'She abandoned the children. She disappeared somewhere so that no one knows where she is.'" On the way from the cemetery, her cousin started the conversation.

"Who did you hear all this from?"

"She told me personally."

"She doesn't know that we are cousins?" For some reason, Miia was surprised by this.

Now she knows. I listened to her politely, then asked, 'What did you tell me all about our Miia? You should have seen her eyes. I told her that you work in Kyiv. In the ministry." Lyuda laughed.

"The ministry only houses the central office of the Ukrainian Farmers Association." Miia interrupted her, smiling.

"And then, I also told her that you were shown on television several times."

206

"It's time for me to get to know her." Miia smiled slyly. "You won't be offended if she finds out that you told me everything?"

"Of course not. If you don't plan to leave by Friday, you can find her at the market on Thursday."

Having entered the market, Miia approached her friend.

"Svetlana, my dear, I congratulate you."

"What a surprise!" The girl was surprised and delighted. "Miia, I'm so glad to see you. What a beauty you are. What do you do that after giving birth to two children, you keep such a model form?" But without waiting for an answer, she quickly continued. "Come on, in half an hour I'll finish work, and we'll go to a cafe. At least we'll chat normally. Just don't say you can't."

"How can I refuse? It's just that it's too early to finish work."

"Do you care about my earnings?" Svetlana smiled. "Don't worry, I work for myself. Are you here for a long time?"

"I was supposed to leave on Tuesday. However," and told her about what she had heard from her sister.

"That's what I heard, too. We are market people here, hear and know everything about everyone. So, your pretzels stopped communicating with me after I told all our mutual acquaintances about you."

"I came to meet her. Where does she sell?"

"That's cool! I'm happy because I can already imagine her face when she sees you, being so beautiful."

"Well, only without the beauty..." Although Miia knew she differed from the local women in her style of clothing and restrained makeup – highlighting the precise shape of her lips and eyes, with no foundation or powder – this all added to her elegance and charm. "I've never seen her. Show me where this 'star' is."

"Let's go."

Miia stood in line the entire time, watching Anton's wife serve her customers. "An ordinary young woman," she thought. "I wish them happiness, but..."

"Good afternoon! What do you want?" she asked Miia.

"I'm not here for goods. I came to introduce myself," Miia said, not rushing to reply. "I'm Anton's ex-wife. And as you can see, I'm alive and haven't disappeared anywhere. I don't understand where you got such accusations against me." It was evident that Miia's appearance had so shocked Vaselina that she couldn't respond. "My advice to you is never to judge people if you don't know them personally. That's what smart people usually do. And also..." Miia's tone was restrained yet confident; a defiant smile appeared on her face. "Also, I suggest you and your mother reconsider your statements about my children. Don't wake a beast in me..." Mykhailo Mykhailovych's voice brought Miia back to the compartment,

"What are you thinking about? What exactly made you think so deeply?"

Miia began to tell this story.

"That same evening, an angry Anton approached me with threats and insults. Seeing him, I thanked God again for the courage and determination He had given me."

"Now I understand your ability to defend yourself like a lioness."

"Very noticeable?"

"It happens. Especially when Konstantin constantly shifts his work onto you and then brazenly accuses you of not understanding something when asked. We have repeatedly discussed appointing you to his position.

"No way!" Miia interrupted him. "On the contrary, I'm always happy to learn something new. But I find it hard to see the inconsistency with which Konstantin handles things. Therefore, I rebel against this very thing."

"Of course," he said, pausing to add with a smile. "And your Ukrainian language is much better."

"Thank you! I have never hidden that I struggle with the Ukrainian language. In school, Ukrainian language and literature only occupied three hours a week according to the curriculum. That's why our attitude as students was carefree. In society, everyone spoke in Russian. At home, surzhyk was the norm. Properly, the older generation, our grandparents, had a dialect that was not a literary Ukrainian one but was brightly saturated with Ukrainian words. I remember, as children, we would sit in a circle and start asking for translations of certain words. And those words that seemed completely strange to us, we wrote down, then

208

repeated them many times to remember. Above all, we loved listening to Ukrainian folk songs.

"I remember when you were coming to us."

"Why are you laughing? I remember that, too." Miia felt ashamed. "One morning, I had to answer the phone. I was ashamed to tell the person who called that I could only communicate in Russian. I quickly expanded my understanding of the Ukrainian language after that incident."

"I praise you! As my grandfather used to say, 'Without a language, there will be no nation.' The Bolsheviks shot him. These words were his last words."

Silence settled in. Outside the window, one landscape gave way to another. Fields and forest belts, rivers and ravines basked in the warm autumn sun, enchanting every passenger who gazed at them from the carriage window: native land, magical land, free winds.

"Those were terrible times – an incredibly distorted story. A grandmother, born in 1922, was pleased when our Ukrainian independence was declared. Afterwards, she often talked about dekulakization, hunger, hard labor, and repression. Her father's two cows, two horses, and all the poultry – geese, ducks, and chickens – were taken to the collective farm, totaling about a hundred heads. The family had eight children, but two of them died. Her mother, my great-grandmother, died right in the field. It was hard work with no days off and no treatment. The Soviet authorities enforced what was essentially slavery.

The echoes of those times also resonated in my generation, when we, schoolchildren, starting at the age of twelve, were sent to work in the fields. First, we dug up beets, and then we collected them. And what's fascinating is that, usually in the middle of the third lesson, the head teacher would come into the classroom and announce the joyful news with a sweet smile: 'Yes, the lessons are over for today. Hurry home and change.' And we were happy. That was all we needed to avoid sitting at our desks. We didn't understand then that this was a criminal use of child labor. We were responsible for unpaid agricultural work, which was deemed necessary for the public good. Only my grandmother, each time, would mutter about the communist devils who have nothing sacred.

209

And she called our father, her only son, the Antichrist. We thought it was because he wasn't baptized. Oh, no. Because he was a communist.

"The trouble is that we have not yet fully gained our independence. Look at what happened after the collapse of the Soviet Union in the Baltic states, Moldova, Georgia, and Chechnya. Who fought there and for what? Who is the main orchestrator of these wars? Ukraine is next. Muscovites will not forgive us for our right to be independent. Remember my words. We will still witness the terrible events that Moscow will bring to our land. By the way, I did not mention the wars in which the Soviet Union actively sent its troops. We need to work hard to be as useful as possible to our country, for the sake of the civilized future of our children, grandchildren, and great-grandchildren. Therefore, do not be sad; we have a lot of work ahead, and we are obliged to do it with dignity."

Noticing the sadness and despair on Miia's face, Mykhailo Mykhailovych continued.

"You can bring the children to your place in Kyiv. We are financially stable now. We have the ability to arrange a dormitory room for you. We will also provide the necessary certificates for kindergarten. And remember, you know very well that you can constantly adjust your work schedule yourself."

Hearing this, Miia burst into tears.

"I was at a loss for words..."

You never said anything like that about yourself. Everyone knew you were divorced and had two kids. So, dare.

Only one day was scheduled for work during the business trip. However, the management of the Poznań Wholesale Fruit and Vegetable Market arranged the guests' itinerary to ensure they could work efficiently at the market and also visit the city's architectural landmarks. Poznań Town Hall, the Imperial and Royal Castles, the Church of St. Mary Magdalene, and the Cathedral of the Holy Apostles Peter and Paul not only pleased the eye but also fostered a sense of peace through their historical significance. The highlight of the walk was the Croissant Museum on the Old Market Square, where they were fortunate not only to taste the famous St. Martin's croissant but also to learn its recipe.

The only thing that puzzled Miia was, "Where to find white poppy seeds in Kyiv, which are the main ingredient in the recipe?" However, these thoughts quickly gave way to more relevant discussions.

On her way to Ukraine, Miia's mind was filled with joyful chaos from her first walk through a European city and her initial interaction with foreigners. At that moment, she wanted Antonchuk and Nikusha to see a beautiful world that is ready to embrace everyone who seeks to touch it with their soul and open their heart.

Upon their return during the week, not only was a concept for building a wholesale fruit and vegetable market prepared, but also a business plan was developed. Additionally, the candidacy of the curator of this project, a former manager of one of Los Angeles's wholesale markets, was approved. The acquaintance with him coincided with the filming of the first talk show about farming development in Ukraine. The inspiration was so strong that it was easy to work from early morning until late at night. Of course, this yielded positive results – an American grant company accepted the business plan and shared it with potential investors for review. All these events, happening rapidly one after another, finally brought their financial rewards. For such productive work, the entire team received a solid bonus, which became a key reason for Miia. She decided to take her children from the village to live with her in Kyiv.

XXVIII

"You have furnished the room so beautifully. Everything has found its place. Do the children like it here?"

"Oh, yes. They already have a lot of friends here. True, they complain about the kindergarten. They say the teachers are mean and the food isn't tasty."

"That's why you don't leave the kitchen on weekends."

"I prepare frozen food for the week. I can survive on crackers and water myself; it's good for the figure. And children need healthy, tasty food."

"Tell me, this is a beautiful place."

The scenery is stunning, with clear, fresh air. The silence is captivating. Only birds singing, bees buzzing, and church bells ringing. Everything feels calm and peaceful.

"During the Chechen war, it was dangerous here for a time. Many unknown individuals hid in the monastery. During the day, they were unseen and unheard, but as soon as night fell, like locusts in monks' robes, they crawled onto the streets. Rapes became frequent. The police only pretended to respond. They couldn't do anything. Someone was covering for them. But after a young woman was murdered, the police managed to restore order."

"Murder?" Miia's voice trembled.

"Yes. Brutal. The body was found under the walls of our building. More than ten stab wounds."

"Horror... Isn't there a man`s monastery across the street? So, who was hiding in the cassocks?"

"Yes, a man`s monastery. It's more than 250 years old. And those "pilgrims" really couldn't be told apart from real monks. To this day, none of the residents knows where they came from or where they went after that murder."

"The Chechen War. But Caucasian men couldn't be hiding in an Orthodox monastery."

"Of course not."

"Have the police found the killer?"

"The killers. The examination showed there were three rapists. They didn't find them, but it seems like they weren't even looking for them. The young woman's husband went to the police but was told, 'You should have met her after work,

212

not stayed at home.' And he was on duty that night. It seems like the killers knew about this."

"Our police. I keep quiet…"

"Have you already been to church service?"

"Not yet. But I want to go. Something is uneasy in my soul."

"Why?"

"I don't know."

"Stay at the church service. Go to confession. It'll get easier… And what about Vlad, whom you met at St. Michael's Cathedral? He brought you home yesterday, right?"

"He. But, Lyudmila Matviyivna, I'm not sure if I want a relationship."

"You don't like him?"

"I don't feel any feelings for him, at least some interest. I'm silent about love."

"But he's handsome. It's obvious that he's well-off."

"That's not the main thing."

"And what? A dorm room? Working from morning to night? Spending every weekend in the kitchen? And instead of lobsters, fried zucchini. Don't be offended.

"I'm not offended." Miia laughed out loud, repeating the phrase about fried zucchini. "Of course, he's handsome and well-off. However, there must be feelings for a man. A desire. A passion. Well, everything must be natural. And I don't have this naturalness for him."

"She doesn't have it… So, eat your natural zucchinis."

Miia laughed again. Looking into the face of her interlocutor, she noticed sadness in her eyes.

"What made you sad?"

"I was just like you. Not as beautiful, but young and with two children after a divorce. I believed that life would fairly reward me for all the suffering I endured with my ex-husband. When I met men who liked me, I also discussed feelings and the concept of naturalness, convincing myself that this was not the person I wanted to share my bed with. And now, fifteen years have gone by. The children have grown up. I've grown old. And no one needs me anymore. Don't make the same mistakes I did."

"Lyudmila Matviyivna, I have no intention of getting married again. Maybe my words seem like those of a woman with a mental illness. However, I repeat – I have no plans to marry again! Let me explain. Look at how Nadezhda Fedorivna lives with her second husband. She once told me that he often reproached her for raising two children who weren't his. He couldn't be a father because of his health. He's been a drinker all his life. They live in a dormitory. And the worst part is that she has the last stage of cancer. The suffering and pain she endures are unimaginable. Even now, he doesn't hold back and argues with her over memories from thirty years ago. It's terrible!" The woman just sighed quietly. "Well, after thinking about such situations, I'm afraid even to consider a second marriage. I'm scared – for myself and for the children. I need them, not another husband. And if I wanted to get married, I would have already done it." Miia smiled and turned the zucchini in the frying pan. "And you and I would never have met. I'd be frying zucchini caviar right now, not zucchini. Well, maybe from eggplants," she said.

"But you need a man for women's health."

"For such a thing, it's not necessary to force yourself into marriage." Miia felt embarrassed. "The main thing is that the man is good-looking and smart, so there's something to learn from him."

"Yes, Vlad is exactly like that." Lyudmila Matviyivna's eyes narrowed.

"Like that. But not like that. He is only good-looking. He needs a homemaker to cook cabbage rolls for him, as this is his favorite dish, and to make sure someone is available to do the cleaning. Regarding cleanliness, I understand him; I love cleanliness myself. But as for cabbage rolls..." waving her index finger, Miia laughed out loud. "Cabbage rolls and I are incompatible things."

"You cook deliciously."

"That's the point. I'm not willing to voluntarily become a cook to take care of my feminine health. I want to develop in life. I crave new knowledge that will open up new opportunities and prospects for me. I want to build my life not on a wealthy husband's wealth, but through my efforts and aspirations." Wanting to stop these discussions, Miia changed the topic of conversation.

"Better tell me what is needed for confession and communion because I don't know anything about it to confess."

"The main thing is a sincere desire. After midnight, don't eat or drink."

"I heard that you can't sing, dance, hug, or make love."

Approaching the window, Lyudmila Matveyevna exclaimed loudly: "My God, Miia, hurry and get them off the tree."

Miia turned pale at what she saw. A moment later, she was already outside. Antonchyk and Nikusha sat at the very top of a young birch tree. The tree was growing by the road. A few inches from it, a concrete curb separated the rammed earth from the asphalt road. Terrible images instantly flooded the mother's mind.

"Why did you climb that tree? Did you forget something there? Apples or tangerines. They don't grow on birch trees." Miia, coming to her senses, started to shout. "Quickly get down!"

"Mommy, we can't." The children answered in unison.

"You managed to climb, but you can't get down? Get down immediately."

"How?" Nika babbled in tears.

"Like on a ladder. Is that how you got to the top? Hold on to the upper branches with your hands, and put your feet on the lower ones." Stomping beneath the tree, Miia was getting ready to catch the children if someone couldn't hold on.

"Nika, get down quickly," the brother grumbled, kicking his sister, who was below.

"Don't push her," the mother ordered, then turned to the children watching the scene. "And tell me, why did they climb this tree?"

"We were pretending to be animals. Tosha thought he was a monkey, and Niki was a bird."

"Logical," Miia said to herself with a sigh. "And what kind of animal are you?"

"Misha is a tiger. Mari is a mouse. Dan is a dog." The neighbor boy started to list, rushing. "And Taras is a mole."

"Anton." Miia turned menacingly to her son. "Taras is a mole, but he didn't burrow into the ground."

"We've almost buried him." Dan was emotionally ahead of all the children.

215

"How?" Miia was surprised by the children's games.

"I brought a shovel from home for this," and waved his hand in the direction of a small hole.

"My God, your whole head is in the ground! Taras, have you been buried all over?"

"I'm a mole," the boy muttered, shaking the ground from his head.

"Who taught you such games?" Miia was surprised, shaking her head in disbelief. "My children, dear ones! We're not sitting; we're going down."

"Mom, take us down," Nika begged. However, Anton laughed at his sister's plea.

"Nika, don't pretend. You were the one who urged me, "Quickly, or the tiger will eat us.""

Having gone to a nearby tree, Miia broke off a stick.

"Listen to me. If you go down by yourself, you'll get one stick. If I take you down, you'll get three." Miia realized she couldn't bring the children down on her own without the firefighters' help. "Niki, you go down first. Anton, you go down second. Don't push your sister. You'll hit her in the face." True, for fifteen minutes, the mother still had to correct the children's process of descending from the tree to the ground. Sighing with relief, she kept her promise about the stick.

"It would hurt more if you fell. Look at the curb..." almost through tears, Miia lamented, leading the children into the room. "You understand that you need to be more careful. How many times have you been told what you can and can't do? Children, why can't you remember this without punishment? What do I have to do to keep you around me all the time, like chained dogs? But you've made such good friends with all the children. You ask to play with them on the street. And I understand you perfectly. However, as soon as I let you out, you're bound to get in somewhere. Occasionally, I drag you off the thin ice. Sometimes I remove you from the fence. Sometimes I chase you off the road. Sometimes I search the entire territory. Why do you do that?" There was silence in response.

After thinking, Miia went to the closet and grabbed a bag of buckwheat. She poured a dozen grains into four piles:

216

"How long did you sit in the tree? Fifteen minutes? I'm sure you'll last a minute on buckwheat. And then tell me your impression." Surprisingly, the children, smiling but slow, knelt on the grains.

"And then we can go outside again?" the boy asked cheerfully.

"Maybe."

Leaving the room, Miia took a few loud steps toward the stairs, then quietly turned back. At first, it was unclear what the kids were talking about. The most terrible images of children falling from that birch tree and the resulting aftermath filled her mind. She was struck with horror at these thoughts. Her heart clenched with fierce pain. Looking at the clock, she wished the minutes would pass quickly, but time seemed to stand still. The children started to speak louder, and every word became audible.

"Niki, do you love mom?"

"I do. And what don't you love?"

"Hmm… Why does she always scold us?"

"Because we don't obey her."

"Does it hurt you to stand?"

"It already hurts."

"And I… Dad never scolded us."

"Dad rarely came. That's why he didn't scold. But Grandpa…"

"I remember how he whipped us with a whip when we went for hide-and-seek and let the chickens out."

"Oh, we all got it from grandpa then."

You could hear the children becoming dizzy from these memories.

"Do you remember when we played with matches and almost burned the hay?"

"Do you remember when you lay down on the threshold, and Great Grandma Motya didn't see you, tripped, and fell? And how you cried next to her because she couldn't get up."

"Oh, I remember."

"Do you remember when Grandfather Khoma and I went to the forest to see the forester's cabin?"

"I remember when we ran away from there."

Hearing about Grandfather Khoma, Miia felt scared. "Did they go somewhere with this local homeless guy? Oh, God… What is the forester's hut? What were they running away from? From what or from whom?"

As Miia entered the room, she told the children they were no longer punished and could get up.

"Does it hurt?" She pointed to the children's knees; the mother tried to keep her calm.

"It hurts." The children answered in unison.

"You are lucky that you didn't fall from that birch tree because you can't even imagine how painful it can be in reality. Can you imagine?" The children were silent in response. Unable to bear the strict teacher's game, the mother sat down next to her little ones and hugged them tightly. Feeling her warmth, the children burst into tears.

"I understand that you want to run, jump, and be naughty because you are children. I remember my antics. At that time, I didn't understand the danger I was exposing myself to. Just as you don't understand this. But I don't want you to cause yourself any harm because I love you very much. Very much." The mother could not help herself; she burst into tears. "I dreamed so much that we would live together. Although it is difficult for me, I believe that together we will overcome all difficulties. Only I beg of you to be more careful. Learn to think about what is good and what is bad."

"We won't do it again," Anton muttered, holding tightly to his mother.

"We promise." Niki picked up his brother.

"I believe you. You are smart in me. If you want to insist on something, you'd better come and ask me what the consequences of your actions may be. Agreed?"

The children nodded their heads in agreement. This was a good moment to ask about the forester's hut.

"I honestly admit, I heard what you were talking about."

"Were you eavesdropping?" The children came to their senses, wiping their tears. "That's not fair!"

"I know, and I honestly told you about it. But did Grandfather Khoma confess to you that he wanted to show you the forester's house?"

"We didn't get there." The boy answered briskly.

"And who else was with you?"

"Taras, Niki, Max, Mari, and I were playing. When Grandfather Khoma came over, he suggested we bring food to the forester. Taras said he'd already taken it, but he didn't see the forester."

"And who were you running from?"

"Nika saw a viper in the grass, screamed, and ran back. We were all scared too and ran after her."

"Viper?" Mother's hair stood on end. "My God, children, stay close to the house when you play. You should have enough time for your games in kindergarten. Almost every weekend we go for walks in the city. Why are you looking for more adventures?"

"Mom, we remembered everything you told us. We won't go anywhere without you." Niki mumbled in a guilty voice.

"Or without my permission. Agreed! And now it's time for dinner."

After these events, for several days in a row, passing by a local homeless man, Miia could not understand why people, even with common sense, submit to life's vicissitudes and end their lives by suicide. At first glance, it might seem that this person never cared about his life. Because it is easier to do nothing, not strive for anything, not achieve anything, but live on alms with an outstretched hand under the church.

But one day, Miia met his gaze. These eyes were full of pain and suffering. At that moment, she remembered the fundamental rule of life that she had known since childhood – the rule that made her ashamed of her judgments about him: do not judge, otherwise you will be considered.

Later, Lyudmila Matviyevna shared the life story of grandfather Khoma and the reasons why he went to the forester's hut. What she heard deeply moved Miia. After that, every time she passed him, she imagined him neat and well-groomed, once he had been a rather attractive man and a financially secure engineer with two higher educations. Why is life ruthless to some and kind to others? Each person finds their own answers. It was clear that Khom's grandfather had not found them. Probably, when it was then, due to the doctors' mistake, he lost his beloved wife and newborn son, which put an end to his hopes.

Miia always believed that her and her sister's childhood had been cruel and cold to them. But when she imagined the childhood of this man, who could not be her grandfather due to his age, since he and her father were almost the same age, she forgave her father for the first time.

However, Miia did not even try to compare her childhood with Khariton Maksimovich's, who was Khom's grandfather. Her parents were not labeled enemies of the people and were not executed. Her grandparents did not die in the Gulag camps. Her childhood was not spent in an orphanage.

This person experienced a lot of suffering and continued to live with memories. Sad. Bitter. Horrible. The forester's house remained his only cozy refuge, connecting him with a happy past and giving his soul a small ray of peace. Not all the old, dirty clothes of a homeless person belong to the unfortunate person, just as not always a righteous nun dressed in a cassock with an apostolic head scarf can be pious.

During the service before confession in the church, Miia focused on her sins, repentance, and desire for spiritual purification...

"Godless woman! Get out immediately! You have no place among holy images. You are a shameless sinner."

This hissing resembled the hissing of a snake's nest. Feeling someone tugging at her skirt, Miia looked around. A nun stood nearby, looking at her with a cruel, hateful gaze. Confused by what was happening, Miia asked quietly and calmly.

"How can I help you?"

"Get out of here immediately, sinner..." Her face burned with hellish anger, and in the snake's eyes, like bloody tongues, the reflections of the candles burning in the temple circled. "Godless woman. Sinner."

Miia was speechless. With her eyes wide open, she watched the nun, who crossed herself over and over, repeating the exact words, like a mantra: "Godless woman. Sinner."

Her whisper attracted the attention of Lyudmila Matveyevna and Nadezhda Fedorovna. The women were not taken aback.

"What are you picking on her for? Go away, for God's sake!" The neighbor's voice, though quiet, still sounded incredibly stern. "Go and repent of your sins."

Surprisingly, without arguing with the women, she went to the opposite side of the church.

"What did she want from you?"

"Nadiya Fedorivna, I don't know. She was pulling at the hem of my dress," Miia whispered, coming back to her senses.

"What's wrong with it, with your dress? And in general, a headscarf on her head, a cardigan to her knees, and a long dress to the floor."

"I think she didn't like that it was tight and had a slit in the back."

Having examined Miia from all sides, the women shrugged.

"A dress like a dress," the defenders said in one voice.

After the service, Lyudmila Matviyivna explained why this woman became a nun.

"She's not, Saint... No, she is a snake. A spider?" Miia was indignant. "A black widow."

All day, Miia couldn't get the image of the nun out of her mind. Her evil face haunted her, and her black lips kept repeating, 'A shameless sinner.' Night fell. The full moon slyly peeked through the lace curtain, feeding her terrible imagination.

"I went to confession... I wanted forgiveness. To cleanse the soul." Miia punished herself.

A swarm of terrifying thoughts, haunted by superstitions, buzzed in her mind like flies on manure.

"A shameless sinner."

Sleep took hold. Miia isn't sure how long she slept, but she woke up feeling a terrible sensation that gripped her body, soul, and heart in its icy hold.

Afraid to open her eyes to see what was pressing down on her chest with a stone heaviness, Miia tried to turn onto her side. But no. There was no way to move. In hope, she felt that only her brain had not turned to stone.

"Who are you? Brownie? Please... there is nothing to breathe..."

In her eyes, darkened.

"Go away... I have nothing to breathe..."

She was seized by wild panic.

She saw a black stone in her soul. A moment later, he started pressing her still body more and more into the darkness of hell.

"What the hell?"

From hopelessness, panic turned into anger.

221

"Step back, you devil..."

With these words, a shaggy black ball started to descend from the ceiling toward her. Something moved inside it, and as the ball got closer, the movement grew more frantic. Anger turned into wild fear.

"Step back..."

Greedily inhaling air, her breathing grew faster and more labored. The encounter with horror was unavoidable.

"Step back..."

The shaggy ball stopped in front of her face, staring. Her eyes were hidden. Miia`s soul sensed this gaze. Then the shaggy ball began to open slowly.

"I close my eyes so as not to see, but the soul sees everything... What is this? Subjects of the Devil."

One. Second. Third...

Three black, hairy spiders, playing with their long legs, hovered over Miia. Three pairs of crimson eyes burned with flame, pulling from the most secret corners of nothingness the horrors of inevitability. The blood froze in her veins...

Shuddering, Miia jumped out of bed.

"Our Father, who art in heaven. Hallowed be thy name. Thy kingdom come, let thy will be done on earth as it is in heaven. Give us this day our daily bread. And forgive us our trespasses, as we forgive those who trespass against us. And lead us not into temptation, but deliver us from the evil one. For yours is the kingdom, the power, and the glory forever. Amen..." Miia crossed herself frantically as she recited the prayer three times. "It is necessary for such a dream to come true..."

Looking around the room, it plunged into complete darkness. Usually, during a full moon near midnight, it's so bright that at least millet can be harvested.

"A complete eclipse..." She leaned against the window in admiration. Watching the celestial miracle, Miia began to forget about the grumpy nun with her evil hissing and found an excuse for the terrible dream. The thoughts that had terrified her also faded away, as if hidden behind the Earth's shadow.

The past carefully guards memories. Memory relentlessly revisits them. Possibly to accept and forgive.

Miia remembered how joyfully children's fantasies sincerely extended their arms to all the beauties of the world, although anger, fears, and pain constantly haunted them.

She recalled how faith painted vibrant dreams on the dark canvases of hardships with magical rainbow colors. She remembered how, in the battles between good and evil, sparks of strength and spirit were forged in her small soul, preparing her for the most unexpected achievements in the future.

She remembered her youth, blown from all sides by cold winds, which, naively seeking warmth and comfort on thorny paths, lost not only hope but also the desire to live.

And how many times has ruthless hopelessness seduced with its subtle charm?

And how many bright dreams have vanished into oblivion without coming true?! Now they dwell somewhere beyond the endless horizon of the worlds, guarding their mistress from vain hopes.

There is nothing to regret. At the crossroads of destiny, you won't veer onto someone else's path, which is smooth and lined with magical flowers.

Everything will be as it should be.

Amid her thoughts, Miia met the sunrise.

A few days later, during a friendly chat with the head of the Ukrainian women farmers' committee, she suggested that Miia join their group.

Miia started to think about it and do calculations. She had more pluses than minuses. One day, she told her coworkers at the office that she planned to return home. This surprised everyone.

Your region is a risky zone for agriculture. Do you understand what that means? "Miia was silent. "You need to talk to the ministerial folks and ask about the dangers you'll face. The first is drought. Do you remember how hot summers can be in the South? Everything can burn out. The second. What Galina advised you is good. But she has a husband and two grown sons. You're alone.

"I can't have a business because I'm alone?" The woman's voice trembled.

"You are smart, and you have calculated everything correctly.

223

And about crop rotation, soil cultivation, and crops to grow. And we will not leave you either – you will receive assistance through the fund as a newly created farm. It's just that your region is unpredictable. Only large farms established on the remains of former state farms and collective farms will be able to survive in it... Consider taking land for farming in the Svyatoshynskyi district near Kyiv, for example. Let it not be fifty hectares, but twenty. You won't grow wheat or barley, but you will produce berries. Raspberries or currants. Or both... Think about it.

Understand me, I don't know anyone here except you. I agree, a berry farm is a good idea. However, for it to start generating income, I need to work on it. And I'm ready. However, if I have to wait two or three years for the first harvest, I need financial resources. I don't have those resources here.

What resources do you have there?"

"I'm at home there!" the woman answered confidently.

But she couldn't foresee that her homeland would bring her difficult trials.

XXIX

Upon returning to the village, she had to live with her parents. Unfortunately, my father's drinking episodes did not go away. They became more frequent and longer. It was reassuring that they were less violent. But this was not the only pain. My mother's illness began to progress. The doctors did not give comforting forecasts. On the contrary, they prepared for painful hours. And this was only the beginning. In addition to family worries, problems that required external intervention were added.

"Mykhailo Mykhailovych, today there was a session of the village council. They are not giving me land for farming." Barely holding back tears, Miia began a telephone conversation without a greeting.

"How do they explain the refusal?"

"By the lack of my financial resources. The letter of guarantee from the association, with venomous faces, was brazenly ignored."

"Go to the head of the village council and take an extract from the decision on the consideration of your issue. It must necessarily indicate the reason for the refusal and send it to us. Let's win it back! It is not right for the village kings or queens to break laws."

Every day, for two weeks, as if for work, Miia went to the village council and was unable to get a decision. On some days, the village council chairman was absent, as if he were ill. On other days, the secretary was absent. Miia understood that it was either some mockery or some envy. However, it was clear to her that cynical stupidity was at work.

"Listen, Miia, it seems to me that Mark's mother thinks that you are bluffing about your capabilities." After listening carefully to her daughter, her mother said in a voice tired from illness. "This applies to both your Kyiv colleagues and the seriousness of your intentions. They think that you cannot cope."

"I may not be able to cope..." The daughter's eyes began to look around the hospital ward in which her mother had been for more than a month. "Mom, I understand that. But I am entitled to try."

225

"And I think…" interrupted Zhanna, "that Mark's mother is taking revenge on you."

"For what? For choosing Mila as her son's wife. It's not my fault that they don't have children, nor is there any harmony between them."

"Well, that's what she's taking revenge for. And they're not allocating land for you because her son works as a driver, her daughter-in-law as a cleaner, and you're going to be a businesswoman. How is that possible?"

"It's good that they have such a job in the village."

Only Miia wanted to continue when, suddenly, the door opened and an excited nurse burst into the ward.

"Borko." Catching her breath, the woman tried to understand which of the two sisters she needed. "Miia. They're looking for you. Dash to the phone."

Returning to the ward, she was surprised and said that she now needed to return to the village.

"Zaminsky has a guest from Kyiv." She hurriedly took her handbag, hugged and kissed her mother, and continued, "Zhanna, you know better than I what to do next."

"Mom and I will cope with both the tests and the ultrasound. Don't worry, sister… Who could it be? Can't you guess?"

Miia was lucky enough to meet neighbors near the hospital who had already finished their business and were on their way home.

"The Creator Himself brought me to you," her voice was slightly excited. "I'm rushing to Zaminsky."

A ten-kilometer road seemed like a lifetime. Excitement was replaced by curiosity. What is it? What awaits her? What to do next? At that moment, she had no idea how everything could turn out in the future. But her inner voice said that a miracle was nearby… The questions that had been bothering her for the past few months will be answered, and in a year, they will no longer be a burden on her soul and thoughts.

"Mr. Zaminsky, from your words, I understood that you are a man of words and deeds. I readily believe you. Help Miia Vladyslavivna get land for farming. We must support young people in their desire to work for their native lands and the state as a whole. On the other hand, I already guarantee that her farm will receive financial assistance for development

226

and all other support of a managerial or organizational nature." Reacting to the solemn intonation of Mykhailo Mykhailovych's voice, Zaminsky was almost trembling. Trying to hide the hopelessness of his situation, he had no choice but to agree.

Life sparkled with all the colors of the rainbow. The head of the district council personally announced a favorable decision to allocate land to her. A month later, the Farm Support Fund provided her with financial assistance. Miia bought a ZIL dump truck, a tractor, a cultivator, a seeder, seeds, fuel, and lubricants, and began farming. Zhanna's husband became her leading assistant. At that time, her family had moved to the sisters' native village a few months ago. The leadership of the regional farmers' association supported her election as the head of the district farmers' association.

Two fellow villagers, whom Miia inspired with her courage to organize a farm, she helped to obtain financial assistance from the Farm Support Fund. In return, they guaranteed to provide her with sowing material on deferred payment and combine harvester services when the time came to harvest.

Everything was set up. And inner voices suggested that something long-awaited and fateful was approaching in her life.

Before the New Year, Miia, as the head of the district farmers' association, received a package of documents for registering the district party organization. The name of the party head was unknown to her. The last time she had spoken in the office, with the former head, she knew that changes were being prepared in the party leadership, but it was said that Mykhailo Mykhailovych was to be elected.

"Hmm... Interesting," she thought, quickly flipping through the folder with documents.

The office address is different. The names of the members of the presidium are unknown to her. She was once involved in preparing for a party conference. The only thing she remembered was the chaos and differences of opinion among the representatives of the organizing committee regarding the correctness of the execution of applications, protocols, and resolutions.

The documents she received were entirely different from

227

those she was already familiar with, in style and design. They exuded modernity. Miia began to examine the majestically sweeping signature of the new party leader, as if she were staring at him like a photograph. A mysterious feeling seized her. Several male images were drawn in her imagination. Different. Small in stature and tall. Thin and fat. Brown-eyed machos and arrogant nerds. She had seen enough of such. She remembered how many such men she had refused to reciprocate with.

"I wonder what this man looks like." At this thought, her heart beat excitedly. "Oh, Miia, stop the flight of your thoughts… Shameless!" But, peering at the signature again and again, the feeling of mystery and enigma only intensified.

Although it was required to submit the documents for registration of the party branch as soon as possible after receiving them, Miia decided not to rush.

"Our congress is in two weeks. I will learn more about those who led the party, and then I will decide whether to lead this branch myself or hand it over to one of the farmers."

Miia enjoyed participating in seminars, conferences, and congresses. These were exactly the events she was happy to prepare for carefully. When buying new clothes and shoes, she had a remarkable talent for finding stylish, high-quality, and rare items at reasonable prices, which not only improved her mood but also boosted her self-esteem and confidence. Financially, she had always faced difficulties. Whenever she spent money on unplanned expenses, she had to cut back on her food budget. To justify her spending, she would always come up with the valid excuse, "I'm dieting." And the golden rule, "God gives a person as much income as he can intelligently master," was the driving force that pushed her toward new knowledge and aspirations.

The university assembly hall was almost complete. The speakers, one after another, came out to the podium, uttered their passionate words, and were loudly applauded. That is, everything was done in accordance with the regulations. During the first part, Miia almost fell asleep. But two men sat down next to her, whose presence dispelled her drowsiness and distracted her from her speeches. They constantly argued: either they thought that the event should have been held in a different place, or they could not decide on their political preferences, or they were embarrassed that, instead of dinner, an ordinary buffet was arranged during a break. Listening to them, Miia already knew that these were not just two neighbors but also two godparents. "I can only imagine how you guys live as neighbors," thought Miia, remembering Chasnyk and Galushka, and, glad that the break had been announced, she ran like a bullet to the exit from the hall.

"Miia, where are you lost? We were holding a seat for you."

"Yulia and I were late counting the participants of the congress. Do you know how many people are present?"

"The hall is full. How many?"

"Four hundred and eighty-four. Twenty-seven did not come."

"This is the first time that there are so many people. But not all of them are farmers here. There are party members here. Did you receive a package of documents for registering a branch of our farmers' party?"

"Yes, I received it. But I haven't submitted it yet – I'm interested in learning more about the new leadership. Can I "go on a reconnaissance trip" with them? Miia smiled, winking at her colleagues.

"Serious people. Aiming to develop the party to the point of being able to bring it to Parliament."

"Wow! The plans are grandiose. Now our farm leaders can't sleep at night but work and dream of deputy mandates."

"A split has already begun within our party. It hasn't come out yet, but it's about to break out."

"I see that something is not healthy happening in the circle of the association's leadership. Today they will elect a new president. But there are only two candidates."

"Is there any certainty that Mykhailo Mykhailovych will gain the most votes?"

"I don't know. However, it would be great if he were to become the president of the association. I worked with him – he is a fair person, has his own opinion, and has his own clear vision. It will be easy for us with him."

"You know, I have been in this field for twenty years, and believe me, fairness is destructive here, just like your opinion

229

with your clear vision. It will be easy for us with him. But those who are higher up…" A sad doubt appeared on Vasyl's face. "Something tells me that it will be so difficult that there are no words to convey it."

"Politics." Nodding her head, Galina shrugged.

"Will you vote for him?"

"If he doesn't withdraw his candidacy." It so happened that the interlocutors answered almost in unison.

"Oh, no." Miia looked at Vasyl, then at Galina, with a confused look.

Announced the end of the break.

"You sit with us." Grabbing Miia by the hand, Vasyl pointed to Miia's place.

"Oh," she exclaimed in response, spinning around in all directions, with passion in her voice, "It's more comfortable and fun here among you."

"Have you read the latest issue of our newspaper?" showing Miia a photo of one of the sexes that took up the entire page. "Who is this?" peering into the face of an unfamiliar man who was surrounded by the president and vice-president of the association, Miia's playful voice changed to an even and calm one.

"This is the chairman of our party, Volodymyr Valeriyovych." Turning back, Vasyl smiled slyly. "By the way, you can meet him right now."

However, Mykhailo Mykhailovych's speech was announced currently. At this, all the attention of Miia's entourage switched to the speech of the vice president of the association. With a confident gait, he walked to the podium. Straightforward, frank, and at times impudent statements about the development of farming in the country elicited a storm of applause from half of the hall. In contrast, the other half, oppositional, launched a disgruntled barrage of criticism.

The reasons and timing of the split in the Farmers' Association leadership were known only to the leaders themselves. They said that Mykhailo Mykhailovych was too demanding, unyielding, and uncompromising in communicating with the head of state's entourage. Of course, they didn't like it because they needed a more loyal leader of the farming community. This tension began to grow all too noticeably a year before the presidential election.

"Just look at what's happening in the hall. This is not normal." Galina looked at Miia and Vasyl, confused.

Some burly men began to break onto the stage. About fifteen of them surrounded the speaker, not allowing Mykhailo Mykhailovych to finish his speech.

"This is sabotage on purpose. Most of those who break onto the stage are not farmers. Galia, prepare your mandate."

Miia, as an invitee, did not have a mandate.

"Someone gives me your mandate." In despair, she began to exclaim, her emotions no longer held back. "My God, someone give me your mandate."

In front of her sat a delegation from the Rivne region. Miia knew that they supported the opponent, Mykhailo Mykhailovych. One of the men looked back and sternly snapped at Miia:

"What kind of a ruckus are you making here? Calm down and accept reality…"

But Miia didn't let him continue:

"The fake people you brought in are making a mess here. Isn't that right? They're running around the stage and around, so much so that even the security can't handle them. How much are they paid?"

At that moment, the mandate flashed before her eyes.

"Miia for you!"

Grabbing the mandate, Miia raised it. After glancing around the hall at those who had voted to support Mykhailo Mykhailovych, she whispered with relief:

"We hope that the new president of the Farmers Association will be Boychenko." At the exact moment, she read the name of the person to whom the mandate that Vasyl had given her belonged. Without saying a word, she looked at her colleague.

"Yes. This is the mandate of our new party chairman."

Miia turned around. She was met with a keen gaze and a sweet, barely noticeable smile from Volodymyr Valeriyovych. "I am pleased to watch you. You own living energies and sincere emotions." As if under the influence of magic, Miia was bewitched by his voice, intonation, and appearance.

231

They looked into each other's eyes. At that moment, everything around disappeared. Amid the stormy noise, silence swallowed them. Somewhere in the subconscious, a confession of the temptation to get to know each other better slipped through. Words were not needed. Only the eyes spoke.

Miia was brought back to reality by Vasyl's alarmed exclamation.

"He is withdrawing his candidacy..."

Coming to her senses, Miia realized that the last minute had fallen out of her life. Panic gripped her. Despair was visible, according to Galina and Vasyl.

"What is he doing?" Getting up from her seat, Miia quickly moved towards Mykhailo Mykhailovych to the opposite side of the assembly hall, forcing almost everyone to get up from their seats to make way for her.

A lot of his supporters had gathered near Boychenko at this point, and they all had similar questions. Pushing everyone aside, not holding back her emotions and tears, Miia grabbed Mykhailo Mykhailovych's hand:

"Why? Your victory."

"You all won. I lost."

"Because you didn't submit?" He understood what the question was about.

"Do you know who owns the security company that works here now?" He didn't give a name; there were too many people around. Having studied Boychenko too well, it was enough for her to look at his expression. Miia approached him so close to make sure that she wouldn't be heard.

"Was a provocation being prepared?" In response, he nodded his head.

Without resisting those around her who sought to communicate with Boychenko, Miia thoughtfully stepped aside.

As if the ground had moved from under her feet. When planning the concept of the Farmers' Association's development, in the event of Mykhailo Mykhailovych's victory, Miia was to head one of the areas that would assist farmers in business planning to obtain state funding and grants. This topic was the closest and most interesting to her. She knew that with each new business plan she would receive new knowledge and experience. Furthermore, having received such an opportunity, she would be in Kyiv more frequently, which would facilitate her studies at the university she planned to attend. And this is what she aspired to most.

Lost in thought, she did not notice how quickly those present vacated the hall. On the opposite side, Galina was waiting for her.

"Yours is a bag." Giving her the handbag, the woman hugged Miia. "I know how shameful the situation is. Such cases kill faith in the 'happy ending in a fairy tale.' But, perhaps, that's how it should be."

"It shouldn't be like this." Despair tore at Miia. She barely held back her tears and, looking around the hall, continued, we are probably the only ones left here. Let's go."

Heading to the exit, Miia began to count the boards on the floor. She had no desire to continue discussing something that had already lost its meaning. Galina tried her best to cheer up her colleague. However, Miia didn't hear her at all.

"Where are you now? "A sharp touch of Galina's hand made Miia look up. "He's waiting for you!"

Miia shifted her confused gaze from Galina to the exit.

"Oh, my God!"

Seeing the person standing at the door, her knees buckled. From excitement, she began to feel how the very boards of the floor were dissolving under her feet. Like a tsunami, excitement covered her so strongly that it took her breath away. Trying to cope with this, Miia slowed down. But with each step, she approached him. His majestic figure exuded a sense of mystery and seduction.

"We haven't met yet," the party chairman said gently, not hiding his passionate gaze. "Volodymyr Valeriyovych."

"Miia." Overcoming her excitement, she confidently looked into his eyes and held out her hand.

"And your middle name?" he asked with a smile.

"Vladislavivna." She laughed. "According to etiquette, I should introduce myself, just like you introduced yourself. That is, by name and middle name." His eyes burned with flames of pleasure. "Miia Vladislavivna."

233

"I understand that you are in despair over what happened."
"In despair. But not everything in life happens the way we want it to."
"Have you understood this for a long time?" Noticing the surprise on Miia's face, he quickly continued. "Don't be offended by the question. I know many people who are much older than you but who live by the thinking of Don Quixote."
"Fighting windmills is not for me," Miia stated with a smile. "Of course, I won't give up without a fight. If this war is mine."
Stopping in front of the stairs, Miia looked around at the company of several men surrounding Mikhail Mikhailovich. Seeing her with Volodymyr Valeriyovych, he winked and bowed his head approvingly. Miia turned her gaze to Volodymyr Valeriyovych. A feeling of peace replaced the relentless sadness.
"That's right! What happened today is not my battlefield. Therefore, I must come to terms… No. I have already come to terms."
"You, Miia Vladislavivna, are not only a beautiful woman. You are intelligent." Their gazes were filled with mutual insight. It seemed that they were reading each other's thoughts.
"It's nice to hear that from you. Thank you!"
"How long do you plan to be in Kyiv?"
"I'm coming back today. The train leaves at 10 p.m."
"Will we have time to drink coffee?" Miia was confused. Volodymyr Valeriyovych noticed this. "Were you staying at the hotel?"
"Yes."
"Are they waiting for you at the exit?"
"Yes."
Volodymyr Valeriyovych took out a business card and gave it to Miia.
"Promise that you will call when you arrive. I need to know that everything is fine with you."
With undisguised pleasure, Miia looked at him intently. She felt that a spark of mutual sympathy had ignited between them: "I promise!"

234

XXX

The tax authorities' audit of financial assistance received from the Farmers Support Fund went smoothly for Miia's farm. At the time of the audit, her colleagues from the region said that opponents of the current head of the fund had initiated tax audits of farmers across Ukraine.

"Mykhailo Mykhailovych, I understand that someone wanted to get this position if they so brazenly, at the highest level, provoked tax audits." The first thing Miia asked at the meeting with the head of the fund in Kyiv.

"They checked all the farms that received assistance under my leadership. This whole company was started against me. They checked me, not you," the head of the fund began in a positively cheerful voice, with a smile on his face.

"Were they looking for bribes?"

"But they didn't find anything." He laughed in response.

"This is so vile," Miia said, grimacing. "The funds we received were for a specific purpose. The value of the property purchased by the farms was significantly lower than its market value.

"No price overestimation was found in any farm, so the Ministry of Finance both started and closed this inspection two months later."

"Should we expect any consequences?"

"I think our opponents will not stop. And in order not to make life difficult for you, the farmers, I have decided to resign from this position."

"For some reason, I am not even surprised. Is everything so serious?"

"The one who wants this place has serious support from the administration of the President of Ukraine. And I confess, I would rather not have cases fabricated against me, as usually happens." Disappointment was visible on Miia's face. "I understand you." Mykhailo Mykhailovych continued. "The elections are on the nose. I don't think I need to explain anything to you."

"And they didn't offer you anything?"

"They offered to be a deputy."

"You refused."

"Of course. Consent will lead to the fact that in all deals, the deputy will become the scapegoat."

"I always remember, 'For me, there is no such multiplication table that would combine state funds with personal ones.' These are your words

"I am not a corrupt person. There is no such person who would say that he bribed me or was involved in any schemes."

"I have known you for three years. During this time, there have been no false intentions behind you. What do you plan to do next?"

"To begin with, I will rest. And then life will show. I am already receiving certain proposals from some political parties. But I am in no hurry to accept them."

"If you are offered a place on the lists in parliament, why not agree?"

"Do you think I want to be a people's deputy?" He laughed out loud. "No way."

"But you have always talked about the pitifully small number of true patriots of the country in parliament."

"New elections will bring new faces to parliament. I would rather leave mine away from parliament. I will be of no use there. By the way, do you communicate with Volodymyr Valeriyovych?"

"I met with him yesterday."

"And how?"

"It seems that everything is fine."

"He also invited me to meet."

"There is a meeting tomorrow; he has a proposal for me regarding the development of the women's wing of the party."

"Did he offer to head it?"

"I can't. To whom will I leave the farm? And the children."

"You'll figure out the household."

"Then let's go together."

"Oh, no! What if Volodymyr Valeriyovych wants to invite you for coffee?" Mykhailo Mykhailovych, he exclaimed, smiling at length. "I would rather not be a hindrance."

"What are you talking about?" Miia was perplexed.

"You're a young, beautiful, intelligent woman. So why wouldn't a man like Volodymyr Valeriyovych invite you

236

for coffee? I would do it myself, but I'm too old for that." Noticing Miia's shyness, he continued in a more serious voice. "Have you already registered a party center in your district?"

"Yes. Registered." Miia laughed. "In two days."

"Wow, how zealous. Typically, the district administration ensures that no one takes any action without their prior permission. How did you manage to do that?"

"I was shocked. As soon as I was elected head of the district farmers' association, the head of the district administration offered me the chance to join the ranks of the pro-government party in the district. But to gently refuse, I had to stick a stupid blonde with a bunch of different nonsense." Miia laughed at these words. "You should have seen the expression on his face! He looked at me as if I were sick. But four months later, when our farmers' party branch appeared, the district leadership was unhappy that I managed to pull off this operation, bypassing their permits."

"Desperate. What did it end up like?"

"The head of the state administration called me 'to the carpet' and declared that the registration of unknown parties could pose a threat..." Miia pointedly emphasized, raising her index finger, "To the state authorities."

"Oh, how!"

"A representative of the regional administration was present in his office. Outwardly, he reminded me of Lavrentiy Beria in some way. A cold, intent gaze. Narrowed eyes. Round glasses, exactly like Beria's. A pampered face." Miia shuddered.

"You don't yet know what a state machine is, at any level. If it grabs your jacket, it will pull you so hard that there may be no chance of escaping. Therefore, be careful."

"What, will they kill me?"

"Will they crush you as a person? Remember how you received the land? Yes, this is the village and district level."

"I remember. Until I connected with the Kyiv offices, the issue was not closed. I understand everything perfectly," she answered evenly. "But when I started listing the names of politicians who are connected to this party, there was nothing to cover for him. And to be honest, the head of the

237

administration himself quickly brought her claims to naught. 'It all depends on the color of her hair,' he said, smiling, and offered help if I needed it."

"Hold on to Volodymyr Valeriyovych and his team. You will be just as comfortable with them as you are with us. Moreover, I noticed their special interest in your active and energetic life position." Miia was pleasantly confused at these words. "I'm telling you frankly."

"It will be seen. The main thing for me is that the next harvest does not disappoint. I won't survive a third year of poor harvest. Neither financially nor psychologically. It's already scary thinking about it."

"Did the dry weather ruin your harvest last year?"

"Yes."

"What are your plans for next year?"

"Winter wheat, 25 hectares. I left the other 25 hectares fallow because I grew sunflowers on them last year."

"Did the farmers you helped receive financial assistance keep their promises? I remember how they swore not to let you down."

"Yes. I got them, just as they promised."

"On what terms?"

"With the harvest, I have to return to them the number of tons of wheat they gave me." After a pause, Miia continued in a quiet voice. "I'm worried. The plants are weak."

"Why?"

"The plants are weak. I went to the Kushchakov field to see how it grows there. So, compared to mine, their winter crop is both greener and taller. Our lands are located some three kilometers away."

"What are your thoughts on this?"

"In mid-January, frosts hit sharply, from minus five to minus twenty. There was no snow. Before the frosts, the winter crop was left completely unprotected. When I arrived at the field in the morning, the plants were black. I don't remember when I cried so much. In the middle of the field."

"Have you been farming for three years?"

"Yes, this is the third harvest. I invested all the money I had, every last penny. And I'm scared."

"The south of the country is a zone of risky farming."

"I remember how they warned me, even at the stage of deciding. However, I couldn't stay in Kyiv at the time. Firstly, it wasn't easy financially. I was constantly bouncing from one paycheck to the next. Secondly, I was torn between children and work. Thank you to all of you who helped with the dormitory. My neighbors were kind and generous people; they always helped me."

"I remember your arguments when you decided to go home."

"I admit, now that I'm in the village, it's not easier for me financially. But I'm at home. My family is my main rear. Because there is food, there is a roof over my head."

"Tell me how another farmer you recommended to the fund helped you?"

"With the fund's money, he bought a combine. He promises to help with the harvest. My fuel is his combine."

"Your fellow villagers should be grateful to you for your help to them. I told you that. Have you forgotten? Because if it weren't for you, they would have received funds from the fund in about ten years. At best. And at worst, they would never have received them at all."

"I remember," she replied with a smile.

"That's good. Let's keep in touch. Always believe in yourself!" With these words, he took out the magazine "AGRO.UA" and, with a thoughtful smile, began to leaf through the pages. Stopping at one of them, he looked intently at Miia.

"You deny the invitation for coffee. Your photo from the last session. A description of your heroism as a young woman who, at the age of twenty-eight, organized her farm and headed the district association of farmers." Giving Miia the magazine, he went to the door to invite people who were waiting to meet and, saying goodbye to her, added. "This is Volodymyr Valeriyovych's idea to have you published in the most popular and prestigious magazine in the country. He is interested in you. And I understand him perfectly."

Full of inspiration, Miia went for a walk in the center of Kyiv, which she missed very much. Her thoughts plunged into memories of Volodymyr Valeriyovych. She remembered every detail of their acquaintance and the beginning of communication. She remembered every word. She felt every look. Her soul was filled with joy and lightness.

"Sinner," she smiled seductively to herself. "However, if it is the will of God, then I will obey it."

Satisfied with the results of this trip, upon returning home, she actively participated in forming the youth district wing of the party. The main inspiration for her was comprehensive support for orphans. This idea became the central concept for the development of the party's youth wing. At the district party meetings, it was unanimously supported, and each farmer decided which children he would take under his patronage, proposing a list of young people who wanted to join the development process.

The active phase of the painstaking pre-election work began. Nine days off for the May holidays provided an opportunity for positive meetings with young people in the villages, useful acquaintances, and interesting ideas.

On Sunday evening, while in her room and working on the next set of notes, Miia saw a car stop near the yard through the window. Her father approached her, and they discussed something before heading into the yard. Miia hurried out.

"They're looking for you," her father said, having already met in the yard.

"They say they have questions about the tax audit."

Miia was surprised.

"Interesting. I'll go and have a chat."

Near the car, she was greeted by two young men, one of whom introduced himself as an investigator from the prosecutor's office and the other as an investigator from the department for combating the theft of socialist property.

"Does socialist property exist in independent Ukraine?" Miia asked with her inherent artistry, without even saying hello. "And what brought you to me, I doubt it, or respectable people?"

Looking at each other, she noticed their confusion and slight irritation from what she had heard. But quickly gathering herself, the prosecutor's investigator said:

"We are authorized to check your accounting."

Miia looked stubbornly from one to the other.

"Authorized by whom and on what basis?"

"Because of the inspection that took place regarding the misuse of funds."

"What funds?"

"Budget funds."

"I have nothing to do with budget funds."

This answer caused both men to become more confused.

"Have you received financial assistance? Please show all the documentation. Contracts, firstly."

"And instead of a table, will you use your knees or the hood of your Zhiguli?" Her face lit up with a sly smile.

"Depending on how many papers." It felt like the interlocutor was trying to speak sternly.

Miia understood their intentions and that communicating with them was a waste of time. However, she joined the game.

"There are many papers; your knees, together with mine, will not be enough. We will have to call all the neighbors."

"You probably do not understand the seriousness of our visit. We are carrying out an assignment," in a commanding tone, the second one said.

"Let me familiarize myself with this assignment."

"We did not take it with us."

"Then, I can't help you with anything – there are no assignments, no accounting documents. I do not say 'Goodbye.' Do you understand why? "Miia smiled, and turning around, she was about to leave.

"Dear, you are playing with fire." After her, the prosecutor's office investigator yelled.

Stopping, Miia took a deep breath and exhaled, and turned to them. Having carefully examined the uninvited guests, she began to speak in a serious tone.

Firstly, I do not keep accounting documents at home. Therefore, you will not be able to review them."

"And where are they?" the interlocutors asked in surprise, almost in unison.

"In Kyiv." Miia's face spread into a smile again. "And secondly, even if they were here, you would not have received them anyway."

"Why?"

"It's banal; I would not have given them to you." Miia began to feel a desire to give them specific standard addresses to which she would gladly send them, but with a smile, she

241

continued her speech calmly. "And thirdly. The tax audit did not reveal any violations in the use of funds received from the fund, which is confirmed by the audit report. Fourthly. The political showdowns that prompted the audit of 130 farms nationwide, including mine, were resolved over three weeks ago. And neither the State Tax Service nor the Ministry of Finance has any claims to the farms that were audited. So, the issue is closed." The two sat and looked at her in surprise. Miia continued. "If you wanted to make friends with me as the head of the farm, as the head of the district farmers' association, and as the head of the district party organization, then you should have chosen another excuse."

"And what is the way to your heart, Madam Head?" the prosecutor's investigator asked flirtatiously.

"My heart is closed to you. Forever." Miia laughed. "And anyway, we've been talking for half an hour, and I still can't understand why you came?

"We said to check your accounting."

"You didn't understand anything at all?" Miia continued, gathering her courage and icy intonation. "Well, listen. Today, in connection with the holidays, is the fifth day off. Sunday. Five in the evening. What did you expect when you came to see me?" The interlocutors looked at her silently, trying to maintain serious expressions on their faces. "You haven't been told yet that I would rather help an orphanage or the seriously ill. And then, if I have such an opportunity. The police and the prosecutor's office are not on the list of those in need. If you wish to communicate with me, please do so in accordance with the law. Provide a summons with the justification for the summons, specifying the date, time, and address where I should arrive. Having put all the pieces together, I concluded that your visit to me is at your whim. Therefore, go home and do not return, and I, in turn, promise that your management, to whom it is enough for me to make one phone call, will not find out about your tour searching for adventure," she added with a smile. "Or money."

She left without saying goodbye. Somewhere deep in her soul, anxiety gripped her. But their impudence outraged her. "Who was it?" asked her father, who had been watching the conversation from the yard all the time.

242

"Orphans. They came for alms."

"Oh, well. They are still those migrant workers."

A few days later, Miia went to the district center on business There was complete peace in her soul. She met with the deputy chairman of the district council, with whom she had established warm business relations. Her career took off and gained popularity in the district, thanks to him.

"Miia Vladystavivna, you know very well that I frankly respect you for your intelligence, courage, perseverance, and tenacity. I have many like-minded people who care about you. You are too bright in our district. And this annoys the district leadership."

"I know. All their smiles with sweet greetings are nothing more than the most ordinary hypocrisy. And it is so disgusting."

"They are forced to do this because they know that there is someone to protect you in Kyiv. You know, everything here is gray. Light gray or dark gray color is allowed. Your fiery-sunny burns their eyes. And they are longingly expecting your failures."

"Gray won't suit me."

"You don't need to. You are like a ray of light in our gray kingdom," he added with a smile. "So, shine, because with you it's brighter for us too."

Miia often recalled this conversation about colors. It happened that her rebellious nature, as a person who valued justice above all, was portrayed in a fiery, sunny color. And it was capable of burning not only the eyes but also causing thunderstorms with lightning.

She remembered one time returning from the store, Miia heard someone calling her.

"Miia, help! Only you can handle this arbitrariness!" Elena, exhausted from running, quickly approached her.

"What happened?"

"The German language teacher rated Stas' knowledge by one point, and she wants to put this grade on the nine-year education certificate."

"One point?" Miia's eyes widened in surprise.

"If she does that, he won't be able to continue his studies."

"The question is why, in five years, the teacher taught the

243

student only 'by one point'? And that's on a twelve-point scale."

"There are two weeks left until the end of the school year. I don't know what to do."

"I know. What time is it? Almost eleven. Let's go. Immediately."

Half an hour later, they were already in the reception room of the district education department's head. Thank God for all the saints; he was there.

"Hello, Dmitry Mikhailovich."

"Good afternoon to you, too, Miia Vladislavivna! What brought you to me?"

"A scandal is brewing."

"What?" He looked at Miia, then at Elena in surprise.

"Meet me. This is Olena Tynko. She is the eldest sister among four brothers. They are orphans. Full orphans. And she is not only their sister but also their guardian. And they are all my protégés as heads of the farm. Do you know about the decision of the farmers of the district to help such children?"

"I know." His eyes lit up with interest. "What brought you to me?"

Elena shared the problematic relationship between her younger brother and the German teacher, where frank disrespect for him and his family prevails. About which, more than once, the teacher allowed herself to express herself openly in front of her classmates.

"Miia Vladislavivna, sit down." After listening to Olena's story, the educator made a suggestion.

"No, thank you!" She went to the window, in front of which a luxurious carpet of pink chestnut candles fluttered. For a moment, there was silence.

"He is handsome." Noticing Miia's frozen gaze on the charms of the flowering tree, the head of the regional education department got up from the table and went to the same window. Olena left the office.

"Dimitry Mykhailovych, as a person, you understand perfectly well that children are not responsible for the actions of their parents. In addition, the mother of these children died of an illness. Olena was only eleven years old. The youngest twin brothers were only three years old. The father

244

tried to provide for the children somehow." Miia felt a lump rise in her throat. "He is not a saint. But what did our society do? What did our local village authorities do to support and help the father of these children? Almost everyone turned away from them. Even the neighbors. Do you know why? Because they are poor. Because they were perceived as being of lower status. No one even considered what the children ate, including whether they had sweets. At the age of eleven, Olena took on the role of mother for her younger brothers. She did not have toy dolls. She had live ones. When their father was shot, by the way, the policeman who did it was never punished. When the children were left as complete orphans, their aunt took custody of them. She has no children of her own because she took care of her orphaned nephews.

"Hmm…" He looks thoughtfully at the floor.

"I told you the story of these children not to somehow make you feel sorry for them. I did it because I encountered the arbitrariness of the history teacher. A long time ago. Furthermore, I have already managed to protect my daughter, a first-grader, from frank humiliations from her class teacher. I understand that the work of a teacher is difficult and important. But teacher arbitrariness is an unacceptable phenomenon that cannot be ignored."

"And how does this man study in general?"

"Judging by the grades, he is below average. Generally, he is a smart individual."

"This is an abstract statement."

"Abstract? Then I'll go on without pretending to be abstract." Miia frowned. "In five years, the teacher rated himself a one. Is that shameful or not?"

"Well, why immediately 'shame'?" Dimitry Mykhailovych began to stammer and blink his eyes faintly.

"You know my sister Zhanna very well. She has a higher pedagogical education, and, as a German teacher, she adequately assessed Stas' knowledge when he came to her for private lessons. And I consider one point in the certificate of a nine-year education unacceptable. I am sure that you can resolve this issue!" The gentle intonation of her voice changed to an expressive and demanding one. "Otherwise, I reserve the right not even to contact the regional education department but to immediately contact the Ministry of Education with a corresponding application for certification of some teachers of our school." He blushed. "Dimitry Mykhailovych, I am not threatening. And I really will do it in order not to deprive Stas of prospects. Twelve years ago, I lost my prospects."

"I will take care of this. Trust me."

"Thank you, and I do not dare to take up your time anymore. Goodbye!"

Returning to the village and walking along the road that led across the river, Miia and Elena saw that the same German teacher was heading towards them

Approaching, everyone greeted politely. Taya Anatolyevna turned to Miia:

"Can we talk in private?"

"If it comes to Olena's brother, I have no secrets from her." Miia's tone was cold.

"Why did you immediately go to the district education department? You could have come to me first."

"Taya, the district education department is the mildest option for you, because I could have immediately turned to the Ministry of Education."

"Are you serious?" Such a sharp statement embarrassed Miia's interlocutor.

"Yes! And you thought about the fact that your children will not always be under your care. The time will come, and they will go into society. Imagine how they will feel when they meet such tyrants as their mother. You have something to think about. Conclude, and in the future, never show such disrespect to anyone. Goodbye."

Leaving, Olena asked in surprise:

"Are you on 'you' with her?"

"I understand that it is not polite. But she is only three years older than I; she studied in the same class as my Zhanna. And then, there is something else, but that is already a story, more than sixteen years old, and you do not necessarily need to know about it."

"Wow! Tell me." Olena's eyes shone. "Please."

"We all did stupid things in our youth. Therefore, you'd better take care that you do not do your own."

246

XXXI

Summer brought Miia hellish disappointments.

Before the harvest, she went to Kushakov's field to look at their wheat. It was full of tall stalks with giant ears. In her field, the grain was three times lower, and it was decorated with the same beauties as the Kushakovs, but very rarely. Selectively, on one square meter, Miia counted about twenty to thirty such plants.

"This is a collapse!" she said to herself, understanding the inevitable bitter consequences.

But at that moment, she did not yet know that in two weeks the next meanness awaited her.

"What does it mean that you cannot?" Hearing the impudent refusal, Miia could not believe her ears.

"I promised to help the guys from Crimea. "He tried to justify himself."

"You promised to help me. Forgot?"

"Sorry!" The interlocutor's eyes ran from one side to the other, trying to avoid Miia's angry gaze.

His excuses were pathetic.

"Oh, Saints, pity him. But if you decide to teach him a lesson – I don't feel sorry for him." Raising her head to the sky and pleading with its azure for strength, Miia felt her anger start to transform into sympathy for her interlocutor, strangely. The hot July air caressed her face as if deliberately holding back her tears. A fantastic calm began to spread through her body. Maybe this was how the heavens worked their magic on her. The wind of impending change embraced her.

Without saying a word, she got on her bike and rode home. On the way, she considered her next steps. "All the farmers are busy now. I clearly understand that it's not worth hoping for anyone. But I need a combine!"

On the way home, she recalled seeing about a dozen modern agricultural machines in the fields of the neighboring district, including combines.

"I will get to them!" With these words came a resolute confidence.

The day was hot. Knowing that in the area where she was going, a canal flows, Miia put on a swimsuit: "I'll at least

247

swim a little. I'll relieve stress," she muttered to herself, grabbed the keys to the farm truck, and drove off.

She loved driving her dump truck. She was proud of this, absolutely deservedly so, because at that time in their village, she was the only woman who drove a car. And it was she who became an example for other villagers.

Finding the fields where the harvest was taking place was not difficult. The steppe was vast with distant horizons. Admiring the beauty of her native land, a fleeting pain squeezed her soul. She stopped and got out of the car. Surrounded by vast fields, through which a playful breeze walked, warmly embracing the not-yet-mown ears of rye, the pain turned to sadness.

"Native land! Do you not love me enough to test me so cruelly? For what?" Tears rolled down her face. "What am I doing wrong?' But in response, both the heavenly distance and the steppe power were silent, and the breeze stopped its breathing.

Gathering her spirit and wiping away a tear, Miia drove on. In the mirrors, clouds of dust rose from under the wheels, breaking away from the hot road, and easily dissolved in the hot, windy embrace. Stopping near the forest strip that separated the canal from the wheat field, Miia went to the combine harvesters who had gathered for lunch.

"Greetings, gentlemen. Enjoy your meal, you."

"Good afternoon, young lady," she heard in response almost in unison.

"We invite you to our table," said the oldest man among those present.

"Thank you for the invitation! But today I haven't earned enough money for lunch. Tell me better, how can I talk to your boss?"

"He will come to us in two hours."

"How will I recognize him?"

"He will be in the white Volga. Where are you from?"

"Forty kilometers. Sincerely grateful. I will wait nearby, by the canal." She was about to leave when someone asked her after her.

"Such a beauty behind the wheel of a ZIL. What brought you here?"

248

Miia didn't answer. Having driven two hundred meters, she noticed a beautiful exit to the water. 'This is where I will swim and sunbathe. When would I ever allow myself something like that again?'

Although the stone weighed down her soul, she felt a mysterious pleasure being here. The fabulously warm water caressed her with its touch. The birdsong filled the air with the melodies of natural voices. One after another, sending airy kisses, the clouds smiled. All this returned peace and comfort to the soul. And this was what was missing most of all.

"The guys told me that you were waiting for me."

Hearing a pleasant male voice, Miia got out of the water and quickly wrapped herself in a towel.

"Probably." Taking off her sunglasses, she approached the car. "If you are the manager."

"The manager." With a glance, he looked at Miia from head to toe.

Noticing this, she felt embarrassed.

"If I had come to your office, believe me, I would have been dressed more decently. "After these words, his gaze stopped on ZIL. "This is my brougham." With pride in her intonation, she continued smiling. "It won't turn into a pumpkin. It's been checked."

"I believe it." It was noticeable that he liked the humor.

"Anatoly." He introduced himself.

"Miia."

"You don't often come across such a name. Where did you come from?"

"Golden groves"

"I know where it is."

"Far away?" Miia understood why she asked that.

"No." It was clear that he noticed Miia's excitement. "What brought you here?"

"I am looking for a combine harvester. I have twenty-five hectares of winter wheat. It has already started to crumble. The countdown has begun to save the rest of the harvest."

"I understand. Don't you have any combines?"

"Since this morning, it has become known that no."

He was silent. He was thinking.

249

"How can I find you in the village?"

"Ostapa Vyshny Street, 12."

"Where is the best place for a combine to go?"

"To the granary. My field is nearby."

"Miia, I have a meeting in half an hour. Now you go home. I'll let the guys rest, and tomorrow at about six in the morning, we'll be at your place."

It can't be said that Miia expected to hear the opposite. These words were heard by all the saints, whom she had begged for mercy on her way here. And she was heard.

"Thank you." Tears filled her eyes. "Thank you very much."

The word was kept.

In the evening, while examining her harvest's size, Miia shared with Anatoly the story of two meannesses in her humanity.

"Yesterday, I nearly became a killer for one. Today, I'm prepared to kill two more people." Her face showed a complex mix of emotions, including sadness, anger, despair, and fear.

"What stopped you?"

"Hope."

"In general, I don't make quick decisions. But your desperation struck me. Stay as brave and determined."

"I will stay."

Over the next four days, Miia was busy selling grain. She couldn't afford to suffer even greater losses due to the approaching rains. She found out during these days that the Kushaks were harvesting over three tons per hectare. Her harvest was supposed to be the same. However, this did not happen. She demanded an explanation.

"This is the entire harvest I harvested. Less than five hundred kilograms per hectare." Roman and Galina Kushak were silent, looking at the small wheat mountain. "And this is to thank that my wheat was mowed by a "John Deere" and not a "Niva" or "Kolos." I have a question for both of you, Mr. Kushak. When you were selling your seed to people, did you understand that in less than a year, those who bought it from you would understand that it is a swindle?"

"Why immediately swindle? The yield can be affected by the technology of land cultivation, the timing of cultivation, the timing of sowing, and the quality of the land." Nervous excitement gripped Galina

"They can!" Miia answered her. "But not to me. You and I cultivated the land and sowed at the same time, and the quality of the land is the same. I have bad news for you. I have laboratory results in my hands that two different varieties of wheat were collected from my field." The couple looked at each other in fear. "Two other farmers have the same laboratory results. And you were lucky with me compared to them. Because, unlike me, they have documents to purchase seed from you. I just believed in your decency."

"And how do we know that you sowed our grain? Maybe you sold ours." Roman joined the conversation.

"No. Didn't sell. You know about it. How much do you have per hectare? Three tons? I should have collected at least seventy tons. And I collected only twelve. Therefore, I cancel my obligations to you! Period." Miia looked at the gloomy faces of her interlocutors with a hopeful look. "Regarding the guys who have the same problem, I'm afraid that your judgments regarding land cultivation technologies, cultivation dates, sowing dates, and land quality will work against you. I'll say more: I don't feel sorry for you."

Miia was once again at a crossroads in her life. She no longer had the means, the strength, or the desire to continue farming. Staying in the village meant returning to the very beginning of her battles for survival. For several days in a row, she didn't recognize herself. Occasionally, she was seized by panic, which degenerated into despair. And the worst thing was that she began to notice how wild rage was taking hold of her. At everything. To everyone.

The most vivid memories that had recently comforted and encouraged her were now maddeningly annoying. She began to feel ashamed of her actions and deeds. "For what?" There was no answer. She began to get angry at God. And this scared her.

"Miia, I heard about your bad business." Uncle Jacob suddenly began, shaking a deck of cards.

"Jacob, why are you picking on the girl? She has enough trouble without you. His wife interrupted him. Pushing him on the shoulder. "You'd better deal the cards; I need to get even. I would rather not make the same mistake twice.

On summer evenings, from time to time, Miia came to her friend, who lived nearby with her mother and children. Lyuba also divorced and had three children. Her mother was an entrepreneur and had a small shop at home. Very cheerful and lively, with a refined sense of humor, Aunt Oksana became Miia's second teacher of trade, after her mother, when Miia, at the age of fourteen, took part in inventories as an intern.

"Nothing, Jacob, I'm sure that she will cope. I know her. "Smiling at Miia, Lyuba's mother cheerfully intervened in their conversation."

"I hope," Miia muttered through sadness.

In the summer, such gatherings dragged on until late at night. The time was approaching midnight. The night customers came to the store. Left alone with Uncle Yakov, playing cards, Miia broke the silence:

"Uncle Jacob, I'm really in bad shape. For the first time over the past seven years, I don't know what to do and how to live on."

"Rumors are circulating in the village about how your friends, whom you once helped a lot, treated you meanly."

"Why is that?" Miia put the deck of cards on the table, and she rubbed her head. "As a farmer, I did the same things on the land as they did. With perseverance, I endeavored to provide more benefits and assistance to those in need. I returned home from Kyiv to be useful here. To my family. To others. After all, to myself."

His expressive eyes looked at her intently and with respect.

"I'm sure you've already eaten up your entire brain with questions that you can't get answers to. Right?"

"I'm tired."

"You have to understand that something like this will happen again. That's why you have no right to give up."

"Uncle Jacob, do you know what thought eats away at my consciousness? It scares me."

"What?"

"The further along in life, the more I am inclined to the idea that living in alliance with the Devil is easier and simpler than living in alliance with God."

252

After these words, silence fell. His gaze became even more attentive. Miia remained silent. The things she was talking about made her soul shiver. And she felt it.

"I'll let you read a book. You'll understand that you're wrong."

"The Bible?"

"No."

"I've read many smart books. Maybe I've already read it? What kind of book is it?"

"The main thing is that you come."

In the morning, Miia was already standing at the door of the Sergienko house. Uncle Jacob was holding a book with a green cover, on which the title was engraved in gilded letters. "The Sorrows of the Lord of Hell." Holding her breath, she looked into Uncle Jacob's eyes.

"I see that the title scared you."

"Not that it scared me..." Miia opened the first chapter. Uncle Jacob noticed her confusion.

"It has the answers to all the questions," he smiled.

"You can feel some secret greatness. Is this book really that powerful?"

"You'll understand when you read it."

"The author who wrote about Count Dracula."

"It's a mistake by the publisher." He pointed to the author's name and surname.

"Thank you."

Miia completely immersed herself in the lives of the characters, imagining herself among them. She had a relatively rich imagination, and it seemed to her that she had drawn with complete accuracy the faces of the novel's characters, their voices, their movements, their clothes, the places where they were, and what they were doing.

Miia read half of the book for two weeks, returning to re-read it again and again. She could not accept some part of the text that she had read but did not fully understand. There were such episodes that seemed to plunge her consciousness into darkness, and to escape them, she had to read aloud to hear her own voice, not the voice of the prince, from whom her blood ran cold.

She read the second half of the book in two days. Reading

was intertwined with understanding not only the text itself. But also, the essence of life. Many questions found their answers.

XXXII

Entering the reception room, Miia greeted politely. The secretary, with noticeable curiosity, informed hir that her boss had an important meeting at the moment. She advised her to come in the afternoon, during the hours when citizens are received. Looking at the clock, which showed eleven, Miia smiled.

"I'll wait until the afternoon here," and looking around, she added. "Here on this stool."

An hour passed. The chief energy engineer was called into the office twice and twice came out red as a boiled crab. Then, the chief economist and the chief accountant were called. Two curvaceous ladies, with an indispensable gait and no less significant expressions on their faces, entered the office just as importantly and left, trying to restrain themselves so as not to show their displeasure.

Another hour passed. Miia waited modestly. She understood that it would be unbecoming of her to interfere with her work by arriving in the morning. Because she had arrived without an invitation, on her own initiative. But the main thing that caused her wild excitement was that Anatoly did not even suspect that she would dare to come to him. However, from the depths of her soul came voices of calm, which suggested that there was no place for excitement.

Miia looked at her watch. Almost two and a half hours had passed. At that moment, she remembered her neighbor, who, having left all his affairs and gone with her, was now waiting somewhere on the street.

"Give me a piece of paper and a pen, please." She turned to the secretary. Having received it, Miia wrote only three words. She folded the paper in four. "Give it to the director. Now." Her attentive gaze and sweet smile forced the secretary to do it.

What was Miia's surprise when, within a minute, the office door opened, two of the people present came out, and Anatoly came out into the reception room after them? With a sincere smile, he invited her in.

"The most pleasant surprise!" he exclaimed in a happy voice. "Why didn't you tell me right away that you were here?" He

255

took her hands.

"I was afraid of distracting you from your important matters."

"She was afraid." His blue eyes lit up with flame. "It's already lunch break. Since you're here, I suggest you take a walk along our magical Dnieper. We have our boat and a chef who prepares real masterpieces on it. We'll have a delicious lunch."

"A wonderful offer," Miia answered happily. "But I'm afraid that I won't have time for this, because I have to go back."

"Afraid again..." A sweet smile did not leave the man's face. "I understand you didn't come alone?"

"Yes, the neighbor agreed to this trip."

"Come, I'll hug you." Without letting go of her hands, he said quietly, and without waiting for her permission, he hugged her tenderly.

She wanted this. Very much. Waiting for this moment. From the first minutes of their acquaintance, she felt his warmth towards her. After their last meeting, nearly three weeks had passed. And all this time, all her thoughts, willy-nilly, were about him. She felt that it was mutual and knew that she would dare to come to him because she understood that she was obliged to pay for the work of the combine harvesters. Therefore, this visit was already planned by her.

"Anatoly, I am sincerely grateful to you for your help. You saved not only the wheat remains in my farm field. You saved my honor."

He looked at her with a sweet look. "I brought money..."

"I won't take a single penny from you," he interrupted her. "Tell me that this is not the main reason for your arrival."

"It's just an excuse," she whispered.

She couldn't take her eyes off him. Anatoly was more than just handsome. He might not be considered a beautiful man, but he possessed such charisma that he resembled Apollo. And he knew it and didn't flaunt it at all. Because of this, Miia felt comfortable communicating with him.

Leaving the office, he asked the secretary in the reception area to call the boat and warn him that he would be arriving. Going outside, Anatoly noticed an unfamiliar car.

"I came with him."

"What will you pay him?"

"I'll just fill up the car."

"I understand. Nikol." He turned to the driver. "I'm going to the pier. And you fill this car to a full tank and wait for us at our pier at five o'clock." He looked at Miia. "We'll take our guest home ourselves."

The drive took about fifteen minutes. On the way, he told her that for more than a year, his wife, having taken her daughter, had gone to another man's house in the city. She would rather not live in the village.

"Is she not local?"

"No. She's from Zaporizhye."

"Are you waiting for her return?" Miia asked cautiously.

"I miss my daughter."

"Are you not divorced?" Even more cautiously, Miia asked.

"I think it's time to resolve this issue."

Arriving at the pier. Miia was speechless when she saw the so-called boat.

"Do you like it?"

"I'm delighted! How old is it?"

"An old schooner. But it is still capable of plowing the vast expanses of the mighty Dnieper."

"A schooner..." She looked at the carved wooden elements on the walls and stairs. Masts with an incredible number of cables and ropes left Miia amazed. "It's a whole science to be able to connect them. And I'm sure that each of these ropes has its task."

"Have you been on ships before?"

"The best ship for us on the river was a wheel chamber from a tractor." She laughed. "Even in three years in Kyiv, I still haven't found time to organize a walk on the Dnieper."

A man appeared on the deck, about the same age as Anatoly. "I welcome you and kindly invite you aboard our "Resolute." The man invited them down the gangway, clearly but kindly.

"Miia, meet me. This is our glorious captain, Serg. He is the deputy director for organizational issues and the most reliable friend since birth."

"We were born on the same day," Serg added.

"That's so sweet." Miia felt light.

"Serg, this is Miia. I told you about her." Anatoly took her hand.

257

"I understood that when Alexandra called, we had a heroically brave, persistent, and fabulously charming lady visiting us." Serg seemed to repeat someone's words. "By the way, my friend, I don't even remember you looking so radiant." Understanding the meaning of these words, Miia looked at Anatoly, whose face showed a slight embarrassment. Serg quickly added. "I invite you!

Going on deck, Miia's imagination took her to the seventeenth century."

"We bought this beauty two years ago. And she got here in April of this year." Anatoly walked along the deck, looked carefully at the set table, and smiled. "Serg, a real captain."

"You can feel the spirit of history here. Maybe she once belonged to pirates?"

"Possibly." Anatoly laughed.

"She hasn't been involved in piracy yet here, but she's already had two weddings," the captain reported.

"Do you imagine pirates on her deck?" Anatoly asked her, hugging her by the shoulders.

"I think…" Miia began to flirt. "With my adventurous nature, I could be a good first officer. But a wedding is more romantic."

Sergey laughed.

"Yes, a wedding is the biggest adventure in life."

"Oh, yes! I agree one hundred percent." Miia's face took on a serious expression.

"Sergey, what are we having for dinner today?" Anatoly approached the table and took a bottle of wine to look at. "The most delicious wine I've ever drunk."

"This Spanish wine arrived with the 'Resolute.' We open it only for the most famous events. Today is the second," turning to Miia, Serg said, and turning to Anatoly, he added. "In fifteen minutes, the surprise dish will be ready. Meanwhile, I offer each of us a glass of wine and a tour of our beauty."

"Since the age of twenty-one, Serg and I have managed to see the world. Sailors." Anatoly's friend interrupted.

"The sea became our life. We were not afraid of storms or calms – neither heat nor rain. We even gave each other a promise not to betray the sea. However, I turned out to be a traitor. And I swore to Sergey to fix it." Having said this, Anatoly smiled guiltily.

Miia looked at Serg.

"He met Elvira."

Miia turned her gaze to Anatoly. She thought he was sad.

"To justify my betrayal, I bought the 'Resolute'." We saw her in a Spanish bay six years ago. It was near her that we made that promise to each other."

From the inside, the schooner turned out to be a magnificent old treasure.

Each of the cabins, although it had its own style, nevertheless had a spirit that distinguished it.

"The steering wheel works," Serg emphasized, climbing onto the captain's bridge. "However," he said thoughtfully, turning to Anatoly. "We need to replace the steering cable. They discovered damage last night. I ordered a new one. They promise to deliver it in three weeks."

"We'll wait. I hope she'll be up and running in a month and a half."

"I hope I'll do everything by our anniversary."

"Anniversary." Miia smiled, glancing from one to the other of her interlocutors.

"Yes... There is a sign that men don't celebrate their fortieth birthday, so we decided to celebrate our thirty-ninth." Serg quickly reported, smiling.

"I promised Miia a walk today, but I turned out to be a liar." He looked at Miia with guilty eyes. "I'll make amends. Definitely." Anatoly pointed at Serg. "Now you're my debtor."

Delicious smells began to waft from the campus.

"Miia, I invite you to visit some of the most beloved dishes of the Mediterranean. Caldo verde – Portuguese soup and Spanish appetizers revolto with ham."

"Wow!" Miia was embarrassed. "I admit, I've never tasted anything like this before."

"His culinary masterpieces have always distinguished Sergey. He taught our chefs himself." Anatoly praised his friend.

"Your wife, probably..."

"Mia, I'm not married." Serg didn't let her finish. "I realized

259

as a child that I didn't want to have a family or children."

Miia didn't answer anything. She guessed that his childhood had its flavors of sadness and anxiety.

Over dinner, the friends recalled their adventures on trips. They explained the various types of sailing ships, ranging from aaks to brigs, and discussed the differences between galleons and caravels, as well as the appeal of schooners and yachts. Three hours flew by instantly. The day was preparing for the meeting of the night.

"It's getting to be evening," Miia said, looking at her watch.

"Yes, let's go." Anatoly picked up. "Nikol is already waiting."

Miia thanked Serg for the fascinating stories and delicious Mediterranean food.

All the way, Anatoly almost did not let go of Miia's hand, holding it in his. He asked her to tell him about her children. About why she had divorced her husband. To some extent, he was surprised that in Kyiv she had not met a worthy man. Miia did not comment on this because she would rather not spread the idea that had taken root in her mind: "I and marriage are incompatible things." She did not count on anything regarding him. Although somewhere far in the subconscious, she admitted to herself that it was from this man that she would risk accepting a marriage proposal. Feeling the warmth of his attitude, at times, she drew parallels with Stefan's attitude towards her, whom she often remembered. From these memories, her soul became lighter because he was in her life.

Having arrived at the yard and seeing Anton and Niki, Miia called them to her. The children ran up joyfully. Anatoly extended a gentlemanly handshake to the boy and then sat in front of the girl, addressing her as "princess." He handed them both packages with gifts and carried the packages with the products they had bought on the way.

"How can I steal you so that we can be alone?" So that the children wouldn't hear, he whispered.

"We'll think of something." Hiding her eyes, she answered him quietly.

The children joyfully began to open their gifts, not hiding their delight.

"This Saturday," as if through Miia, he watched the smiling

Anton and Niki. "If you don't have other plans."

Miia looked at him sweetly. She wanted his hugs, his kisses, and his body.

"This Saturday," she repeated, unable to take her eyes off Anatoly's fabulous blue eyes.

"In the afternoon," he whispered again.

"In the afternoon," she repeated.

"I'll steal you." Miia feels that someone was watching us from the neighboring yard.

"These are my ex-husband's parents."

"Do you live next door?" He was surprised.

"All our disagreements are in the past. They are my main help with the children." Miia looked at the children, who started arguing. "What didn't they share?" The children immediately quieted down.

"Do you have a good relationship with them?"

"They are mom and dad for me."

"Unbelievable. You rarely meet someone like that. You've been divorced for so long, and…" He was shocked to hear that.

"It's been eight years."

"You said your parents live here too."

"Yes, two streets away." Here, Miia seemed to come to her senses. "I'm so hospitable. I'm inviting you for tea."

"Thank you, dear, no tea. I'm letting you go; otherwise, I would have kept you with me all day anyway."

Anatoly turned out to be a real man. His care for Miia and the children knew no bounds; he always kept his word and did not allow himself to indulge in fantasies, and an incredible sense of humor accompanied all this. These qualities, again and again, pleasantly impressed Miia. She felt that not crazy love had covered her head. She deeply respected, appreciated, and protected his warmest and brightest attitude towards her.

His appearance in her life brought her real peace. She did not bother with everyday issues. With his eagle eyes, he saw everything that needed to be fixed or done. In the past, they used to do it together. For more serious matters, specialists came to him and made the necessary repairs.

As they anticipated new meetings, time gently protected

their expectations, fostering new gratitude for each other's presence.

When they were left alone, it was the sweetest, most secret, most divine time.

However, at the anniversary celebration, Miia refused, explaining that she could not bring herself to do so, as it would somehow discredit Anatoly's reputation in the eyes of distinguished guests. At the same time, she did not want to feel uncomfortable as a friend of a married man.

Miia did not set any conditions and did not demand any decisions regarding their future. She did not understand why. Either she was afraid of losing what she had. Or she entrusted Anatoly with their future. Or maybe she wasn't sure.

One day, when Miia was on "Resolute" again, Serg told her that Anatoly had sent his lawyer to his wife with a divorce application with favorable terms for her. And everything seemed to be going to a happy ending. But...

Three in the morning.

Waking up to the sound of a car stopping near the yard, Miia was amazed to see that it was Anatoly.

"I want to be with you." Hugging her tightly, he began. Miia immediately understood that something had happened.

Anatoly looked at her with wide-open, sad eyes. The despair on his face was not even hidden.

"I wasn't so confused when she left me. I knew that she had gone to another, and for some reason, I wasn't even jealous or embarrassed. To some extent, I was happy..." Miia was silent, hugging him. "The only thing is, separation from my daughter was painful. But I quickly coped with this pain because I received permission from my wife, so to speak, to see her. For each meeting with Sofiyka, I paid Ellie $500. That was her condition. Otherwise..."

Miia could not gather her thoughts to understand what had happened.

"Is everything okay with the girl?" Miia asked quietly.

"Yes, okay."

"What happened?"

"Miia, I fell in love with you. From the first minutes of our acquaintance, you have always been on my mind, wherever

262

I am and whoever I communicate with. I perceived your appearance in my life as a gift of fate." Miia believed his every word, and not because he spoke words pleasant to women's ears, but because his actions were more eloquent than any verbal confessions. "I am in wild despair because... I don't want to lose you." Without saying a word, she took his face in her hands and looked tenderly into his eyes. "Ella admitted that her beau didn't need someone else's child."

"She brought your daughter to you? That's good." Miia smiled cautiously.

"That would be so. But he doesn't need Elvira anymore." Anatoly hugged her.

"Listen, I have a proposal. Just don't say no, please. I've already filed for divorce." I require some more time to sort everything out."

"Does she not give you her consent?"

"She doesn't."

There was silence.

"Morning is wiser than evening." She gently took his hand. "Let's go."

There was no night. There was love. Pleasure. Sadness.

"You were planning to go to your mother's hospital one of these days."

"The day after tomorrow."

"I promised I'd take you, but if you go with Serg, you won't mind, right?"

That was even better because Miia had the opportunity to learn more than she could have heard from Anatoly personally.

Without hiding behind male solidarity, Serg said that he didn't like Ella, which is why he didn't communicate with her. He told her that she had constant complaints about his friend, who arose "out of the blue." He also told her that, instead of attending Anatoly's mother's funeral, she had gone to her parents' house for a month. Furthermore, he told her how she blackmailed him for money to see her daughter and a separate monthly allowance so that she wouldn't have to depend on her boyfriend.

"That's terrible." Miia couldn't help herself. "Is she so incapable of anything that she would resort to such

263

humiliating steps?"

"When they met, I immediately told Anatoly that she was both too beautiful and too empty."

"However, they have a child, and Anatoly loves the girl with all his heart. She won't leave her to him, will she?"

"He offered Ella in exchange for a divorce, an apartment, a car, and a monthly allowance."

"She didn't agree?"

"She came back after finding out about you."

Miia thought for a moment. She found it strange that Serg's stories about Anatoly's wife made her feel sorry for this woman, and her first thoughts at that moment were that, despite everything, she could not allow the family to break up. And even more so, she would rather not be the cause of it.

XXXIII

The next day, Miia went to her in-laws.

"I decided to move back to Kyiv. I see no future for myself or my children in the village. My fellow farmers suggested I set up my farm in the Kyiv area. But I believed that among my people, here in my home village, I could more confidently grow my small farm business. However, I was wrong."

"Your kindness and trustworthiness have become a hindrance, child," her mother-in-law interrupted. "If it weren't for your connections in Kyiv and the help you gave to Leszyk and the Kushaks, would they have what they have? And what is their gratitude?"

"Yes." Miia smiled. "With poor-quality seeds and lies about a broken combine. However, I'm no longer angry with them. I'll even say more: I don't wish them anything bad. It was all supposed to be that way! I had to go this way. Because there is a powerful will of the Almighty for everything. I gained valuable experience that will be beneficial to me. I believe."

"You will still get a lot. However, we are now certain that you are on the right path in life. You can achieve your goals. And you know for whom…" The mother-in-law began to cry.

"Our children, Anton and Niki, have only one hope," the mother-in-law tried to calm down. "You are their hope and their future. Because when I think about it, what will await them here? In our time, when jobs were available, no one even considered leaving. And now what? The village is half-empty."

"Leave the children with us. Let them go to school here. Our teachers are just as good as those in the city. Grandma and I will manage. We will get help and have more fun. And you there… Yes, I know you will carve the path for yourself and the children. So, Miia, grandma is right: you are their hope and their future!"

The next three weeks went by almost unnoticed. Miia had enough on her plate. To raise more money, she, as before, wasn't afraid to work in the fields.

One evening, tired but cheerful as he returned home from fieldwork, Mark stopped near her and, getting out of the car,

265

blocked her path.

"Miia, I am worried that you are working in the fields."

"Your wife also goes to these jobs. So why is it that my work in the fields worries you?"

"Listen to me, please. I already suggested that we go. Let's get ready right now and go."

"Where?" She raised her eyebrows, surprised.

"Nothing is holding us here anymore. I'm alone. You're alone."

"You're confused, dear." Miia stopped him. "None of us is alone! You're married; I have two children."

"I meant no one is holding me back, and the path to you is clear."

"A clear path to me? Hmm... how is that?" She looked at him with prejudice.

"You and Anton divorced. I'll file for divorce tomorrow. I would have done it today, but today everything is closed."

"You know, if you were divorced today, your offer would be tempting. And if you're ready tomorrow, then it means I'll break up the family. And I won't let that happen."

"There is no family." Grabbing her by the shoulders and looking her in the eyes, he shouted. "What family? I would rather not be left alone in my old age. It's scary to think that there won't even be anyone to bring me water."

"Well, you still have to live to be old." Black humor flickered in her eyes. "When did you manage to think that my children should take care of your old age? Do you think your proposal is attractive?"

He looked at her silently.

"You have changed. Not on the outside. On the outside, you've blossomed even more."

"I'm not seventeen anymore. I'm already thirty. That girl who froze at the thought of you is gone... Yes, I loved you."

"I can't forgive myself for abandoning you like that without knowing what happened next."

"And you wanted to know?" Her voice trembled. "Was it easier for you to adopt the pose of an ostrich, invent some excuses for yourself, and obediently go to bed with Mila, as your mother and sister wanted?" Her demanding gaze acted on him like fire. "Why are you silent?"

266

"My mother and sister?" He was surprised.

"Wow!" Moving away from him, she looked him up and down. "You are lucky that your grandfather, Danilo, is alive. Go and ask him how it happened that he married not Varvara but your grandmother, Dunya, whom he mercilessly beat all his life. And why does he despise her so much? By the way, just like you did, Mila."

"He loved her…" he said hesitantly, thinking.

"If he beats, then he loves. But for some reason, your father doesn't beat his mother. Doesn't he love? Mark, our destinies intertwined that distant evening. But they broke off. You still don't know why?"

In her memories, Nona's lying words about Mila's nonexistent pregnancy surfaced. She recalled the remorse of the postmistress's assistant, who, at the request of Mark's mother, destroyed his letters addressed to Miia.

Her thoughts stopped moving. Her gaze froze. Furthermore, her eyes looked through him, into nowhere. She felt how he stared intently into them and found neither questions nor answers. There was a desert in them.

In those distant years, Miia could not tell why their fate broke off. The two most important people created a chasm in his life. "I would rather not stir up the past. But you are entitled to know." Taking a deep breath and exhaling quickly, she came close to him. "Ask your mother about the fate of the letters you wrote to me. And also, ask Nona why, a couple of weeks after you were drafted into the army, Mila had a miscarriage. Timko can help you."

His wide-open eyes were filled with what seemed like endless surprise.: "Letters. Miscarriage. Wait."

"Our fate with you was cut short by those people with whom I will never be able to try on. Too much has been experienced and put at stake in life." She carefully studied the despair and sadness in his eyes. "My life and the lives of my children are at stake. Many years ago, for the sake of the two of us, you failed to figure it out. And now, I don't need it anymore. Goodbye."

He watched her and punished himself for the fact that on that distant evening, he had not found the perseverance to stay with her forever.

Her thoughts, like pieces of a puzzle, began to fall into place, forming a clear picture. 'It's terrific. How quickly events started to unfold! There is no longer any fear in my soul. It was replaced by inspiration. I didn't stop, no matter how tired I was. I didn't despair because God himself was nearby. Furthermore, I am walking along the path of future changes. I am waiting for them. I do not have any plans. However, I have a desire to leave so that I won't return.

My native land, you did everything to push me away. Now I am not with you because you do not associate my life with yourself.

Well, I am ready to prepare another lemonade of my destiny. Tomorrow, on the road.'

There had been no news from Anatoly for the last three weeks. Miia began writing a letter to him. She did not despair because everything could have worked out for her with him, but it did not. She humbly accepted her fate because she was grateful to him for showing her that, among men, there are caring and sincere ones.

According to her reasoning, she did not hear either the car that stopped near the yard or the gate that opened. She was alerted by a soft knock on the door.

Opening it, she froze. Anatoly stood on the threshold with a luxurious bouquet of roses. They looked at each other in silence.

"You are on time." Miia broke the silence.

Having walked through the rooms, Anatoly understood everything.

"I was gone for a long time. You probably thought that I had forgotten you."

"No. I did not think. Each of us has our path."

"Ella has a tumor. The doctors say they contacted them in time."

"She needs you."

Silence fell again. Hugging, they could only hear each other's breathing and the beating of their hearts.

"I'm sorry," he whispered.

"Don't be sorry." Looking intently into his eyes, she replied with a slight smile. "I'm grateful to you for us."

"We were happy."

"We were?" she repeated. "It will be tomorrow. And today, we are…"

In the morning, Miia went to say goodbye to her in-laws. Anton and Nika were already awake. They were waiting.

"Be obedient. Study well and help grandma and grandpa." Miia hugged the children. "I will come to you. And for the holidays, I will take you to my place in Kyiv. Everything will be fine with us."

"Everything will be so. "You know, child," barely holding back tears, said the mother-in-law, "your life can turn out differently. You can meet a better man than our son. We ask for only one thing: do everything so that the children do not suffer." Nevertheless, unable to bear it, she burst into tears.

"Mom, I am not going to search for a new father for the children." Miia's voice was firm but gentle. "I am going searching for prospects and opportunities. I am going to stay there forever. For the sake of my future and the future of the children."

Returning to the car, Miia found Anatoly leafing through the pages of a book.

"And how do you like it?" he asked.

"This book should be a desk book for every living person on the planet."

"Wow!" Anatoly's eyes lit up. "Really?"

"If it were so, then there would be less evil in life."

He looked at her in surprise. Her tone seemed harsh to him. However, he agreed with the statement.

"I will miss you. I will miss your optimism, openness, and courage."

"Don't miss me, and let's live and thank God for the time that was allotted to us. A happy ending only happens in fairy tales. And you and I had a small story that had a happy beginning. It's not our will. But we must humbly accept it… With gratitude!" In a moment of silence, as she looked at the sad Anatoly, Miia decided that she needed to cheer him up.

"I am not emigrating abroad. It is scary to imagine what it is like to go to foreign lands, languages, traditions. However, having gathered with the will and the need to survive, people master the terrain, learn languages, and respect traditions. It isn't easy. What kind of determination do you have to have?

269

What circumstances do you have to go through when deciding to emigrate? Therefore, I am glad that I am not leaving my country. Only the administrative unit will change. I am home."

On the way, Miia asked Anatoly to stop near the Sergienkos. Returning the book, with shining eyes and a sweet smile, Miia sincerely thanked Uncle Jacob.

"Child, the only one who leads us along His unspeakable paths is God! Remember forever, no matter how endless the life's off-road paths may seem, the thirst for life will always open new life horizons. No matter how hellish the darkness of life may be, it will always be replaced by the divine light of faith, hope, and love. And you, thank the past. Bless the present. Trust the future."

"No one lives my life for me. So, let everyone I have wronged or offended forgive me, just as I have learned to forgive."

The clouds were quietly drifting towards those lands where significant changes awaited her.

Overcoming dozens of kilometers, the train raced, frightening the night darkness with its metallic power. The rumble of the wheels, again and again, like a lullaby, hummed the same song: "The bitter lessons of the past are the keys to a bright future! That is why memory preserves them, carefully and without compassion."

"No, not grief…" she told herself, looking into the sad eyes of the full moon. He was the only one who saw her tears. "How can I think that living in alliance with the Devil is easier than living in alliance with God?" Covering her face with her hands, Miia hid from her thoughts, through which the question wandered confusedly: could she have turned the other way, at least at one crossroads in life?

However, in the deepest corners of her soul, a mysterious lightness awakened the first sprouts of gratitude for all of life's storms, adversities, and trials, recognizing that even their strength did not break her character, her spirit, or her faith.

This is the Destiny.

And Miia with hers – one whole!

Made in the USA
Middletown, DE
12 January 2026

23554073R00155